Momentous

Events,

Vivid

Memories

Momentous Events, *Vivid* Memories

David B. Pillemer

*

HARVARD UNIVERSITY PRESS

Cambridge, Massachusetts, and London, England

First Harvard University Press paperback edition, 2000

Library of Congress Cataloging-in-Publication Data

Pillemer, David B.
Momentous events, vivid memories / David B. Pillemer.
p. cm.
Includes bibliographical references and index
ISBN 0-674-58205-5 (cloth)
ISBN 0-674-00418-3 (paper)
1. Memory. I. Title.
BF371.P63   1998
153.1′2—dc21
97-47043

TO

Jane, Michelle, and Julianna

*

AND IN MEMORY OF

Jean, Louis, Bernice, and Oliver

*

Acknowledgments

*J*HAVE MANY thanks to offer. Two grants from the Spencer Foundation and a Brachman Hoffman faculty award from Wellesley College funded my research on personal event memories. I began writing this book during a sabbatical leave supported by Wellesley College, and the College provided additional financial assistance through the Edith Barenholtz Child Study Program and the Class of '32 Social Science Research Fund.

Friends, colleagues, and relatives provided intellectual and emotional support: Jerome Bruner, Carol Feldman, Michel Grimaud, Dick and Pat Light, Clare McMillan, Michelle and Stephen Parker, Karl Pillemer, and Mary Ucci. My Wellesley colleagues Jonathan Cheek, Laurel Furumoto, Maggie Keane, Elissa Koff, Margery Lucas, Julie Norem, and Paul Wink cheerfully tolerated my frequent interruptions, gave generously of their time, and made valuable suggestions. Alison Hickey, Lawrence Rosenwald, and Vernon Shetley helped me make connections between psychology and literary studies. My former students Sharon Bhandari, Julienne Brackett, Frances Chao, Amy Desrochers, Caroline Ebanks, Lynn Goldsmith, Lisa Haueisen, Anneliesa Beebe Law, Sandra Lee, Rebecca Morton, Abigail Panter, Mimi Picariello, Colette Dumont Rather, Jill Reichman, and Arla Zions, and research associate Lynne Krensky, generated ideas and conducted research. Kathryn Hughes helped prepare the manuscript for publication. Angela von der Lippe at Harvard University Press was very supportive during the initial stages of writing. Tamiko Jones, President of Tamiko Productions, graciously provided a tape of music and commentary by Smokey Robinson and granted permission to quote from it.

Several people provided extensive commentary on the manuscript. Roger Brown and Robyn Fivush reviewed the manuscript for Harvard University Press and their comments were most helpful. Blythe Clinchy, Michelle DeSimone Leichtman, Jane Pillemer, Sheldon White, and my

Harvard editors Elizabeth Knoll and Anita Safran gave extraordinarily insightful and detailed feedback. The book was improved immeasurably by their efforts. Shep White's influence on my thinking and writing has been profound and has spanned almost 25 years—I am very fortunate to have his continued friendship and mentorship. The value of Jane Pillemer's contribution cannot be expressed adequately in words. Only she and I can know how central she was to writing of this book, and how central she is to my life.

*

Contents

1 Personal Event Memories 1

2 Memorable Moments 25

3 Memory Directives 63

4 Image, Narrative, and the Development of Self 99

5 The Living Past in Everyday and Clinical Contexts 136

6 Gender, Culture, and Personality 177

References 213

Index 235

Momentous Events, *vivid* Memories

Chapter 1

*

Personal Event Memories

𝒜 HUMAN LIFE is composed of an unending stream of particular instances. As I write this sentence, my behavior and thoughts are influenced by attitudes and skills that grew out of an accumulation of countless past learning experiences, experiences that are for the most part no longer identifiable as individual lived episodes. But *right now,* the writing is taking place in a particular location (my office), at a particular time (2:30 in the afternoon), accompanied by a particular set of feelings, perceptions, and bodily sensations (blue sky and sun visible from my window, sore jaw from recent surgery). Will this singular moment, marking the beginning of writing the first chapter of a book, be preserved in memory, or will it suffer the fate of most experiences and drift from consciousness into oblivion? More generally, what determines whether a pinpointed life event will persist in memory, will remain accessible to conscious awareness, and will continue to influence the life course days, months, or years after its initial occurrence?

For truly momentous events, memory longevity is expected. A person is likely to remember, for example, an episode in which his or her life was in danger, even if the event occurred long ago. Howard Hoffman's oral history of his experiences as a soldier in World War II included a life-threatening encounter that happened 35 years earlier:

> I was in a truck and I was sitting in the cab of the truck, and we were driving along a road, our whole convoy, when I looked straight in front of me, and I see a plane coming down to make a strafing run, and it's a German plane, and it's coming down very, very low, just exactly like what you always see in the movies. . . It made two runs, and between the first and the second run a lot of the guys ran into a house that was right by the side of the road. I was planning to run to the house, but for some reason I didn't, and the plane made a second run and this time I just maybe took one shot at it when it was pretty far in front of me and then I could see the bullets coming down. . . I saw a

1

puff of smoke six inches from my foot. . . It made that run and then disappeared, and I went on into the house and the guys in there had been watching through the window, and they said, "Jesus Christ, I thought you were hit. I saw those shells coming down right next to you and I thought I saw one hit you." That's how close it was, but I hadn't been hit. (Hoffman and Hoffman, 1990, pp. 113–114)

When extraordinary danger or death strikes a loved one rather than oneself, memories can be similarly vivid and long-lasting. Henri Benchoan traveled to Auschwitz, the Nazi concentration camp, some 50 years after his mother was sent to her death there. He was 8 years old when he saw his mother for the last time: "We were at the police station all morning. There was lots of confusion. Suddenly my mother, sensing the danger, said to me, 'Take your brother and get out fast.' [From a nearby doorway, Henri and his brother watched his mother board a bus that took her to the train to Auschwitz.] She saw us and waved. I will never forget the look on her face" ("French Jews' Kin Retrace Rail Journey to Auschwitz," 1992, p. 12; no author).

Just as one would expect to be revisited by vivid mental images of a direct threat to one's own life or the life of a significant other, it is commonplace to remember the death of a beloved public figure. The assassination of President John F. Kennedy in 1963 is the most celebrated example, but it is by no means unique. The renowned social reformer Jane Addams recounted how as a young child she heard the news of Lincoln's assassination:

> Although I was but four and a half years old when Lincoln died, I distinctly remember the day when I found on our two white gate posts American flags companioned with black. I tumbled down on the harsh gravel walk in my eager rush into the house to inquire what they were "there for." To my amazement I found my father in tears, something that I had never seen before, having assumed, as all children do, that grown-up people never cried. The two flags, my father's tears and his impressive statement that the greatest man in the world had died, constituted my initiation, my baptism, as it were, into the thrilling and solemn interests of a world lying quite outside the two white gate posts. (Addams, 1992, pp. 507–508)

Not all vivid and persistent memories involve intense shock, danger, or death. Most graduates can recall specific influential episodes from their college years (Pillemer, Picariello, Law, and Reichman, 1996), most women can recall the details of their first menstrual period (Pillemer, Koff, Rhinehart, and Rierdan, 1987), and most married couples can recount the moment when they first met (Belove, 1980). At an interview for a special tribute to Benny Goodman, Helen Ward, a vocalist with the famous swing band led by Goodman, reported a vivid memory of a marriage proposal she had received decades earlier:

> I remember my date taking me to the Brown Derby and we're sitting there talking and Benny [Goodman] leans over to Bill—that was my date's name—and says, "You know I'm going to marry that girl." And I'm sitting there like this. And my friend looks at me—What the heck's going on there? Bill took me home. Before I knew it, there's a ring at the doorbell. And it's Benny. And I let him in. And I'll never forget this. I'm, I'm sitting on the couch and Benny's standing in front of me and he's saying, "I want to marry you." And now no prelude, no inkling, no, out of left field, "Want to marry you." He convinced me to go East with him.   (O. Jacoby, 1986)

Still other memories record personal milestones or turning points. A select few episodes come to be perceived as "originating events" (Pillemer et al., 1996) or "self-defining memories" (Singer and Salovey, 1993), moments that are believed to have profoundly influenced the life course. Photographer Margaret Bourke-White experienced such a moment in childhood:

> Now and then Father put the drafting tools aside and took me with him on trips to factories where he was supervising the setting up of his presses. One day, in the plant in Dunellen, New Jersey. . .I saw a foundry for the first time. I remember climbing with him to a sooty balcony and looking down into the mysterious depths below. "Wait," Father said, and then in a rush the blackness was broken by a sudden magic of flowing metal and flying sparks. I can hardly describe my joy. To me at that age, a foundry represented the beginning and end of all beauty. Later when I became a photographer, with that instinctive desire that photographers have to show their world to others, this memory was so vivid and so alive that it shaped the whole course of my career.   (Bourke-White, 1992, p. 425)

Although the topics represented in this sample of memories are diverse, the narratives share several basic characteristics: they each describe a circumscribed, one-moment-in-time event rather than an extended time period or series of repeated experiences; they focus on the rememberer's personal circumstances at the time of the event, including what was seen, heard, thought, and felt; they contain many specific details, such as direct quotations and descriptions of physical surroundings; and they have retained their vivid, life-like quality through the years The term *personal event memory* captures these general characteristics, and it will be used in a somewhat informal sense until a more formal definition is offered in Chapter 2.

All readers will be able to identify events from their own pasts that fit this characterization. Indeed, when in our everyday lives we say that we clearly "remember" a specific past event, we usually mean that we can produce a detailed narrative description of the episode as it was personally experienced. Considering the ubiquitous nature of this type of remembering, one might expect it to be a primary research topic for cognitive psychology in general and the study of memory in particular. This is not the case. Another shared characteristic of personal event memories is that they have until very recently been neglected by much of the scientific community. Before developing a case for increased scientific emphasis on memories of specific life events, this pervasive earlier neglect must be addressed.

*

Neglect of Specific Life Episodes
in Cognitive Psychology

Although studies of memory have long been a part of cognitive psychology, specific life episodes have rarely been the focus of these efforts. Rather, the primary goal was, and for the most part still is, to discover general rules about how people learn, solve problems, and form concepts. Cognitive psychologists can certainly point to hundreds of experimental studies of episodic memory, but the to-be-remembered "episodes" in these studies typically are words, numbers, or nonsense syllables presented to undergraduate students under controlled laboratory conditions. According to Endel Tulving (1983), perhaps the world's leading authority on experimental studies of episodic memory, "Experiments done in the past *can* be interpreted as episodic- rather than semantic-memory experiments . . . but they were not designed as part of a grand plan to understand how people remember personal experiences" (p. 129). Tulving observed that "It looks almost as if there was something basically incompatible between human cognition as seen by contemporary cognitive psychology and the human experience that characterizes one of the most advanced forms of cognition, episodic memory" (p. 125).

Why have mainstream cognitive psychologists been content to study memory for stimuli presented experimentally, without broadening the scope of investigation to include personal event memories? Many cognitivists share the belief that psychological phenomena should be examined under controlled laboratory conditions; only then can underlying memory processes or mechanisms be isolated and described. "Everyday memory research . . . may alert psychologists to new phenomena, but progress in understanding them will depend on what experimental control is brought to bear, whether inside or outside the laboratory" (Roediger, 1991, p. 40).

The emphasis on experimental control is accompanied by an almost exclusive focus on memory accuracy as the outcome of interest. When the experimenter chooses the to-be-remembered materials and presents them to the "subject" in a laboratory setting, memory can be assessed "objectively" by comparing the stimulus input to the memory output. In contrast, personal life episodes are idiosyncratic, emotion-laden, and messy, occurring as they do within the ongoing flow of daily activities. They are uncomfortably similar to psychoanalytic case descriptions, a frequent object of disdain within scientific psychology. According to this view, personal memories are interesting as anecdotes and are a valuable component of autobiography, literature, and some forms of psychotherapy, but they lack the necessary qualities for truly scientific study.

Another reason personal memories have been given short shrift is the higher priority psychologists place on acquiring general knowledge than on remembering and learning from particular episodes. The dominance of the general over the specific led Jacoby, Marriott, and Collins to name the last 20 years the "abstractionist period" in the history of psychology (1990, p. 111). Once one adopts the commonsense view that "many of the important things in human experience are ongoing situations rather than single events" (Neisser, 1985, p. 274), or that "knowledge of the world, by and large, is more useful to people than are personal memories" (Tulving, 1983, p. 52), then the most important subject of scientific inquiry is how the ongoing flow of particulars that confront consciousness becomes transformed into useful abstractions: "even undergraduates understand that the truly interesting question is how we ever come to represent abstractions from the particular world in which we live—to develop categories and impressions of *types* of people, *types* of situations, and so on" (Srull and Wyer, 1990, p. 166).

The emphasis on learning that is general rather than situation-specific is reflected by the research focus in cognitive psychology on abstract knowledge structures, including schemas and scripts (Abelson, 1981). Much of the time our behaviors are indeed guided by generalized, over-learned expectations or scripts for how to act in particular settings, such as restaurants or classrooms, not by memories of specific past experiences in those settings. One would expect the human memory system to reflect this priority of the general: "the basic episodic memory system is part of a general mammalian learning-memory adaptive function for guiding present action and predicting future outcomes. The most useful memory for this function is generic memory for routines that fit recurrent situations, that is, a general event schema (or script) memory system" (Nelson, 1993, p. 11).

Information-processing approaches to understanding the mind, with their reliance on the computer analogy, have given top priority to explaining the acquisition of abstract knowledge structures. Because memory in computers is limited, it is necessary to economize on storage rather than keep detailed records of specific instances (Smith, 1990). From this perspective, the theoretical and programming challenge is to explain how particular episodes can be transformed into generally applicable abstract knowledge structures, such as prototypes, concepts, and schemas. Because the information-processing approach coincides with our intuitions about how an efficient memory storage system should work, the priority of the abstract has gone unchallenged. "If we see a hundred dogs and each has four legs it just seems like common sense to 'store that information only once'. . . To change our thinking and consider memory storage as virtually unlimited is not easy" (Smith, 1990, p. 25).

The dominance of the general over the specific is not limited to academic theory-building. The acquisition of abstract, general-purpose knowledge structures is a primary research topic within applied psychology. Although most readers will be able to identify particular educational experiences that influenced their lives— words of support from a valued teacher, a harsh reprimand, an inspirational lecture or assignment, or an unusually successful or disastrous performance on an exam or paper—educational researchers have paid scant attention to such "educational episodes," specific moments of learning or insight that occur in educational contexts (Pillemer et al., 1996). Research preferences in education reflect instead the high value placed on the acquisition of general knowledge: "Children and people of all ages go to school in order to learn skills and knowledges that they need for life. They do not go to school in order to acquire a storehouse of temporally dated personal memories" (Tulving, 1983, p. 51).

A final underlying reason why the idea that specific episodes can profoundly influence the life course has captured only a modest amount of scientific interest and attention is that this idea runs counter to the prevailing (and reassuring) view that life is thematic, continuous, and predictable. For the most part, the core of personality and progression of the life course are believed to be consistent over time, resilient to abrupt changes and unforeseen events. Yet this book contains abundant and multifarious examples of singular events that are represented in memory as profoundly life-affecting and even life-altering. If one scathing comment from a professor can appear to prompt a change in a student's choice of a major, if one colossal mis-step on the baseball field can send the life of a professional athlete into a downward spiral, or if one forceful social rejection in childhood can linger in memory and cast a negative tint over subsequent interpersonal interactions, then life plans are alarmingly vulnerable to unexpected and disquieting interruption and people may inadvertently affect others' lives in negative ways. The potential power of the specific may be an unpalatable idea to many, but it is an idea that is nevertheless worthy of serious scholarly attention and scientific investigation.

*

The Specific Episode in Memory Research

The scientific status of personal event memories has risen in recent years as a result of new theoretical and empirical advances in several research domains: memory in natural contexts, narrative studies, and experimental psychology.

Memory in Natural Contexts

Two publication events were central to the growth of interest in personal memory among cognitive psychologists: Roger Brown and James Kulik's famous paper on "flashbulb memories," published in 1977, and Ulric Neisser's influential edited volume, *Memory Observed,* published in 1982. Brown and Kulik's paper was unique in several respects. They analyzed memories of a number of different shocking and consequential public events, such as the assassination of President John F. Kennedy in 1963. Brown and Kulik were centrally interested in people's memories of their own personal circumstances when they "heard the news," rather than memory for factual, verifiable public information about the newsworthy events. The researchers obtained memories and quantitative ratings of reactions to the remembered events from 80 adults. Almost all of the respondents remembered how they learned that Kennedy had been assassinated, and the vivid details that characterized the memory narratives suggested the photographic "flashbulb" metaphor. Even though it was not possible to assess memory accuracy, Brown and Kulik accepted the respondents' recollections as data worthy of study in their own right. The relatively large sample size enabled Brown and Kulik to go beyond anecdotal reporting and to conduct statistical tests of several hypotheses; for example, events that respondents rated as more consequential (such as the Kennedy assassination) were remembered in greater detail than events they rated as less consequential (such as the 1975 assassination attempt on President Gerald Ford).

Because Brown and Kulik's paper was published in the respected journal *Cognition*, it received attention from cognitive psychologists even though it broke sharply with the usual emphasis on laboratory control and assessment of memory accuracy. Moreover, flashbulb memories were so easily recognized, so universally experienced, that they were difficult to dismiss out of hand. Virtually every American who was at least of school age in 1963 had his or her *own* flashbulb memory of the Kennedy assassination. Famous and ordinary people alike were dramatically affected by the news, and their memories persisted for years with little loss of clarity. Opera singer Robert Merrill, for example, remembered being in a restaurant. "The waiter said, 'Sir, I must tell you that your President Kennedy has been killed.' I choked. His shaking hand dropped the chocolate on Marion's white dress" (Peyer and Seely, 1993). Marylyn Moore, homeless when the following memory was elicited 30 years after the assassination, was a Boston homemaker in 1963:

> I was at a drugstore in the South End getting an ice cream when the radio announced that Kennedy was shot. Right away I started praying and ran home to the Lennox Street projects where I lived. I started crying and everyone came into the halls crying. I went downtown to Filene's Basement [discount retail store] afterwards to do some shopping, and everyone's eyes were puffy. It was like going to a wake. I was pulling on a piece of clothing that another woman was holding onto. We both looked at each other and started crying. She was white. We had heard that Kennedy had died, and we started holding hands.   (Tlumacki, 1993)

Surely there must be a scientific explanation for this ubiquitous phenomenon, and examining personal memories of contemporary public tragedies was an obvious research strategy to follow.

Brown and Kulik's paper was followed closely by Neisser's provocative *Memory Observed* (1982). Neisser presented examples of research conducted outside the laboratory and case studies of interesting memory phenomena. His criticism of traditional laboratory-based memory research included this highly publicized charge: "If X is an interesting or socially significant aspect of memory, then psychologists have hardly ever studied X" (p. 4). Neisser's stature made the claim difficult to dismiss out of hand. It was not leveled by a representative of "soft" psychology, but by a leader in the field of cognition: in 1967 Neisser had written an extremely influential book, *Cognitive Psychology*, which helped to establish the field as it currently exists. Cognitive psychologists who had closeted their interest in memories of personal life episodes or had struggled to translate their unconventional ideas into acceptable research designs welcomed Neisser's bravado and his manifesto was readily adopted. Researchers who continued to believe in the inherent superiority of traditional laboratory approaches did not remain silent for long; the counterattack in Banaji and Crowder's 1989 paper, "The Bankrupcy of Everyday Memory," had an edge as sharp as Neisser's contentious statements.

Narrative Studies

The sudden rise in research on memory in natural contexts, including remembered personal life episodes, has not occurred in a vacuum. The study of narrative has experienced a similarly dramatic increase. The virtues of examining life narratives or stories have been extolled in recent books (Britton and Pellegrini, 1990; Bruner, 1986, 1990; Josselson and Lieblich, 1993; McAdams, 1993; Schank, 1990; Singer and Salovey, 1993) and academic journals (Bruner, 1987; Connelly and Clandinin, 1990; Howard, 1991; Vitz, 1990). Human experience is conceived as a process of constructing and reconstructing a life narrative: "'Life' in this sense is the same kind of construction of the human imagination as a 'narrative' is" (Bruner, 1987, p. 13). If one accepts the premise that "a life is not 'how it was' but how it is interpreted and reinterpreted, told and retold" (Bruner, 1987, p. 31), then the ground rules for scholarly analysis are shifted. According to Singer and Salovey (1993), "What is most intriguing to us about the self is that identity may be as determined by events we believe happened to us as ones that did" (p. 157). The concern with the *accuracy* of memories, so prevalent in experimental cognitive psychology, gives way to an emphasis on the person's *beliefs* about what happened: psychic reality is as important as historical truth.

The narrative movement also has strong adherents within the psychoanalytic and psychotherapeutic communities (see White and Epston, 1990). Donald Spence's influential book, *Narrative Truth and Historical Truth* (1982), identified two views of memory as it is expressed in therapy. The first view assumes that objective truth is discoverable in the patient's life story, and that a goal of the therapy is to get closer and closer to this historical truth. The second view assumes that the patient's story is a construction in which the teller *creates* a coherent and convincing personal history. Spence argued that the patient's created narrative account is "truthful," but that its truth value does not lie in its historical accuracy. "There seems no doubt that a well-constructed story possesses a kind of narrative truth that is real and immediate and carries an important significance for the process of therapeutic change. Although Freud would later argue that every effective interpretation must also contain a piece of historical truth, it is by no means certain whether this is always the case; narrative truth by itself seems to have a significant impact on the clinical process" (pp. 21–22). Narrative truth is defined as "the criterion we use to decide when a certain experience has been captured to our satisfaction; it depends on continuity and closure and the extent to which the fit of the pieces takes on an aesthetic finality" (p. 31). When we arrive at the historical truth, our description of a prior event is based on the "facts"; when we arrive at the narrative truth, our explanation carries "conviction."

In the psychotherapeutic milieu, creating narrative truth may be more important than establishing historical truth: "narrative truth has a special significance in its own right . . . making contact with the actual past may be of far less significance than creating a coherent and consistent account of a particular set of events" (Spence, 1982, p. 28). In a similar vein, Howard (1991) characterized psychotherapy as "exercises in story repair" (p. 194). If a life story can be truthful even if it does not conform perfectly to the historical past, then personal memories composing a life history are psychologically valid objects of analysis in their own right. "Once a given construction has acquired narrative truth, it becomes just as real as any other kind of truth" (Spence, 1982, p. 31).

From an applied standpoint, narratives describing personal experiences can offer valuable truths or lessons for practitioners (Pillemer et al., 1996). Sarason (1993) argued that descriptions of personal experience could enrich analyses of educational policy: "In fact, in the entire literature, reference to personal experience is very rare. I'm quite aware of the arguments against using personal experience to prove anything or as a basis for a policy recommendation. But what if there are certain types of personal experiences that are so general, so illuminating, so important that they should not be dismissed on grounds of subjectivity?" (p. 10). Similarly, Carter (1993) extolled the educational value of personal narratives, their lack of quantitative rigor notwithstanding: "these stories capture, more than scores or mathematical formulae ever can, the richness and indeterminacy of our experiences as teachers and the complexity of our understandings of what teaching is and how others can be prepared to engage in this profession" (p. 5).

The force of the narrative movement has been strengthened greatly by the stature of its outspoken proponent, Jerome Bruner, within the field of scientific psychology. Narrative analysis itself is not new; Labov, for example, had conducted detailed analyses of memories of specific life episodes decades earlier (Labov and Waletzky, 1967). But Bruner, like Neisser, was not an outsider; he was a prominent player in the cognitive revolution of the 1960s and 1970s. Bruner had a track record of anticipating major shifts in interest and practice within psychology. He and the prominent experimental psychologist George Miller had co-founded the influential Harvard Center for Cognitive Studies in 1960. In recent publications Bruner strongly endorsed the study of lives through autobiography—"an account of what one thinks one did in what settings in what ways for what felt reasons"—in which belief rather than accuracy is the primary consideration. "It does not matter whether the account conforms to what others might say who were witnesses, nor are we in pursuit of such ontologically obscure issues as whether the account is 'self-deceptive' or 'true.' Our interest, rather, is only in what the person thought he did, what he thought he was doing it for, what kinds of plights he thought he was in, and so on" (1990, pp. 119–120). Within this conceptualization, memories of specific life episodes are psychologically real entities that are worthy of study independently of their objective truth value.

Episodic Models of Cognitive Processing and Social Behavior

Just as research on remembering in natural contexts has challenged traditional assumptions of laboratory-based memory research, so recent experiments within cognitive and social psychology have challenged the dominance of the abstract—including schemata, scripts, categories, and prototypes—over the particular. The abstractionist view is so well established that it presents a formidable barrier: "the prevailing view is that cognition is largely controlled by abstract data structures. The belief has become so entrenched in modern thought that it is hard for many to see that anything else is possible. People see no room for the effects of specific experience" (Logan, 1990, p. 147). In a provocative and far-reaching essay, Smith (1990) argued forcefully and convincingly for a re-balancing in theory and research: "social cognition may have devoted a disproportionate amount of attention to one class of mediators: schemata and other abstract, generic knowledge structures. Many phenomena appear to depend on other types of mediators, particularly memory traces of specific experiences. . ." (p. 2). In his comments on Smith's paper, Logan (1990) stated the case even more strongly: "The priority of the specific should be obvious. We live life in the particular. . . Moreover, we remember the particular. Our memories are filled with details of particular experiences with particular people in particular settings with particular purposes and cross-purposes. The question should not be whether specific experience is important but rather, how anything other than specific experience is possible" (p. 147).

The evidence for the importance of specific experiences is not merely anecdotal; the influence of particular instances on later behavior has recently been measured using controlled experimental procedures. For example, Lewicki (1985) demonstrated that momentary past encounters can affect choice behavior in social settings. Participating high school students first interacted with an interviewer who asked a series of questions. For one of the questions, the interviewer acted in either an "unkind" or a "neutral" way. In the next part of the experiment, students were presented with the choice of approaching one of two new experimenters, one of whom physically resembled the first interviewer. Only 20% of students who had had an unpleasant brief encounter during the interview approached the experimenter who physically resembled the interviewer, whereas 57% of students who had had a neutral interaction with the interviewer chose the physically similar experimenter. Although the influence of the single unfriendly prior episode on students' choice behavior in a separate encounter was apparent, the influence apparently operated outside of conscious awareness. When asked, most students believed that their choice of experimenter was completely random. Lewicki concluded that "the memory representation of even a single instance relevant in some respect to the present situation is capable of influencing the final decision" (p. 573).

Perris, Myers, and Clifton (1990) reported a more spectacular experimental demonstration of the long-term impact of a singular episode. Children had participated in an experiment on auditory localization on one occasion when they were 6.5 months of age. The experiment involved reaching for a sounding object in the light and in the dark. Two years later, the children (now 2.5-year-old toddlers) returned to the experimental setting. Their behaviors in the situation were compared to a control group of children who had not participated in the original experiment. Children who had participated in the auditory localization study two years earlier showed clear evidence of memory; for example, they were more likely to reach out in the dark toward the sound than were the inexperienced control group children, and their reaches were more accurate. The effects of prior experience were also apparent in children's affective reactions to the test situation: children who had participated in one 20-minute experiment two years earlier were much less likely to show discomfort in the dark and to request to leave. The authors concluded that "one unique experience at 6.5 months of age was sufficient to establish a memory of both action and meaning that became accessible upon reinstatement of the event in the third year of life" (p. 1806).

Research findings such as these call into question the universal priority of general rather than specific influences on human behavior. Suppose that the same children had participated in Perris et al.'s study at 2 1/2 years of age, but that the researchers had been unaware of some children's prior exposure to the experimental situation. The skilled performance of some of the children may very well have been attributed to their general intelligence or perceptual acuity, and their calm demeanor in the test situation may have been attributed to their underlying emotional character, rather than to the one similar experience of two years earlier. How often in everyday life are behaviors and feelings attributed to general characteristics, tendencies, or traits, when a key contributing influence is a specific past event of which the person is no longer consciously aware?

Experimental demonstrations of the importance of particular instances also exist within applied cognitive psychology. For example, Brooks, Norman, and Allen (1991) examined how medical doctors diagnose skin disorders. Doctors did not rely solely on canonical "dermatological rules" (p. 284); their diagnosis was also influenced by prior exposure to specific visual examples of skin lesions. Whittlesea and Dorken (1993b) concluded that experimental studies clearly demonstrate the potential influence of specific episodes: "there is considerable evidence that people do preserve the mass of past experience, whether or not they additionally compute information about the regularity of each experience . . . irrelevant and trivial detail of experience is preserved and influential in later encounters" (p. 402). These empirical findings have led some researchers to adopt an "episodic view of cognition" (Jacoby, Marriott, and Collins, 1990), or to develop an "episodic-processing account of implicit learning" (Whittlesea and Dorken, 1993a), in which specific instances play a central role. Although these views may not as yet be shared by the majority of experimentalists, the episode appears to have a promising future in cognitive psychology.

General learning is also the main focus of applied research in education. Achievement tests, for example, are designed to measure general knowledge that is broadly applicable rather than to assess long-term memory for specific instances of illuminated insight. Yet even within the domain of educational testing, the central importance of particular learning experiences is beginning to surface. Nuthall and Alton-Lee (1995) asked elementary and middle-school children to talk aloud as they answered test items, and to explain how they learned or knew the answers. The most common explanation was "recall of directly relevant information or classroom experience. Students reported recalling both the specific classroom experiences from which they learned the answer as well as details of the answer itself" (p. 195). For example, one child described how she learned that a thermometer contained mercury:

> C: Mr. B. said, what's in a thermometer? And Tony put up his hand and said it was mercury. And it was right, and since then I have remembered.
> Interviewer: What did you think at the time?
> C: I thought, you [Tony] have got to be wrong. I thought mercury was sort of a jewel or something like that. Or just a planet.
> Interviewer: So you thought he was wrong?
> C: Mm. I thought it was ink or water.   (pp. 195–196)

Another child recounted, 12 months after a unit on science, how she had learned the names of four types of clouds:

Interviewer: You remember Mr. B talking about those clouds. . . . Do you remember any pictures of them?

    C: He drew some on the blackboard all red (laugh). He didn't do them in white, he did them all red. He did pigs' tails, big fluffy one, feathery-tailed one, flat layers, and a stormy one. . . . We had to do them on a piece of paper and hand them in to Mr. B. We had to do, it was on a red piece of paper, but we had to do it in pencil . . . and we had to remember what the clouds were 'cause he would rub it off the board, but he would leave the names. (p. 196)

Nuthall and Alton-Lee concluded that "an achievement test item does not simply measure a student's ability to recall the correct answer" (p. 219). Rather, "memory for a concept or idea defined by an achievement test item usually consisted of parts or fragments of the original learning experiences" (p. 216). Furthermore, the data suggested that "being able to answer achievement test items is strongly related to the ability to recollect the original learning experiences" (p. 204). Conway, Gardiner, Perfect, Anderson, and Cohen (1997) obtained similar findings in a university setting. They asked students in psychology lecture courses to describe how they had known the answers to final exam questions. A substantial proportion of students reported remembering specific circumstances in which the information was learned, and students who received higher grades "were able to engage episodic memory more effectively than their colleagues" (p. 408). Clearly, any model of achievement test performance that fails to take into account the episodic roots of learned information is incomplete.

This revised view of the importance of specific instances of learning also finds support in the recent work of Schank and Abelson (1995), who, as principal architects of script theory, encouraged the current emphasis on abstract knowledge structures in cognitive and social psychology. Schank and Abelson identified specific episodes, and stories that are created about those episodes, as an additional important source of general information about the world.

Many psychologists have claimed that memory for facts must be organized hierarchically in a semantic memory. Others have argued for a memory that is more episodically based, and still others have suggested combining the two. A neatly organized hierarchy of semantic concepts is easy to imagine, but the world is full of oddities and idiosyncratic events that fail to fit neatly into a pre-established hierarchy. For example, we may "know" from semantic memory that female horses have teats, but we may more readily access this fact from an episodic store if we witnessed our pet horse giving birth and then suckling its young. Our first memories of playing ball may very well come to mind when the word "ball" comes up, and the properties we ascribe to "ball" may well be the ones that a particular ball we remember actually had. (p. 37).

Successful models of cognitive processing within applied domains, such as education, must complement the usual emphasis on abstract knowledge structures with a new focus on the specific.

∗

Organization of This Book

Scholarly advances in episodic learning, narrative studies, and memory in natural contexts have created a favorable intellectual climate for scientific analysis of personal life episodes. In the chapters that follow, I draw freely upon the resources of a diverse set of methodological approaches and fields of study, including episodic models of cognition and social behavior, narrative, communications, language studies, clinical psychology and psychiatry, cross-cultural psychology, gender studies, and personality. The analysis of personal event memories is organized around five overarching themes or perspectives: (1) an emphasis on memory *function* rather than accuracy—how personal memories are used in everyday life; (2) an emphasis on memory *development*—how the ability to construct and share personal memories is acquired during childhood; (3) the portrayal of memory as a *complex interactive system* rather than as a singular entity—how conceptualizing the organization of personal event memory as involving multiple levels, systems, or modes of expression helps to explain diverse phenomena from both clinical and experimental domains; (4) an exploration of *individual and group differences* in memory function and performance, including the influence of gender, culture, and personality; and (5) a persistent focus on the life impact of specific, one-moment-in-time events, and corresponding *memories of specific instances,* rather than on cognitive summaries of repeated happenings.

Memory Function

A distinguishing characteristic of this book is the pervasive and overriding emphasis on memory function. Following Bruce (1989), function refers to "the real-world usefulness or adaptive significance of memory mechanisms" (p. 45). Bruce's definition identifies two different senses of function. An analysis of *adaptive significance* would focus on how and why human memory would have evolved into its current state. In the case of flashbulb memories, for example, what is the adaptive significance of remembering minute details of personal experience when one hears the news of a public tragedy? Why would a memory system have evolved in this fashion? An analysis of *real-world usefulness* would focus on how personal event memories influence people's daily lives, for better or for worse. For example, how does a vivid memory of a serious childhood injury, or a moment of special encouragement from a favorite teacher, influence subsequent behaviors, goals, and attitudes?

Memory accuracy is part of the functional equation. To get through one's daily life, it is adaptive to recollect past events in reasonably veridical form. But accuracy is only one part of a functional explanation of personal event memories, and in some circumstances it plays a relatively small part. Consider an 8-year old's memory of having been kidnapped over 4 years earlier:

> My Mom let me take my nap in my blanket tunnel. I heard footsteps. I woke up. I went into the tunnel thing. I didn't have time to put my pants on. The man aimed a revolver at Mom. She lay on the floor. He took me in a car. On a hill I said, "I want to go back to my mom," and the man said, "You will." He asked me if I wanted Coke or 7-Up and I said, "7-Up," and we went to his apartment. He let me call Mom lots of times. I pushed over his bed. I went to sleep. The next morning he took me to the airport—pushed me out of his car. A lady came. The FBI takes me in. The FBI man takes me in a car. I see Channel 2 news. He takes me to my house. I watched the news. Dad was smoking a cigarette. Then I saw Channel 8 News with my neighbor. Then I went out to play. Nobody let me watch TV after that.   (Terr, 1990, pp. 5-6)

The absolute truth value of this memory would be the critical concern in one real-world domain: legal testimony. A crime was committed, and the young child was the key witness. An arrest and conviction could ride on the child's ability to pick out the abductor in a line-up, or to describe the physical features necessary to produce a realistic composite picture. Concerns about memory accuracy would be heightened by the child's young age at the time of the kidnapping (Ceci and Bruck, 1993).

What issues besides accuracy are central to understanding how the child's memory of being abducted has affected his behavior, attitudes, and life course, and also how its retelling has affected others? For the child, the event was shocking, difficult to comprehend, and highly traumatic. Remembering the event, and recounting it to others, will serve *emotional or psychotherapeutic functions*. Models of psychotherapy often posit that consciously remembering and recounting the details of trauma is an essential part of the healing process. For psychiatrist Judith Herman, detailed remembering is a necessary step to recovery from trauma: "the survivor tells the story of the trauma. She tells it completely, in depth and in detail. The work of reconstruction actually transforms the traumatic memory, so that it can be integrated into the survivor's life story" (1992, p. 175). Note that the memory is *reconstructed* and *transformed* in the retelling; the survivor's beliefs are more important than any objective measure of veridicality. (The emotional functions of remembering personal event memories are explored in Chapters 4 and 5.)

The kidnapping undoubtedly provoked more than a negative emotional reaction: basic, life-or-death lessons about how the world works were also transmitted. The memory of a life-threatening encounter can serve a *directive function:* it captures in vivid detail what is safe and what is to be avoided in the future. Momentous past events continue to influence our lives for months or years in part because we repeatedly revisit the events in memory and adjust our current behaviors accordingly. It would be understandable for a child who was abducted at a young age to deliberately take special precautions, rational or extreme, to secure his own safety and, much later in life, the safety of his own children. These precautionary activities may be triggered by conscious, detailed recollection of the past trauma; what sort of current situation will trigger a precautionary response may be determined in part by its surface similarity to the circumstances of the original trauma. The guiding influence of the memory may also be expressed in a more general fashion: it would not be surprising if the survivor's story of his life began with this most salient episode of childhood, and thereby colored his perspective on subsequent events. The use of a traumatic memory as an example should not imply that memory directives are invariably associated with negative events; positive moments, such as dramatic and unexpected successes, are often remembered in vivid detail and can provide inspiration and guidance in the pursuit of a particular career or life course (Pillemer et al., 1996). (Directive functions of remembering particular events are the focus of Chapter 3.)

Although emotional and directive memory functions do not require absolute veridicality in recall, the child's spoken memory narrative is convincing and believable, and its telling elicits emotional or empathic responses from the listener. What gives it this communicative power? The *form* of narrative expression supports an essential *communicative function*. Explicit details contribute to its believability and emotionality. We will never know if the child actually selected 7-Up over Coke, or if his father was really smoking a cigarette, but these minute details paint a life-like scene nevertheless, with the urgency and immediacy of an ongoing event. Another subtle but important communicative device is the verb tense shift from the past into the present at a key point in the narrative ("The FBI takes me in. . ."), consciously or unconsciously suggesting that the child is not merely remembering the event—he is *reliving* a salient aspect of it (Pillemer, Desrochers, and Ebanks, 1998). (The communicative functions of recounting personal event memories are described and analyzed in Chapter 5.)

From a functional perspective, it is permissible and often valuable to view personal event memory as a belief system rather than a mechanistic entity filled with traces that are objectively true or false. This should in no way imply that it is unsuitable for rigorous scholarly analysis. The study of contemporary religious beliefs provides a useful analogy to the study of belief structures represented in autobiographical memory. With respect to Christianity, questions about historical truth include "Was Jesus a real person?" and "Does the Bible accurately portray historical events?" But the formal study of religion does not hinge on establishing historical accuracy. Functional analysis of religion would focus on a different set of questions: "What is the form and content of current religious beliefs?" "What psychological functions do religious beliefs serve in people's lives?" "How are people's career paths and life decisions influenced by their religious beliefs?" "How are people's feelings and mental health influenced by their religiosity?" "How do religious beliefs change in relation to changes in life experience?" In these questions, as in similar questions posed about memory functions, the analysis focuses on current beliefs and personal meaning rather than on historical truth.

Development

A special interest in development follows naturally from a functional perspective on personal event memories. Autobiographical memory does not unfold in a stereotyped and mechanistic fashion with growth;

rather, memory functions are acquired and elaborated as the child learns to use memory in the service of everyday tasks. How does the child learn the social rules of memory sharing? How early in childhood are emotional, directive, and communicative functions operative, and what are their developmental trajectories?

Two phenomena in particular suggest that personal event memory undergoes dramatic changes with development: childhood amnesia and parent-child memory talk. Childhood or infantile amnesia, identified by Freud (1905/1953), refers to the inability of most adults to recall specific episodes from the first years of life. The average age of the earliest memory reported by adults in Western cultures is between 3 and 4 years (Kihlstrom and Harackiewicz, 1982; Mullen, 1994; Pillemer and White, 1989), and few individuals are able to recall even landmark childhood events, such as the Kennedy assassination (Winograd and Killinger, 1983), the birth of a sibling (Sheingold and Tenney, 1982), or the death of a family member (Usher and Neisser, 1993), if the events occurred during the first 2 or 3 years of life. Had the child survivor of an abduction, described above, been even 6 months younger than his 39 months when the kidnapping occurred, it is unlikely that he could have produced a coherent narrative description of his capture and release; in a study of 20 childhood trauma victims, Terr identified 36 months as the earliest age at which children "have the capacity for full verbal recollection" (1988, p. 103). The inaccessibility of personal event memories from the earliest years, despite the abundance of salient and emotional experiences during this time, poses a puzzle that has drawn the focused attention of memory researchers and clinicians alike.

One well-known psychoanalytic explanation for the inaccessibility of early memories is repression: because the memories are connected to infantile sexual and aggressive impulses, they are blockaded from adult consciousness. Modern theorists have instead favored cognitive-developmental explanations for childhood amnesia (Fivush and Hamond, 1990; Howe and Courage, 1993; Neisser, 1962; Nelson, 1993; Pillemer and White, 1989; Schachtel, 1947; White and Pillemer, 1979). Infants and toddlers lack developed language, have a limited cognitive sense of self, and only a primitive and ever-changing understanding of social and cognitive events, so they cannot construct personal event memories in a form suitable for purposeful retrieval many years later.

Developmental accounts of childhood amnesia are supported by a groundbreaking collection of recent empirical studies on the evolution of memory talk between parents and children (Fivush, 1991; Hudson, 1990; Nelson, 1993). According to the "socials interaction model" of memory development, "children gradually learn the forms of how to talk about memories with others, and thereby also how to formulate their own memories as narratives" (Nelson, 1993, p. 10). It would be a mistake, then, to characterize autobiographical memory development as the simple unfolding of a fixed, uniform information processing system; rather, distinctive strategies for representing and sharing personal event memories are *co-constructed* during parent-child interactions. From a functional perspective, the central research issue is to illuminate how memory comes to be *used* rather than to define what memory *is*. Autobiographical memory *becomes* the operations that it is encouraged or required to perform.

A fascinating implication of this work is that individual differences in the form and content of parent-child conversations about the past can affect the organization of personal event memories; as parents differ systematically in the ways that they engage in memory talk with young children, so they contribute to marked individual variations in autobiographical memory style. If, as Bruner (1987) says, "a life is not 'how it was' but how it is interpreted and reinterpreted, told and retold" (p. 31), so that "we *become* the autobiographical narratives by which we 'tell about' our lives" (p. 15), then the particular modes of expression that children acquire to narrate and recount their lives could have profound implications for the types of people that they will become. These developmental issues are examined in Chapter 4.

Individual and Group Differences

New work in the areas of gender studies, cross-cultural psychology, and personality all point to substantial individual and group variations in the value placed upon sharing personal memories with other people, and in the way that past events are actually talked about. Gender studies show that women often appear to be more comfortable recounting intimate details of personal experiences than are men. Cross-cultural comparisons suggest that Caucasian-Americans share personal event memories more readily than do Asians, whereas Asians may rely more strongly on nonverbal modes of emotional expression. Research in personality also has identified stylistic differences in the ways that past events are remembered. For example, depressed people appear to be overly general when describing their personal pasts; they report general memories even when the situation calls for a specific response (Williams, 1996).

Group differences in memory sharing behaviors could simply reflect stylistic preferences. If that is so, then men and women, Asians and Caucasians, and depressives and nondepressives would have the same underlying memory organization and an identical battery of strategies for narrating past episodes, but members of different groups might simply choose to express their memories in different ways. A bolder and more provocative hypothesis is that early differences in the ways that people are socialized in the uses of memory actually lead to enduring and fundamental (although potentially modifiable) differences in autobiographical memory itself. Do differences in social circumstances associated with growing up female rather than male, or growing up in a primarily collectivistic rather than an individualistic culture, reach into the domain of memory talk and, ultimately, memory function and organization? This topic is the focus of Chapter 6.

Multiple Levels of Representation

Just as autobiographical memory development cannot be adequately described as following a single, universal trajectory, so personal event memories cannot be adequately described as occurring within a single level of mental representation or as involving a single mode of expression. Consider again the memory narrative provided by the 8-year old kidnapping victim. The verbal, consciously produced narrative is detailed and impressively coherent, but it almost certainly does not represent the entire scope of the child's memory of the event. Vivid personal memories, including memories of traumatic experiences, often have a strong sensory, and particularly visual, component. According to Terr (1990), "horrible experience creates permanent mental pictures" (p. 170). A person who wishes to recount a past trauma must translate nonverbal, affect-laden, sensory images into an understandable, coherent, verbal narrative. This difficulty of translation routinely confronts patients undergoing psychiatric treatment: "visual data are among the primary data of an analysis . . . in their natural state they are seen *only* by the patient . . . the large part of an analysis must make do with an approximate and largely makeshift verbal translation" (Spence, 1982, p. 56).

In addition to narrative and sensory levels of representation, specific past events may be represented behaviorally. Terr (1988) reported that although children are usually not able to give a full narrative account of a traumatic experience that occurred before the age of 3 years, the original event is frequently represented in children's play activities: 18 out of 20 traumatized children "demonstrated in their play, fears, or personality changes what they had retained from their traumas" (P. 98). In the study by Perris et al. (1990) described earlier, preschool children who were exposed to a single laboratory experience two years earlier demonstrated unmistakable behavioral memory of the prior experience.

Multiple levels of representation are also demonstrated by the degree to which memories are available to conscious awareness. The representation of a specific past event may be readily obtained through purposeful retrieval efforts; it may be currently inaccessible, but be potentially retrievable and available to consciousness; or, it may not be accessible to purposeful address and narrative expression. Memories need not be expressed as explicit, conscious, fully-formed narratives in order to be influential. Implicit memories can also have a profound impact on a person's thoughts, feelings, and actions, although they exert their influence outside of conscious awareness. Different levels of conscious representation in memory are examined in Chapters 2, 4, and 5.

The description of multiple levels of representation in memory need not imply that corresponding independent structures exist in the brain; the description is functional rather than neurological. Nevertheless, increased emphasis on functional analysis of personal event memories may ultimately inform efforts to construct models of underlying memory mechanisms or systems. New memory systems evolve in response to new environmental demands: "we would be hesitant to postulate a new memory system to accommodate a particular experimental finding or pattern of findings unless a good case could be made that the proposed system performs a function that cannot be performed by another memory system" (Sherry and Schacter, 1987, p. 449). Systematic functional analyses can "specify more clearly the range of functions that a system can serve and, hence, set the stage for meaningful analyses of functional incompatibilities" (p. 450). Identifying multiple, nonredundant memory functions would support the possibility of a corresponding set of distinctive memory systems. Through its focus on the adaptive significance of remembering, functional analysis can illuminate the practical uses of memory and at the same time provide clues about underlying mechanisms.

The Power of the Specific

Although the four overarching themes presented above—function, development, individual differences, and multiple levels of representation—could inform an analysis of almost any aspect of memory, the focus here is squarely on the specific. Researchers have shown increasing interest in personal memories, but we have as yet no comprehensive theory of particular instances: how they are remembered and how they influence the life course. I will make a case for the centrality of specific episodes in human thought and action, in part by presenting many and varied illustrations of influential life events and accompanying personal event memories, and in part by tying the illustrations to systematic empirical research and memory theory.

Emphasizing the power of the specific in no way negates the crucial role that general knowledge structures, including scripts, concepts, and prototypes, play in the unfolding of the life course. It is important, however, to reset the empirical and theoretical imbalance between the general and the specific. Rather than focusing almost exclusively on how episodes become transformed and incorporated into scripts, psychologists could accept a more demanding and potentially more valuable scientific challenge: developing a broader psychology that also respects the integrity and potential power of the specific episode.

Under some circumstances the power of the specific is directly evident, as when a child's sense of the world is changed by horrific personal trauma or when a successful professional athlete's career and life course are suddenly and dramatically altered by one colossal mistake, and by the lingering collective memory of that mistake (both in Chapter 2). In a happier instance, during a period of indecision a student unexpectedly receives unsolicited feedback from a respected professor that suggests a new career path, and the enduring memory of the spoken interaction serves as a continuing source of redirection and support (Chapter 3). Under other circumstances, the power of the specific is more subtle: memories of particular instances also exert their influence on feelings and behaviors outside of immediate conscious awareness (Chapters 4 and 5). In each of these cases, a memory of a specific episode is more than an emblematic surrogate for a long-established life script—it is an active force in forming, redirecting, and sustaining the life course.

Chapter 2

*

Memorable
Moments

*I*N THE PREFACE to her book *Too Scared To Cry,* Lenore Terr recounted a personal memory of a Saturday movie matinee she attended when she was 9 years old:

> One Saturday . . . I watched a newsreel of the U.S. Army entering Hiroshima. The Americans were wearing space suits not unlike what the actors wore on *Green Lantern* and other such Saturday serials. I remember how Hiroshima looked on the screen—I can see it now as I write. The city was scorched white and leveled to the ground. . . The newsreel people had found a foot bridge at ground zero or near to it—and the bridge had been bleached of all color. But a man's shadow lay obliquely across the bridge. He must have been walking there, the movie announcer said, when the bomb vaporized him. . . We know he was there, however, the announcer went on, because the man's shadow had protected the bridge at the instant of highest intensity. . . I took it all in. . . It was either the most horrifying thing I have ever seen—or I was young enough to more fully absorb the horrors. At any rate, Hiroshima entered me by way of the eyes, by dint of a shadow. That shadow still lives today in my mind. (1990, p. ix)

According to Terr, this singular moment in a movie theater had a profound and continuing impact on her life. One way that the event continued to express itself was through psychological symptoms of traumatic stress:

> From the moment I saw that newsreel, if a light was turned on in the middle of the night or if a sudden noise awoke me from sleep, my heart would start pounding at once even before I awoke. I would breathe in gasps, sweat, and say to myself, "This is it. The bomb." I would lie there for a minute—until I could orient myself—and I would wait to be vaporized. I still have that symptom today. I suppose it's not so bad anymore. . . But the symptom still exists—and at least once a year that same horror comes to me, "This is it! The bomb!" (pp. ix–x)

Terr's memory of the Hiroshima newsreel also influenced her life plans. She became a psychiatrist whose specialty is children's reactions to trauma, and she traced her professional development in part to her own trauma in the movie theater many years earlier: " as soon as I began my training in psychiatry, I started doing research on childhood trauma . . . part of it, I must confess, was in order to better know myself, the self I had become after Hiroshima. I write this book as a child psychiatric researcher. . . But I was impelled to the book as a fourth grader at a Saturday afternoon movie matinee" (p. x).

This event, so vividly represented in memory, exerted a lasting influence on Terr's life. What other types of experiences are likely to produce similarly vivid memories and similarly dramatic effects? To begin to address this question it is helpful to distinguish between two components of Terr's experience: the original event as she perceived it; and the characteristics of the memory itself, including its particular form, content, and mode of expression, the circumstances in which the memory comes to mind, and the ways that it may influence feelings and behaviors outside of conscious awareness. These two components—event and memory—are of course intimately connected, because the characteristics of the event are inferred from Terr's memory report. Nevertheless, it is possible to distinguish between questions that focus on properties of events—"What kinds of events are likely to be long remembered and to have a lasting impact?"—and questions that focus on properties of memories—"How is the episode represented in memory? How does the memory come to influence the life course? What psychological functions are served by remembering the event, and how are these functions revealed in thought and behavior?" In the sections that follow, these two components—events and memories—will be considered in turn.

*

Momentous Events

Terr's memory of the Hiroshima newsreel illustrates several key characteristics of personal event memories. The original event was delimited: it occurred at a particular moment in time and a specific place. Terr's personal circumstances in the movie theater are clear in her mind, even though the event occurred many years earlier. A striking and somewhat paradoxical aspect of Terr's traumatic episode is its perceived strong impact on her life despite its short duration. The experience was brief and circumscribed, yet the memory persisted and its influence was apparently felt for decades.

The adjective *momentous* captures the sense of importance, definiteness, and brevity that is characteristic of memorable episodes. In everyday usage, "momentous" is synonymous with "very important" (*Webster's New World Dictionary*, 3rd College Edition, 1988). The noun *moment* commonly refers to a definite point in time ("She entered at that very moment"), although it can also convey a sense of importance ("This was the moment we had been waiting for"), and, at least historically, could indicate a determining influence or turning point in a course of events (*The Oxford English Dictionary*, 2nd Edition, 1989), or an originating cause or moving force (*Funk and Wagnall's New "Standard" Dictionary of the English Language*, 1954).

How did importance or influence come to be linked with brevity of occurrence? According to Noah Webster's original 1828 edition of *An American Dictionary of the English Language* (Volume II), the word "moment" "is contracted from motamentum, or some other word, the radical verb of which signifies to move, rush, drive, or fall suddenly, which sense gives that of *force*. The sense of an instant of time is from falling or rushing." Hence forceful motion implies brevity and suddenness. By extension, special influence may be attributed to an event that occurs suddenly or "all at once" rather than over an extended period of time. When a car travels 100 yards at high speed before crashing into a wall, the time of occurrence is brief and the impact is great; when another car travels the same distance at a slower speed, the time of occurrence is longer and the corresponding impact is less. Similarly, when a life-altering event happens suddenly rather than gradually, the personal impact may be intensified. For example, Charles Darwin's worldview was suddenly altered after he witnessed a major earthquake in Chile: "[in] one second of time [the earthquake] has created in the mind a strange idea of insecurity, which hours of reflection would not have produced" (Janoff-Bulman, 1992, p. 55).

Psychological reactions of survivors of the atomic bombing of Hiroshima and Nagasaki provide clear, although extreme, examples of the connection between suddenness and impact. Decades after the bombs landed, the survivors (*hibakusha*) continue to confront major problems, including "learning to live with their memories and learning not to fear the future. Some people refuse to leave their houses, some can't hold

jobs, some suffer from nightmares, some experience depression or anger" (Silberner, 1981, p. 297). These persistent, intensely negative effects
are not simply the result of the large number of deaths—a comparable
number of people died in the fire-bombing of Tokyo, but the long-term
psychological devastation appears to be far less. One explanation why
the atomic bomb attacks were especially devastating is that "the de-
struction occurred all at once, in such an unexpected and incomprehen-
sible manner and wiped out all social structures. . . 'The damage was not
limited to August 6,' says a Hiroshima social worker, 'The life cycle was
destroyed beyond repair'" (Silberner, p. 297). Horrible memories of that
life-altering moment have persisted for decades. Toyoko Sugano was in a
military factory sewing officers' uniforms when the bomb exploded: "I
tend to forget so many things these days, even money spent just a few
minutes ago, so I tie things around my waist. But I still remember my
experience" (Silberner, p. 298).

If Terr's second-hand exposure to the horrors of Hiroshima had occurred gradually, say over the course of a fourth-grade unit on World
War II, rather than in one sudden viewing experience, would the impact
on her psychological functioning and approach to life have been as
intense? The notion that singular moments, such as the horror experienced indirectly by Terr during a Saturday movie matinee, can strongly
influence the life course appears to conflict with Tulving's commonsense assessment that "knowledge of the world, by and large, is more
useful to people than are personal memories" (1983, p. 52). From this
perspective, the directive force of Terr's Saturday afternoon trauma pales
alongside the lifetime of general learning experiences that prepared her
for a career in psychiatry. Nevertheless, it would be premature to dismiss the potential influence of particular events summarily, without
first achieving a more advanced scientific understanding of the specific
episode.

The idea that brief, pinpointed episodes are potential, even likely,
underlying causes of profound and lasting alterations in the course of
events is not without scientific precedent. Two prime examples come
from the natural sciences. The universe is now thought by many to
have originated out of the Big Bang. According to astrophysicist Michael Turner, scientists claim to know what happened seconds after the
Big Bang occurred, but the first 1/100,000 of a second following the Big
Bang is the key to understanding the universe's ultimate fate ("A Very
Brief History of Time," 1993, p. 36; no author). Similarly, a viable expla-

nation for the disappearance of dinosaurs is the impact of a huge mete-
orite which dramatically lowered the temperature on earth, rather than
a prolonged evolutionary process of extinction. Although the critical
incident is thought to have occurred 68 million years ago, paleobotan-
ist Jack Wolfe used fossil records to identify the probable time of year
when the impact took place: "Reproductive stages reached by the fossil aquatic plants at the time of death suggest that freezing took place
in approximately early June" (Wolfe, 1991, p. 420). Summer turned into
winter on that spring day, which led to a chain of environmental
changes that eventually killed off the dinosaurs. Clearly, research and
grand theory in the physical sciences are able to incorporate the notion
of momentous events; there ought to be a place for similar ideas in the
scientific study of human lives.

Momentous events have been studied extensively in two psychological domains: experiencing trauma directly, and learning about shocking, public events. These two categories of experience in no way exhaust
the possible types of influential life episodes. In the psychological literature, both personal traumas and public tragedies have been defined by
external criteria. Most people would agree that wartime horrors or rape
qualify as genuine traumas, and that a presidential assassination is a
public tragedy. But many, perhaps most, of the momentous events in
people's lives are neither devastatingly traumatic nor newsworthy. The
events are influential because of the way in which they intersect with a
person's particular circumstances at the time of occurrence. Terr was not
the only person who viewed the Hiroshima newsreel. Although the film
was undoubtedly moving for many viewers, its impact was not uniform
on all who saw it. For Terr, at age 9, the movie struck a deep and reso-
nant chord; when memorable events fall within the boundaries of ordinary human experience, part of the puzzle is determining why they are
momentous.

Momentous events are defined by retrospective evaluations of the
people who experienced them. We may accept Terr's claim that the
Hiroshima newsreel changed her life, but we cannot conduct a controlled experiment in which her life plays out in the absence of this
critical incident. The reliance on retrospective reports raises questions
about both accuracy and causality. Do memories of momentous events
closely resemble the original events, or are grossly inaccurate personal event memories commonplace? What is the causal relationship
between the original events and the perceived life changes that fol-

low? These questions will be addressed after momentous events and personal event memories have been described, defined, and illustrated more fully.

Trauma

On rare occasions, people suffer a terrible and devastating experience that has a far-reaching effect on their lives. Psychotherapist Shelley Neiderbach was driving to her Brooklyn Heights home when she paused at a red light. Two teenagers approached the car: "One guy stood in front of the car; another pointed the gun at my head through the window. I only fully comprehended what was going on when he tapped on the window and said, 'Move over or I'll blow your head off'" (Goleman, 1992, p. 66). The men entered the car. One drove off while the other held her by the neck and repeatedly smashed her skull with a revolver. Before losing consciousness, Neiderbach opened the door of the car, now traveling at 30 mph, and leaped out.

This harrowing experience left deep psychological scars. Neiderbach felt compelled to recount the episode to friends repeatedly. She was hospitalized for severe depression and was treated by a series of therapists. Years later, the trauma of that shocking one-time confrontation on a routine ride home still played a role in Neiderbach's life: "There is always a little piece hanging around. I just recently became able to tolerate the New York street-corner window washers. I was driving down the West Side Highway one day, and it was pouring, I looked and saw only a solitary figure in the road. The paranoia started again" (Goleman, 1992, p. 66).

Neiderbach's experience fulfills psychological definitions of a traumatic event:

> At the moment of trauma, the victim is rendered helpless by overwhelming force. When the force is that of nature, we speak of disasters. When the force is that of other human beings, we speak of atrocities. . . Traumatic events are extraordinary, not because they occur rarely, but rather because they overwhelm the ordinary human adaptations to life. Unlike commonplace misfortunes, traumatic events generally involve threats to life or bodily integrity, or a close personal encounter with violence and death.   (Herman, 1992, p. 33)

For Terr, "'psychic trauma' occurs when a sudden, unexpected, overwhelmingly intense emotional blow or a series of blows assaults the person from the outside. Traumatic events are external, but they quickly become incorporated into the mind. A person probably will not become fully traumatized unless he or she feels utterly helpless during the event or events. . . Externally generated terror, or trauma, often continues to exert a specific, ongoing influence on attitudes and behaviors—sometimes for the remainder of the person's life" (Terr, 1990, pp. 8, 35–36).

Traumatic events have a "bigbang" quality: the survivor's life is abruptly and violently altered. The effects are not subtle; they can permeate the entire fabric of existence. A survivor of the Cambodian holocaust was continually plagued by depression, suicidal thoughts, sleep disorders, and thoughts of killing her children. Three years after leaving Cambodia, she "did not want to hear, see, or be reminded of anything that happened in Cambodia. . . Everything she heard brought back bad memories. She had noticed no changes in these symptoms over 3 years. Any exposure to these events brought back her symptoms as intensely as if she were experiencing them for the first time" (Kinzie et al., 1984, p. 647). Another survivor, who was 13 years old when Hiroshima was bombed, vividly remembered the hideous details decades later. She commented on the devastating long-term impact: "Frequently, we survivors find ourselves responding to situations in our present life with emotions rooted in an experience that is now nearly 40 years old" (Thurlow, 1982, p. 645).

Sexual attacks leave similarly long-lasting emotional scars. Many rape victims experience months or years of anxiety, fear, depression, sleeplessness, and sexual disturbances. Adults who were sexually assaulted as children by former Catholic priest James R. Porter described deep and prolonged depression, suicide attempts, drug abuse, broken marriages, and loss of all religious beliefs (Franklin and Matchan, 1993). Victims of "acquaintance rape" may take years to recover from the experience. According to one survivor, "now I have a really hard time trusting any men. My red flags go up if a man shows any interest in me, even the man who strikes up a conversation with me in the grocery store" (Bass, 1991, p. 6). Another woman is continually plagued by the memory of being raped and physically assaulted by her husband. "It never goes away. If you read something in the paper about someone being raped or see a movie, you go into your memories and begin removing yourself from the people around you" (Bass, p. 6). In a study of ten preschool children who were reportedly sexually abused in a day-care setting, seven "evidenced sudden acting or feeling as if the traumatic event were re-occurring due to environmental stimuli," and nine "demonstrated an intensification of symptoms by exposure to events that symbolize or resemble the traumatic event" (Kiser et al., 1988, p. 647).

Nine months after hurricane Andrew devastated southern Florida in 1992, children still showed symptoms of post-traumatic stress disorder. According to a school principal, "Every time we have high winds, children start to cry. A few weeks ago, we had a tornado watch and I had fifth- and sixth-graders coming into my office in hysterics. We have some children who talk about dying and have retreated into themselves. Other children are constantly burning themselves, and it almost seems intentional" (Boyd, 1993, p. 25).

A defining characteristic of momentous events is brevity or suddenness. Yet some of the traumatic experiences described here appear to have loose time boundaries. Sexual abuse or physical torture, for example, can occur repeatedly, and the physical discomforts brought about by natural disasters can persist for weeks or months. Yet even in instances when trauma is prolonged, specific moments appear highlighted in victims' memory narratives, embedded within the broader tragedy. According to Herman (1992, p. 187), "For survivors of prolonged, repeated trauma, it is not practical to approach each memory as a separate entity. There are simply too many incidents, and often similar memories have blurred together. Usually, however, a few distinct and particularly meaningful incidents stand out."

Survivors are plagued by detailed images of particular instances, which protrude from the global misery and despair of the extended time period. A survivor of the Nazi holocaust recounted this detailed memory:

> I had a brother, he was 16 or 17 years old. He was taller than I, he was bigger than I, and I said to him, "Son, brother, you haven't got no working papers, and I am afraid that you will not be able to survive. Come on, take a chance with me, let's go together.". . . When I came to the gate where the selection was, then the Gestapo said to me. . . "You go to the right." I said, "This is my brother." He whipped me over my head, he said: "He goes to the left." And from this time I didn't see anymore my brother. . . I know it's not my fault, but my conscience is bothering me. I have nightmares, and I think all the time, that the young man, maybe he wouldn't go with me, maybe he would survive. It's a terrible thing, it's almost 40 years, and it's still bothering me. . . God forgive me!   (Langer, 1991, pp. 32–33)

Other memorable moments are superficially less consequential, but they seem to capture a horrible truth. An Auschwitz survivor remembered a brief encounter: "And I remember I was standing there after five or six days that we arrived, and somebody tapped me on the shoulder, and looked at her, and I burst into crying. It was my sister-in-law! There were one million women [an exaggeration, of course], there were about 35 blocks [barracks], one million women all looked alike, no hair, some of them naked—and my sister-in-law says hello to me!" (Langer, 1991, p. 24).

Japanese-Americans who spent extended periods of time in U.S. internment camps during World War II remember particular instances of fear and sadness. Fifty years later, one survivor "recalled the day she came upon the evacuation notice nailed to a telephone pole in the California town, now called Fremont, where she was born and raised. 'It sure made me feel like I was an enemy,' she said." Another victim recounted a specific indignity: "When a friend outside the camp sent [the victim] a package of sanitary napkins, a military police officer felt every pad with his hand, searching for something. 'Those are the things that rankle,' she said" (Adams, 1992, pp. 1,4).

For victims of extended periods of trauma, intrusive memories pose a major barrier to achieving a sense of well-being and normalcy. A survivor of the Nazi holocaust described her continuous struggle with memory: "I feel my head is filled with garbage: all these images, you know, and sounds, and my nostrils are filled with the stench of burning flesh. . . It just won't go away. . . I talk to you and I am not only here, but I see Mengele . . . and I see the crematorium and I see all of that. And it's too much; it's very hard to get old with such—so ungracefully, because that has anything but grace, those memories, you know. It's very hard" (Langer, 1991, pp. 53–54).

Any serious attempt to understand the psychological experience of survivors must address the persistence and impact of detailed memories of particular instances as well as more global psychological manifestations of trauma.

Hearing the News

Not all memorable moments focus on trauma directly involving the self. Following a shocking and consequential public event, such as a presidential assassination, natural disaster, or even a dramatic turning point in professional sports or the arts, people frequently remember not only factual information about the event but also their own personal circumstances at the instant they "heard the news." In 1899 Colegrove interviewed people about their recollections of the assassination of President Lincoln. Although 33 years had passed since the shooting, the event was vividly remembered. One respondent reported:

> My father and I were on the road to . . . in the state of Maine to purchase the "fixings" needed for my graduation. When we were driving down a steep hill into the city we felt that something was wrong. Everybody looked so sad, and there was such terrible excitement that my father stopped his horse, and leaning on the carriage called: "What is it, my friends? What has happened?" "Haven't you heard?" was the reply—"Lincoln has been assassinated." The lines fell from my father's limp hands, and with tears streaming from his eyes he sat as one bereft of motion. We were far from home, and much must be done, so he rallied after a time, and we finished our work as well as our heavy hearts would allow.   (pp. 247–248)

A memory of hearing about the assassination attempt on President Reagan, given 7 months after the 1981 shooting, reflects world changes in the intervening century, but the general form of the narrative is very similar to the Lincoln example:

> On the afternoon it occurred, my husband and I were returning from a holiday in the Caribbean and had reached the Miami airport. We were standing in line to check baggage or tickets or something, with other people near and people passing to and fro. I heard a man next to me say to his companion "You heard about the President," and the other one say something like "Yes, have they got the guy who shot him?" I cannot recall the exact wording but I know that I had learned someone had shot President Reagan and some news about it already existed. My immediate reaction was "Oh, God, here we go again," and then a feeling of resignation, depression, we have been through this before and it was terrible, and an ironic recall of the superstition that Presidents elected in years 00, 20, 40, 60, 80, etc. will not finish their terms alive. We boarded the plane before we heard any more, and then I was asked by a young couple, visably shaken, if I knew anything. Shortly after the plane took off the captain made an announcement giving all the information he had up to that time.   (Pillemer, 1984, p. 64)

Although researchers may differ in their assessments of the accuracy of these "flashbulb memories" (Winograd and Neisser, 1992), the phenomenon of sharply delineated memory of personal circumstances is widespread. Almost everyone has a personal story of the shooting of President Kennedy or of some other major news event. Researchers have examined how people heard the news of the Kennedy assassination (Brown and Kulik, 1977), the assassination attempt on President Reagan

(Pillemer, 1984), the 1986 explosion of the Space Shuttle *Challenger* (Bohannon, 1988; McCloskey, Wible, and Cohen, 1988; Neisser and Harsch, 1992; Warren and Swartwood, 1992), the 1986 assassination of Swedish Prime Minister Olaf Palme (Christianson, 1989), the 1989 California earthquake (Neisser et al., 1996), the 1989 Hillsborough football disaster in which spectators were crushed (Wright, 1993), the 1989 bombing of Iraq by the United States (Weaver, 1993), and the 1990 resignation of British Prime Minister Margaret Thatcher (Conway et al., 1994). Conway (1995) recently reviewed this expanding corpus of research.

In their original "flashbulb memory" paper, Brown and Kulik (1977) hypothesized that any event that is shocking and is judged to be highly important or consequential will be recorded initially in sensory rather than narrative form. If the event is subsequently thought about or talked about, a narrative description of one's personal circumstances and reactions will be constructed and preserved through repeated retellings. As the authors specifically acknowledged, personal shocks—including the death of a close relative or a serious accident—also share the qualities of surprise, high consequentiality, and frequent verbal and mental rehearsal. Brown and Kulik speculated that one and the same underlying memory mechanism accounts both for vivid memories of events in which we are centrally involved and memories in which the central action takes place elsewhere. "Probably the same 'Now Print!' mechanism accounts both for the enduring significant memories in which one has played the role of protagonist and those in which one has only been a member of an interested audience of millions" (1977, pp. 98–99). What gives flashbulb memories of public events their unusual quality is their content, which focuses on mundane personal circumstances that are not linked in a meaningful way to the facts of the newsworthy event itself. Colegrove's respondent was traveling in Maine when he heard the news of Lincoln's death, and his long-lasting memory image was far separated both in location and meaning from the fateful events in Washington.

Brown and Kulik's speculations notwithstanding, similarities and differences between direct and indirect exposure to a shocking occurrence have yet to be studied fully. Comparisons of "experienced" and "reported" events suggest that memories of these two types of occurrences do in fact differ in some respects (Larsen, 1988). For example, flashbulb memories of how one heard the news of a public tragedy appear to be factually less consistent over time than memories of tragedies experienced personally. People who directly experienced the 1989 California earthquake had highly consistent memories of this event a year and a half later, whereas people who only heard the news of the earthquake showed more evidence of memory distortion or loss (Neisser et al., 1996).

Although highly celebrated examples of flashbulb memories involve landmark public tragedies, memories of hearing the news more commonly focus on important personal rather than national events. The news of a personal misfortune frequently comes indirectly rather than through immediate exposure. I was not actually present when my mother died, but my memory of receiving the phone call still has a distinct flashbulb quality—my immediate surroundings are vividly represented—not unlike my memory of hearing about President Kennedy's death or the Space Shuttle explosion. Other events that are newsworthy only within a circumscribed context include serious illness of a loved one, wedding and birth announcements, and college acceptances.

The distinction between public and personal newsworthy events is further blurred by the fact that reactions to, and memories of, a public tragedy are colored by the strength of one's perceived personal connection to the target event. Brown and Kulik found consistent differences between African-American and Caucasian respondents in the incidence of flashbulb memories: many more African-Americans than Caucasians remembered hearing the news of the assassination of Malcolm X, and African-Americans rated this event as more consequential than did Caucasians.

Similarly, the murder of Boston police officer Walter Schroeder in 1970 was generally newsworthy, but especially meaningful for police officers. When Katherine Ann Power pleaded guilty to manslaughter in 1993 in connection with Schroeder's death, memories were vividly reinstated: "For many police officers who still recall where they were on Sept. 23, 1970, when Schroeder was shot in Brighton, Power's 23-year flight has spanned the life of their careers—at once an angry shadow and a bitter memory." Said one officer, "The memory of a fallen brother is a hard one. It is a memory we live with forever" (Ellement and Coakley, 1993, p. 1).

Baseball players were greatly moved by the shocking 1994 news that Philadelphia Phillies player and World Series hero John Kruk had been diagnosed with cancer. Boston Red Sox pitcher Ken Ryan has a sharp memory of when he heard the news: "I found out last night. I was lying in bed. The TV was on, but the sound was down low because the baby was sleeping. I look at the screen and I see John hitting a home run. Then I see his picture. Then the word 'cancer.' By the time I turned the sound up, they were on to another story" (Ryan, 1994, p. 41).

The disastrous Cocoanut Grove nightclub fire of 1942 is a well-known landmark in Boston history, but news of the disaster held special significance for people whose lives were connected in some way to the tragedy. A doctor recounted this memory some 50 years later: "I remember well that Thanksgiving day. We had a wonderful meal in the hospital, and then I came down with [food poisoning]. I was still in bed on Saturday night, when I got a call from Dr. Charles Lund, chief of surgery, and he told me no matter how I felt, I had to get to ER [emergency room] immediately, something terrible had happened." For this doctor, the news reception event was quickly followed by the direct experience of trauma: "By the time I got there, two house officers were already at the door, sorting the patients into living and dead, stacking the dead along one side of the hall, the living on the other" (Montgomery, 1992, p. 34).

Although hearing the news is not the same as "being there," it would be a mistake to assume that getting the news second-hand necessarily saps an experience of authenticity, emotional intensity, and meaning. Public tragedies such as the Kennedy assassination have strong emotional effects on large numbers of people (Wolfenstein and Kliman, 1966). Similarly, children who are exposed only indirectly to violent crimes by viewing televised news accounts may show clinical manifestations of trauma. A study of children's reactions to media coverage of the 1993 kidnapping and murder of 12-year old Polly Klaas in California documented that many children were still haunted by lingering thoughts of the crime two months later. According to Sara Stein, the Stanford psychiatrist who conducted the study, theories of trauma must incorporate the notion of indirect or vicarious influences: "This kind of rocks our perception of trauma—kids can be affected by being exposed to the news of a traumatic event, not just by being directly involved" (Bass, 1995, pp. 1, 9). Similarly, Terr (1990) identified symptoms of vicarious trauma in children who were informed about other people's misfortunes. One 9-year-old girl only heard about an injury suffered by her grandmother during an earthquake, but the event had a strong psychological impact nevertheless: "And Lois did not see anything, not Grandma's bandaged nose, not the collapsed house, none of it. But Lois *did* see the picture in her 'mind's eye.' And the event, vicariously experienced as it was, had made its mark" (p. 317).

In a recent study of the psychological impact of direct versus indirect exposure to a violent crime, victims of a life-threatening restaurant hold-up were interviewed along with close family members or intimates with whom they had discussed the event. Significant others as well as victims manifested signs of emotional distress months after the event occurred (Rierdan, Losardo, Pillemer, and Penk, 1995). In a parallel vein, therapists who regularly treat victims of trauma may themselves experience distress symptoms, including intrusive thoughts and acute emotional discomfort, that closely resemble their patients' distress (McCann and Pearlman, 1990). Therapists do not listen passively to the news of their patients' traumas; they actively process and internalize a good deal of what they hear. So violent or traumatic events experienced secondhand, whether the actual victim is a world leader, a patient, or a loved one, can have psychological effects that rival the impact of direct experience.

When a newsworthy event receives intense and detailed media coverage, the general public vicariously shares in the flashbulb memories of celebrities. In 1991 basketball superstar Magic Johnson abruptly announced that he was retiring because he had contracted the AIDS virus. Because of the extensive media exposure, the public had access to the initial reactions of Johnson's famous friends. Fellow superstar Michael Jordan heard the news directly from Johnson on his car phone: "I'm almost driving off the road because I couldn't handle it as well as he could. I told him I loved him and my family's with him, and whatever we can do, we're willing to do that" (Romano, 1991, p. 30). Johnson himself described how his celebrity friends received the news: "Larry [Bird] cried. So did Arsenio [Hall]. Isaiah [Thomas] just didn't want to believe it. Pat [Riley] and Michael [Jordan] listened in stunned silence" (Goodwin, 1991, p. 41). Even sportswriter's initial reactions were public knowledge: "My heart was still thumping. My stomach was still upside down. Two hours after I heard the news and my body was telling me something was terribly wrong" (Madden, 1991, pp. 51, 55).

The fascination with sharing stories of "how we heard the news" is so widely recognized that it is a target of parody. In Gary Larson's *The Far Side,* a caption to a 1993 cartoon reads: "More facts of nature: All forest animals, to this very day, remember exactly where they were and what they were doing when they heard that Bambi's mother had been shot."

Each animal tells its own story: the snake was "under a rock, getting ready to shed," the rabbit was "in the glen, just finishing a new burrow when I got the news," the raccoon was "looking for crawdads in my favorite creek," and the possum was "just getting ready to cross the interstate."

Media sensationalism creates defining moments not only for the general public but also for the newsmakers themselves, sometimes with tragic consequences. In 1986 Donnie Moore was a pitcher for the California Angels baseball team. The Angels were playing the Boston Red Sox for the American League championship. At a critical point in a pivotal game Moore threw a pitch that opposing player Dave Henderson hit over the fence for a home run, and California went on to lose the series. Moore was booed by his home fans for the rest of his career. Three years later, in 1989, he killed himself with a gunshot to the head.

Was Moore's tragic death linked to one fateful pitch in a baseball game? His friends and acquaintances believe so. The *Boston Globe* article on Moore's suicide began, "Donnie Moore, the man who threw The Pitch, is dead," and an Associated Press story led with "Tormented by the memory of one pitch. . . ." As Moore's agent commented, "Ever since Henderson's home run, he was extremely depressed. He blamed himself for the Angels not going to the World Series. . . Even when he was told that one pitch doesn't make a season, he couldn't get over it. That home run killed him." A teammate's bitterness was directed to the media coverage of the event: "He wasn't treated fairly. . . Nobody remembered the great things he did. All they remembered was that one pitch. And it ruined his life" (Shaughnessy, 1989, p. 33).

Some people will question the post-hoc identification of one pitch, however important the baseball game, as a causal factor in Moore's death. Henderson, the player who hit the momentous home run, believed that other contributing factors existed: "I guess there's a connection [with the pitch]. I heard he had a lot of family problems and everything. I'll tell you what—baseball can't be that serious that you'd take your life. There's got to be a lot of other stuff" (Shaughnessy, 1989, p. 33). Yet it was not simply "one pitch," it was a pitch made momentous and memorable by the negative national attention it drew.

Although the Donnie Moore incident was unusually tragic, it is not an isolated occurrence. In the 1986 World Series Boston Red Sox player Bill Buckner committed a fielding error at a critical moment. In 1993 Buckner decided to move from his home in Massachusetts, in part because of the lingering memory of his blunder: "It's been almost seven years since his error ended the apocalyptic, cataclysmic Game 6 of the 1986 World Series, and Buckner says he's tired of hearing about The Error. . . 'I'm definitely out of there. I don't want to hear it anymore.'" Buckner attributed a large part of the blame to media sensationalism: "You guys are the worst. Media. Television. You bring it up all the time." But from the sportswriter's perspective, there is simply no escape: "The reality is that Buckner is doomed to spend the rest of his life hearing about *it*. There is no safe house when you are a symbolic figure of a singular, whopping moment of failure. There is nothing fair about it, but this is the way it works" (Shaughnessy, 1993, p. 53). Buckner, like Moore, is held prisoner by the collective memory of one ill-fated momentous event.

Critical Incidents

Most momentous events are neither devastatingly traumatic nor newsworthy. They simply occur as part of the ongoing flow of life events, and their special significance is identifiable only by examining the belief systems they inspire. McAdams has written about *nuclear scenes,* defining moments that stand out from the backdrop of usual experience:

> Our lives are punctuated by certain incidents—some of them seemingly critical or formative and others seemingly mundane—which we draw upon to define who we are, who we were, and perhaps who we are to become. . . These incidents may be highly positive or negative. They may mark perceived transformations of self—identity turning points—or they may affirm perceived continuity and sameness. They may involve things we did or things that were done to us. They may entail private moments or a shared experience with an entire community.　(McAdams, 1988, p. 133)

Life-changing insights can be triggered by unlikely circumstances. In 1992 Morris Smith was the whiz-kid 34-year old manager of the largest mutual fund in the United States, Fidelity Investment's 20-billion dollar Magellan Fund. In 1994 Smith was living in Israel, his days as "the single most visible portfolio manager in America" (Bronner, 1994, p. 25) left far behind. Smith traced his career shift to a stroll up a grocery store aisle: "the idea of leaving high finance and spending a year in Israel came to Smith while shopping on the day before Passover . . . as he was working his way up the supermarket aisles—it was Good Friday so the financial markets were closed—Smith realized how long it had been since he had done something as satisfyingly mundane as shopping" (Bronner, 1994, p. 28).

Basketball superstar Michael Jordan had a low-point or "nadir" experience (McAdams, 1988, p. 141), as a sophomore in high school. When the roster for the varsity basketball team was posted, Jordan's name was absent: "It was embarrassing, not making that team. They posted the roster and it was there for a long, long time without my name on it. I remember being really mad, too, because there was a guy who made it that really wasn't as good as me . . . Leroy Smith." The image of that embarrassing moment of defeat had a continuing effect on Jordan: "Whenever I was working out and got tired and figured I ought to stop, I'd close my eyes and see that list in the locker room without my name on it, and that usually got me going again" (May, 1991, p. 105). Leroy Smith, the player who took Jordan's place, also has the scene clearly in mind: "I can still remember that day, when we looked at the names. I really thought I'd make the JV [Junior Varsity] team, and when I saw my name on the [Varsity] list, and I didn't see Mike's, I was totally surprised. It really hurt Mike and he was definitely dejected, because he should have made it" (p. 110). The seemingly unfair rejection could have pushed Jordan away from basketball, but instead it became a powerful and persistent motivator.

Not all critical incidents are linked directly to life plans. Some events are special because of the symbolic meaning they communicate. As a high school student, Tom Brokaw, anchor of NBC *Nightly News,* experienced a striking moment of personal connection with his father. Brokaw's family had driven 8 hours to see him play in the state basketball tournament, but the coach had chosen to keep him on the sidelines. Brokaw remembered his parents' reactions to his misfortune:

> I glanced up at the huge crowd and by chance made eye contact with my mother. She offered a silent expression of great sympathy. My father, sitting next to her, began to smile, then looked left and right to be sure no one was watching. When the coast was clear—how to put this delicately?—he subtly, but clearly, flashed a prominent middle digit of his right hand. We shared a hearty laugh, just the two of us, a very private moment amid the thousands caught up in the frenzy of the game. Father and son connected as surely as if he had carried me around the arena on his shoulders.   (Brokaw, 1991, p. S 9)

A memory of an influential college experience recounted by a participant in a questionnaire study (Pillemer et al., 1996) demonstrates the potential symbolic meaning of an activity as mundane as getting a haircut:

> I had really long hair when I first came to Wellesley. I had always wanted to try having my hair short, however. After breaking up with my boyfriend and feeling like I really needed a change in my life, I got enough courage to do it. I went downtown with a picture of a girl in a magazine and showed it to my hairdresser. I closed my eyes and just listened to the radio while she cut all of my hair off. I remember her accent, she was from the Soviet Union, and she had long curly black hair. I remember talking to her about her family and how they came over to the States and had been separated for so long. I couldn't believe I was letting someone do something so drastic to my hair. I remember walking back to campus, feeling very good and smelling the leaves that had fallen from the trees and listening to the wind rushing past my face (not blowing any hair around!). I felt like a *new* person and I was excited about all the changes I was finally making in my life.

These events are difficult to categorize or taxonomize as a group, precisely because their meaning is defined locally by particular circumstances. Nevertheless, some common characteristics are discernible. Morris Smith's leisurely shopping experience illuminated a troubling aspect of his current life style, whereas Michael Jordan's failure to make the varsity team spurred him on to excel in basketball. In both instances the event was momentous, at least in part, because it suggested a direction for future activities; when the event was revisited in memory, the directive was reinstated. Memories of critical incidents can provide a number of different types of directives: they can originate a plan of action (an originating event), point to a new direction (a turning point), provide the basis for a continuing set of beliefs or feelings (an anchoring event), or provide a useful analogy for understanding and responding to new situations (an analogous event). (Directive functions served by remembering momentous events are described more fully in Chapter 3.)

Extreme trauma does not require a special vulnerability on the part of the victim in order to have a lasting impact. In contrast, understanding why selected everyday incidents prove to be momentous for particular people is more difficult. Not all basketball players would see a moment of failure as a motivating challenge, nor would most stock portfolio managers find inspiration for a career change in the supermarket. Although it is hard to identify a priori which everyday life occurrences are likely to be memorable and influential, it is possible to identify general life circumstances or "critical periods" when people are especially susceptible to the influence of specific episodes (Bandura, 1982; Pillemer et al., 1996). During times of persistent dissatisfaction about a current life path, a specific incident may instigate an action that was imminent. Morris Smith's revelation in the supermarket probably did not come out of the blue; he may have been ready for a change, and the supermarket incident triggered it.

Psychologist George Miller provided another example of a triggering incident. Miller was the overworked and disenchanted chair of Harvard's Psychology Department when he had a momentous encounter with his colleague B. F. Skinner: "One day I ran into Fred Skinner in William James Hall. I must have looked pretty bad. 'Are you all right?' he asked. 'I'm exhausted,' I said. And then, in a sudden burst of candor, I told him how exploited and overworked I felt. Maybe I hoped he would volunteer to help. Fred listened with patient interest. 'Yes,' he said, 'you are something of an empire builder, aren't you?' That was when I decided to leave Harvard" (Miller, 1989, pp. 413–414).

People also are highly susceptible to external influences when they are in a period of transition or uncertainty. Situational cues—how others behave, what others say—may provide prescriptions for behavior. Unlike triggering events which precipitate an imminent course of action, the direction of change often does not appear to be predetermined.

Major life transitions, such as entry into college, are fertile periods for casual yet highly influential incidents (Pillemer, Rhinehart, and White, 1986; Pillemer, Goldsmith, Panter, and White, 1988; Pillemer et al., 1996). Decisions may be made abruptly, in direct response to external suggestions. In a pilot study conducted at Wellesley College, a student explained her choice of a major: "When I was coming in as a freshman and they asked for a tentative major, my mother spotted psychobiology. 'That would be good for you,' she said. 'Okay,' I said, relieved at not having to make the choice all on my own. I have just stuck with that choice." Another student recounted how her academic focus shifted:

> I had been interested in psychobiology and there were no psychology nor biology classes that I was really interested in taking. So I was a little upset and I talked to a good friend of mine, who said, well, since I'm not interested in any, any of these majors, why don't I create a major? And I couldn't think of anything to create, so she took into account my personality, and she decided for me that I would major in Middle Eastern Peace Studies . . . putting together everything that, that I'm interested in. So I thought that sounded

good and I'd give it a shot. So I went to and I spoke to two professors and my dean, and they all loved the idea. So . . . I did it.

One has the feeling that the outcome could have been very different had the mother of the first student or the friend of the second student made different suggestions, or had the sought-after input come from other quarters. (The idea of critical periods during which people are especially susceptible to episodic influences is explored in Chapter 3.)

A dramatic example of how a critical incident can help to resolve uncertainty comes from the world of politics. In 1990 Boston University President John Silber and William Weld were engaged in a spirited contest for Governor of Massachusetts. Although the polls identified a Silber lead shortly before the election, voters were wavering in their convictions. One week before the election, Silber was interviewed in his home by a highly respected and well-liked television news anchor, Natalie Jacobson. Silber responded angrily to a seemingly innocuous question, giving the public a startling glimpse of a troublesome aspect of his character: "'It was clearly one of those definitive moments,' said Arnold Zenker, a local media consultant. . . 'My wife was leaning toward Silber, but after that interview, she said, Not on your life!. . . Nobody thinks of Natalie as a barracuda-type interviewer. For Silber to jump on her was like jumping on an 88-year-old grandmother'" (Reidy, 1990, p. 59). Silber lost the election by a slim margin. The troublesome and memorable incident involving Jacobson may have influenced voters who were highly attentive to even peripheral events that could help to resolve their uncertainty.

Insight

Some memories record a moment of internal illumination or sudden insight—an epiphany, to use a term from literary studies (Abrams, 1988). Episodes of personal revelation punctuate the narrative flow of contemporary autobiographies. Filmmaker Leni Riefenstahl experienced an epiphany the first time she heard Hitler speak, when he gave a public address in 1932: "The instant she heard his voice, she tells us, 'I had an almost apocalyptic vision that I was never able to forget. It seemed as if the earth's surface were spreading out in front of me, like a hemisphere that suddenly splits apart in the middle, spewing out an enormous jet of water, so powerful that it touched the sky and shook the earth. I felt quite paralyzed'" (Simon, 1993, p. 27).

Novelist Ellen Glasgow described the thunderbolt of attraction that she felt for a stranger whom she had not yet met, and the dramatic change in world view that followed:

> It was in [a friend's] charming drawing room (how vividly I can still see it!) that the flash came from an empty sky, and my whole life was transfigured. Like all other romantic episodes, great or small, in my life, this began with a sudden illumination. . . One moment the world had appeared in stark out-lines, colorless and unlit, and the next moment, it was flooded with radiance. I had caught that light from the glance of a stranger. . . I remember shrinking back, as I entered the room; and when we were introduced, I scarcely distin-guished him from the man with whom he was talking. Then, gradually, I noticed that he kept his eyes on me . . . however hard I tried, I could not keep my glance from turning in his direction. . . What I knew, through some vivid perception, was that the awareness was not on my side alone. . . In the years before my youth was clouded by tragedy, I had known an attraction as swift and as imperative; but not ever the permanence, and the infallible certainty, as if a bell were ringing, 'Here, now, this is my moment! (Glasgow, 1992, pp. 390–391)

Moments of illumination frequently have a self-reflective quality. The people affected appear to be self-consciously aware of and even startled by the intensity of their ideas and feelings. A participant in a study of influential college experiences (Pillemer et al., 1996) described one such event:

> I remember one day in late October. It was a Saturday. It was a beautiful crisp autumn day. I remember that it was Saturday and that I was walking to the Science Center from [my dorm] to do a calculus problem set. I remember that I was extremely depressed because a friend of mine had just gotten raped. I felt very angry, very upset, very helpless and I remember that as I was walking a leaf fell off of a tree and floated down near my head and I remember realizing at that moment that no matter what kind of terrible things happen in the world, leaves still fall off of trees, and seasons still change, and every-thing always goes like that, and there I was going off to a problem set. I remember feeling all that when I saw that falling leaf. It was an overwhelm-ing feeling that sometimes comes back to me now.

Self-reflection is the focal point of a memory of an insight that psy-chologist Fritz Heider had in early childhood: "I must have been about two years old when I had a flash of insight about having a *self*, about being a person. I was sitting on a little footstool in a sort of nook formed by the doors between two rooms. My father was reading to my older brother, and I felt left out, frustrated. I remember the awareness that it was *I* who was frustrated, and this discovery of the self made it an exciting experience" (Heider, 1989, p. 127).

Psychologist Margaret Washburn reported a similar childhood revelation: "It seems to me that my intellectual life began with my fifth birthday. I remember a few moments when I was walking in the garden; I felt that I had now reached an age of some importance, and the thought was agreeable. Thinking about myself was so new an experience that I have never forgotten the moment" (Washburn, 1992, p. 131).

Creative discovery or invention frequently involves an intellectual breakthrough experience, what Simonton (1988) has called "unexpected illumination" (p. 29). Like flashbulb memories of newsworthy events, recollection of the discovery includes not only the substance of the insight, but also the precise physical circumstances when the breakthrough occurred: "So dramatic are such spontaneous revelations that the precise moment in which the successful permutation emerges is commonly remembered in unusual detail. We see this . . . in Darwin's *Autobiography* when he reminisced about when he arrived at his solution to the problem of the origin of species: 'I can remember the very spot in the road, whilst in my carriage, when to my joy the solution occurred to me'" (Simonton, 1988, p. 30).

Sometimes the insight appears in the presence of new data. Russell Hulse, winner of the Nobel Prize for physics in 1993, "never forgot the moment the odd new pulsar showed up on the radio data. 'It was a very exciting thing to have happened as a graduate student,' said Hulse" (Chandler, 1993, p. 8). Neurobiologist Gary Lynch recalled a similar moment of discovery: "Gary Lynch clearly remembers the evening in 1971 when Sarah Mosko came to him in the hallway with one of the slides. He held it to the light and saw a band that, if his interpretation was correct, represented newly grown neural connections. 'I absolutely couldn't believe it,' Lynch said some fifteen years later. 'You could see the effect with the naked eye. It was that big'" (G. Johnson, 1991, p. 34).

In many other instances, the idea surfaces outside the usual context of scientific work. Linguist Noam Chomsky described the sudden realization that his analytical approach was misguided:

In retrospect I cannot understand why it took me so long to reach this conclusion—I remember exactly the moment when I finally felt convinced. On board ship in mid-Atlantic, aided by a bout of seasickness, on a rickety tub that was listing noticeably. . . It suddenly seemed that there was a good reason—the obvious reason—why several years of intense effort devoted to improving discovery procedures had come to naught, while the work I had been doing during the same period on generative grammars and explanatory theory, in almost complete isolation, seemed to be consistently yielding interesting results. (Newmeyer, 1986, p. 30)

Simonton (1988) discussed an early questionnaire study (Platt and Baker, 1931) in which episodes of unexpected illumination were commonly recounted by distinguished scientists. This example is typical of the kind of responses received: "Freeing my mind of all thought of the problem I walked briskly down Tremont Street, when suddenly at a definite spot which I would locate today—as if from the clear sky above me—an idea popped into my head as suddenly and emphatically as if a voice had shouted it" (Simonton, 1988, p. 30). Although such insights may be subjectively experienced as coming "out of the blue," Simonton has argued that subliminal environmental cues may play a role:

Once a scientist has entered into an incubation period with respect to a certain problem, extraneous stimuli in the environment may introduce new elements into the permutations, either directly or indirectly through a divergent train of associations. . . Because most of this haphazard influx is subliminal, the scientist may not realize that the insight that appeared apparently without warning may actually have been elicited by some recent external stimulus. . . This possibility may help explain why the illuminations so often come when the scientist is engaged in some totally irrelevant activity, such as a walk in the woods or vacation travel, for just such circumstances would offer new input into the permutations in the guise of diverse recollections. (1988, pp. 36–37)

The genesis of an idea can be momentous even for those witnessing it at second hand. Barbel Inhelder, frequent collaborator of famed child psychologist Jean Piaget, described one of Piaget's moments of scientific discovery:

Apart from our effective collaboration, I had also sometimes the rare joy of being present at the birth of new ideas. Piaget often needed a (not necessarily competent) listener, since he felt that his ideas became clearer when he explained them to somebody else. I remember with excitement a hike along a glacier at sundown, both of us proceeding with the slow gait of the mountaineer, when Piaget developed his central ideas of what was to become the three volumes of the *Introduction à l'Epistemologie Genetique*. (Inhelder, 1989, p. 222)

Moments of scientific insight can occur in childhood as well as in adulthood. Noted astronomer Cecilia Payne Gaposchkin vividly remembered the time when, as a child, she discovered a rare flower:

The Bee Orchis was growing in the long grass of the orchard. . . Instantly I knew it for what it was. My mother had told me of the Riviera—trapdoor spiders and mimosa and orchards—and I was dazzled by a flash of recognition. For the first time I knew the leaping of the heart, the sudden enlightenment, that were to become my passion. I think my life as a scientist began at that moment. I must have been about eight years old. More than 70 years have passed since then, and the long garnering and sifting has been spurred by the hope of such another revelation. . . These moments are rare, and they come without warning . . .   (Gaposchkin, 1992, pp. 249–250)

Although the examples of sudden insight presented here are taken primarily from scientific autobiographies, similar experiences occur in other domains of invention and creation. Popular singer and songwriter William "Smokey" Robinson recounted a moment of inspiration that had occurred decades earlier, when he finished the hit song, "Tracks of My Tears." Robinson had obtained a sound track, but he was stuck on the lyrics:

I couldn't get an idea for it so I went and actually recorded the [sound] track. I still had no song, no idea, and I would just listen to the track over and over again. So one day I was listening to it at home alone and the chorus came to me: "Take a good look at my face. You'll see my smile looks out of place. If you look closer it's easy to trace." I had no ending. Easy to trace what? I toyed with that for a few days. One day I was in my car and I was driving along and it just came like out of nowhere: "The tracks of my tears."   (Robinson, 1993)

Robinson also recounted how another hit song was inspired by a friend's misstatement:

"I Second That Emotion" was started during the Christmas holidays. The guy who wrote the song with me—Al Cleveland—and I were good friends and we were just Christmas shopping one day. . . And there is an old saying, "I second the motion." . . . So we're in the department store and we're shopping and we're having a conversation with one of the salesgirls . . . somebody said something during the course of that conversation and Al Cleveland said, "Oh, I second that emotion." And we laughed because he had gotten the thing wrong. He said, "I second that *emotion*." . . . We walked away from the counter and I said, "Hey, man. I second that emotion. What a great title for a song." So we went home and started to write it.   (Robinson, 1993)

Why are personal circumstances accompanying a sudden insight often remembered so vividly? The insight is accompanied by strong feelings—emotion terms abound in the descriptions. It marks an intellectual or artistic turning point and, as such, is frequently mulled over and shared with others. In addition, pinpointing the exact moment of discovery allows one to claim intellectual ownership: the discovery was a tangible event and it happened to me at a particular time and place, even if there is no external marker of the moment of achievement. Recounting personal circumstances when the idea was born is one way of documenting that "I made the discovery."

*

Memory Representations

The broad question posed earlier—"How are momentous events represented in memory?"—is the focus of the rest of this chapter. Momentous events include dramatically different types of life experiences, ranging from violent physical assault to the sudden birth of a scientific idea, but the memory representations of these disparate events share certain core, defining qualities. The characteristics of personal event memories as defined here are an expansion of Tulving's (1983, 1993) conception of *episodic* memory, Brewer's (1986, 1988) *personal* memory, and Nelson's (1993) *autobiographical* memory.

Tulving (1983) defined episodic memory as involving "unique, concrete, personal experiences dated in the rememberer's past" (p. v.). Recently, he updated this conception by adding an emphasis on conscious awareness in remembering: "Episodic memory . . . makes it possible for a person to be consciously aware of an earlier experience in a certain situation at a certain time. . . The act of remembering a personally experienced event, that is, consciously recollecting it, is characterized by a distinctive, unique awareness of reexperiencing here and now something that happened before, at another time and place" (1993, pp. 67–68). Thus, knowing that you arrived at college on a particular day, or correctly identifying an item from an experimentally presented word list as one that appeared on an earlier list, may not qualify as episodic memory unless the act of remembering is accompanied by a conscious awareness of having arrived at college or having previously seen the target word.

Brewer's (1986, 1988) concept of personal memory expands upon the core concept of episodic memory. A personal memory is "a recollection of a particular episode from an individual's past" (1988, p. 22); it approximates a "'reliving' of the individual's phenomenal experience during the earlier episode" (p. 22); it usually involves visual imagery and affect; it represents an event that occurred at a specific time and place, whether or not the event can be dated retrospectively or located precisely; and it is accompanied by the beliefs that the event was personally experienced and that the memory is veridical.

Nelson (1993) identified autobiographical memory as a subcategory of episodic memory. Certain events have a privileged status in memory because they matter to the individual's evolving "life story." In contrast to mundane episodes that are quickly forgotten, autobiographical memory is "specific, personal, long-lasting, and (usually) of significance to the self-system . . . it forms one's personal life history" (p. 8). Consistent with Brewer's definition, event representations need not be accurate to qualify as autobiographical memories: "Memories do not need to be true or correct to be part of that system" (p. 8).

These overlapping definitions provide the basis for the description of personal event memories adopted in this book. The term *personal event memory* was favored over other contenders on several counts. In cognitive psychology, episodic memory often refers to accurate memory for a specific test item, such as a word from an experimentally presented list, without any reference whatsoever to the subjective experience of remembering. Flashbulb memory has come to be associated primarily with memories of learning about newsworthy events, and the term misleadingly suggests an all-inclusive record (Pillemer, 1990). Autobiographical memory and personal memory are general terms whose common meanings do not capture the emphasis on specific events. Brewer (1996) recently attempted to resolve the ambiguity in terminology by suggesting that researchers adopt the term "recollective memory," but recollect is a synonym for the general term "remember," and it too fails to reflect the emphasis on specificity.

The defining characteristics of personal event memories are as follows:

- The memory represents a *specific* event that took place at a particular time and place, rather than a general event or an extended series of related happenings.

- The memory contains a *detailed* account of the rememberer's *own personal circumstances* at the time of the event.

- The verbal narrative account of the event is accompanied by *sensory images*, including visual, auditory, olfactory images or bodily sensations, that contribute to the feeling of "reexperiencing" or "reliving."

- Memory details and sensory images correspond to a particular *moment* or moments of phenomenal experience.

- The rememberer *believes* that the memory is a truthful representation of what transpired.

Two additional characteristics described by Nelson—that the memories are long-lasting and important for the self system—will apply to most memories of momentous events, but these concepts are too labile to be included as part of the formal definition. How long must a memory last in order to be considered autobiographical? What if the memory is consciously accessible at some life periods and not others? How should we classify a long-lasting memory whose importance for the self system is unclear? Memory persistence and significance will be addressed throughout the remainder of this book, but they can be omitted from the definition of personal event memories with little cost.

The definition of personal event memories may seem at first glance to apply to a narrow set of vividly remembered events, but in fact the five qualities are defining characteristics of what is usually meant by "remembering" any particular episode. Consider the question, "Do you remember any specific events that occurred during your college years?" Respondents will know where and when they attended college, what courses they took, who their friends were, what the campus and familiar faculty members looked like, and other general information. But to give a convincing response to a question about specific college episodes, one must remember and recount a detailed memory of personal circumstances at the crucial moment: where and when the event occurred, what was seen, heard, and felt, and so forth.

An experience recounted by a Wellesley College alumna provides a vivid illustration of the core qualities of personal event memories:

> I remember sitting in X's class on the day that a midterm . . . was handed back. I was a freshman and felt that I was in over my head. The professor gave a stern lecture on the value of good writing before she handed back the papers. As she reproached us, my terror grew because her remarks seemed to be personally directed at *me*. I was from a small town, did not have the same background as anyone in my class, and had immediately felt my inadequacies when class began in September. Suddenly she turned and looked directly at me—I thought I would die of humiliation. Then she said, "But Y has answered the question well and has an unusual lyrical and personal style that enhanced her answer." I couldn't believe that she was talking about my pa-

per, but she was. I can still envision that dimly lit little room in the bottom of Z and smell its peculiar musty odor. I can still picture her stern but kind face and feel the relief and pride that I felt at that moment.   (Pillemer, 1992b, p. 252)

Not all personal event memories are as detailed and fully elaborated as in this example. Nevertheless, the basic characteristics of personal event memories are still identifiable. The description of personal circumstances may be highly selective, and the imagery (accounts of what was seen, heard, smelled, or felt) may focus on one sensory modality only, "but remembering some fragment of personal experience is probably necessary to feel and believe with conviction that 'I was there'" (Pillemer, 1992b, p. 239). In order to qualify as a personal event memory, it must be clear that the memory represents the phenomenal experience of a specific, one-moment-in-time event, even if that moment is embedded in a more general description of related experiences. Distinguishing between specific personal event memories and more general autobiographical memories is in most cases relatively straightforward: when independent raters are asked to divide personal memories into specific and general categories, they can do so at an acceptable level of agreement (Pillemer et al., 1986; Pillemer et al., 1988; Williams and Broadbent, 1986).

Several aspects of the definition of personal event memories invite further analysis and explanation. First, personal event memories appear to involve two levels of representation: image and narrative. What is the relationship between these two modes of memorial expression? Second, personal event memories need not be accurate representations of objective reality, so long as they are *believed* to be veridical. What are the consequences of eschewing concerns about absolute accuracy in favor of belief? Third, personal event memories document not only central themes or meanings of past episodes, they also contain idiosyncratic peripheral details of personal circumstances. What is the adaptive significance of remembering minutiae in addition to core information? These three issues are addressed below.

Memory Images

The usual communicative form for sharing personal event memories is the narrative: people talk and write about them. But the phenomenal experience at the time of a momentous occurrence is not primarily verbal; things are seen, heard, and felt. Telling the story of what happened requires that the primarily nonverbal, imagistic input be *translated* into a coherent, story-like, verbal memory narrative.

Clinical studies repeatedly point to the presence of an underlying sensory component of highly emotional memories. Janoff-Bulman (1992) observed that trauma survivors vividly reexperience past episodes: "These thoughts and memories are involuntary, persistent, recurrent, and psychologically disturbing, and they are virtually universal among those who have experienced extreme, negative life events" (p. 104). The memories are represented imagistically: "Intrusions in daily thoughts are typically visual memories and images of the traumatic event" (p. 108). Similarly, Terr (1990) reported that "psychic trauma victims are cursed with an unstoppable tendency to 'see' their traumas" (p. 140). The presence of imagery is pervasive: "After traumatic experiences, children repeatedly 'see' what happened to them. These visions, accurate or inaccurate, are brought on when the child visits a place where the event occurred, when someone else mentions the traumatic episode, when something connected with the trauma comes to mind through association, and when the smells, the atmosphere, and the season renew a sense of 'being there'" (p. 138).

Gold-Steinberg (1994) analyzed women's abortion narratives. Regardless of whether the abortions were legal or illegal, the memories were replete with sensory details. The women "could recount experiences fifteen to twenty-five years in the past and provide compelling, precise, and often visceral detail" (p. 26); they remembered "sounds, smells, the quality of pain, and the words spoke to them on the day of the procedure. One woman recalled eating doughnuts afterward, others described the noise of the machinery or the feel of someone holding her hand as a gesture of support" (p. 264).

Memories laid down under less extreme circumstances are also commonly characterized by the presence of visual or other forms of sensory imagery. Most people who remembered the assassination attempt on President Reagan 1 or 7 months after the shooting had a visual image of what they were looking at when they heard the news; about one-fourth of the respondents described other forms of sensory imagery (Pillemer, 1984). Rubin and Kozin (1984) analyzed undergraduate students' clearest autobiographical memories; most respondents reported sharp images. Brewer (1992) summarized the research on flashbulb memories and concluded that "most and perhaps all flashbulb memories are associated with strong visual imagery" (p. 285). Goldsmith and Pillemer (1988) asked undergraduate students to describe vivid memories of spoken statements heard at any time in their pasts. A majority of respondents reported having both visual and auditory images associated with the memories: most could visualize the situation when they heard the statement, and they claimed they could still "hear" the words being uttered.

Brewer (1988) conducted an extraordinarily detailed study of memory for randomly sampled events. College students wore beepers for 13 days. The beepers sounded at random intervals and students recorded information about the ongoing events in their lives at those instances. Several weeks later, memory of the sampled events was assessed using cued recall or recognition. The results indicated a strong relationship between belief in the veridicality of the memory and sensory imagery: "when subjects are confident of their memory on autobiographical memory tasks of this type, they give strong reports of phenomenal experience during the recall process" (pp. 66–67). Students who were highly confident of their recall always reported strong visual imagery. When students were less confident in their memories, ratings of visual imagery were lower. In addition, accurate recall was associated with high levels of visual imagery. Neisser and Harsch (1992) examined memories of the space shuttle disaster and also found a strong positive relationship between the vividness of visual imagery and memory confidence.

Research studies on the whole have shown that memories of momentous events are almost always accompanied by visual imagery, and quite often with other forms of relived sensory experience. They support Johnson's (1988, p. 391) claim that "thinking about events . . . typically involves activation of perceptual (especially visual) qualities," and Rubin's (1995b, p. 157) assertion that "imagery is a central feature (as close to a defining feature as one can get) of what most people mean by the term autobiographical memory." A person recounting a momentous event does not simply present a narrative account of what was seen, heard, or felt; he or she can "see" the situation, "hear" what was said, and "feel" the accompanying emotions. The empirical findings cited support the idea that personal event memories, although communicated to others in narrative form, have a core imagistic component. Brewer's linking of memory confidence to strong visual imagery supports the conjecture made earlier, that people evaluate the quality of their own memories in part by the availability at recall of detailed information about how the original event was personally experienced. If visual or other sensory images are readily available, enabling the rememberer to mentally reexperience the event, then the event is judged to have happened and to be a veridical record. Nevertheless, vividness does not guarantee accuracy; for example, the perceptual characteristics of delusional memories recounted by psychiatric patients are extremely strong, and their very vividness may mislead the patient into believing that they really happened (David and Howard, 1994).

The common presence of perceptual, imagistic representation alongside narrative suggests that personal event memories are the blended productions of two functionally distinct but interacting memory systems. Speculatively, an early-developing memory system which records perceptions, images, and feelings may provide the raw material for a later-developing, higher-order, narrative memory system. (The idea of dual memory systems is examined in Chapter 4.)

Accuracy

Do vivid memories of momentous events accurately represent actual experiences? Most of the memory functions examined in this book do not depend on absolute veridicality, and it is not feasible to undertake here a definitive and exhaustive review of the scientific literature on memory accuracy. But it is safe to say that memory researchers do approach a consensus on some issues. There is widespread agreement that memory is an active, reconstructive process rather than a passive, reproductive process. In the process of constructing a memory narrative, errors can occur. At the same time, memory, for the most part, does its job; that is, memory descriptions usually are consistent with the general form and content of past experiences, even if particular details are lost, added, or distorted in the act of remembering. Schwarz and Gilligan (1995, p. 22) provided an apt summary: "Most memory research . . . is really about the distortion of details, not central events. A person hit by a car may misremember its color, or the day of the week, but will rarely confuse being hit by a car with, say, falling down a mountain."

Heuer and Reisberg (1992) reviewed laboratory and naturalistic studies of vivid memories of highly emotional events. They concluded that emotional memories, although not infallible, are often broadly accurate: "Emotion leads to the exclusion from memory of some information. . . What *is* remembered about emotional events, however, seems to be remembered fully and well. . . . Emotion provides no guarantee of permanent or perfectly accurate recall—emotional memories will contain errors and will eventually be lost. Nonetheless, we believe it likely that we can largely trust our vivid memories of emotional events" (p. 176).

Individual studies of memories of important life episodes are generally consistent with this conclusion. One might expect, for example, that adults' memories of early childhood would be especially vulnerable to gross reconstruction. Although examples of memory distortion do exist, including the creation of false childhood memories through suggestions made by a family member or therapist (Loftus, 1993), studies in which memories are elicited without strong outside interference indicate that those memories that do persist into later life are likely to be generally truthful. Usher and Neisser (1993) elicited college students' memories of salient childhood events—a hospitalization, sibling birth, death of a family member, and making a family move. They also contacted the students' mothers and asked them to rate the accuracy of their children's memories. Although the data demonstrated the usual pattern of "amnesia" for the earliest childhood years, with little information remembered before the second birthday, "most responses were judged to be accurate and only a small fraction [12%] were definitely wrong" (p. 163). Sheingold and Tenney (1982) also found that children's memories of a sibling birth generally agreed with mothers' recollections.

Howes, Siegel, and Brown (1993) asked college students to describe their earliest childhood memories. Another person or "verifier" who had been present at the time of the event was then asked to confirm the accuracy of the memories. Many of the recollections were in fact corroborated: "The majority of earliest childhood memories emerged here as apparently accurate recollections of real events. Thus the assumption of a standard or frequent distortion factor in infantile recall was not supported" (p. 108). The high level of verification may have been due to the salience of the experiences; most of the memories involved "striking external events" that were memorable for the verifier and the rememberer alike.

In an extensive review of the scientific literature on the validity of memories of early childhood experiences, Brewin, Andrews, and Gotlib (1993) concluded that, although autobiographical memory can be flawed, "the evidence supports the view that adults asked to recall salient factual details of their own childhoods are generally accurate, especially concerning experiences that fulfill the criteria of having been unique, consequential, and unexpected" (p. 87). The authors noted that some psychotherapeutic models "assume some basic integrity to autobiographical memory," and that "it is reassuring that this assumption is supported by the research we reviewed" (p. 94).

Naturalistic studies of memory for salient events occurring in adulthood also point to a considerable degree of memory integrity over time. For example, Yuille and Cutshall (1986) evaluated the accuracy of eyewitness reports of a shooting that had occurred 5 months earlier. In contrast to the experimental literature on eyewitness testimony, in which witness fallibility has been emphasized, the authors concluded that "most of the witnesses in this case were highly accurate in their accounts, and this continued to be true 5 months after the event. . . The salience and uniqueness of this event probably played a major role in producing vivid memories. . . We suggest that the relatively high accuracy rates found in this study may have been due, in part, to factors usually absent in experimental research: a particularly salient event with obvious life and death consequences, and the opportunity for active involvement by some witnesses" (p. 299).

Brewer's (1988) mammoth study of memory for randomly sampled autobiographical events, described earlier in this chapter, also supported the idea that memories are generally trustworthy: "The qualitative analysis of autobiographical recalls found few overt recall errors and thus supports a partly reconstructive view of autobiographical memory . . . which suggests that recent personal memories are reasonably accurate copies of the individual's original phenomenal experiences" (p. 87).

It has not been possible to assess the accuracy of flashbulb memories of newsworthy events, because what "actually happened" rarely can be confirmed independently. Instead, researchers have measured a related characteristic: memory consistency over time. Most studies reveal some instances of memory distortion, but at the same time have shown reasonably high overall levels of consistency over months or years (Bohannon and Symons, 1992; Conway et al., 1994; McCloskey et al., 1988; Pillemer, 1984).

In contrast, Neisser and Harsch's (1992) study of memories of the explosion of space shuttle *Challenger* in 1986 showed substantial inconsistencies over time. College students recounted their memories the morning after the explosion and again approximately 2 1/2 years later.

A quarter of the respondents gave a completely different memory at time 1 and time 2, and many other memories were only partially consistent. A possible explanation for the unusually high incidence of incorrect memories in this study involves what Brewer (1988, 1992) has called "wrong time slice": "The subject remembers a real event, but that event was not the occasion on which he or she first heard about the explosion" (Neisser and Harsch, 1992, p. 27). For example, a respondent may have heard something initially about the explosion in a college class, and then gone back to her room and witnessed the vivid details on television. Because Neisser and Harsch administered the first memory questionnaire more quickly than was done in other flashbulb memory studies (within one day of the explosion), initial sources of incomplete information, such as the classroom discussion, could still be recalled. Years later, however, the student may have forgotten the initial, unconfirmed mention of the explosion in class and instead clearly remembered viewing the tragedy on television. In this instance, the memory is accurate even though preceding events were forgotten. The fact that a number of Neisser and Harsch's participants shifted the source from a non-TV informant to a TV informant over the intervening years supported the "wrong time slice" explanation.

A second possible explanation for the relatively high incidence of memory inconsistency in Neisser and Harsch's study, and for inconsistencies in other flashbulb memory studies, is that only some of the participants perceived the target event as consequential or personally meaningful. Conway et al. (1994) examined flashbulb memories of learning that British Prime Minister Margaret Thatcher had resigned in 1990. People who reported strong affective reactions and judged the resignation to be highly important often had memories which remained consistent over an 11-month time interval. In contrast, people who attached less emotion and importance to the event exhibited memory inconsistency and reconstructive errors. Participants who lived in the United Kingdom were much more likely to have consistent memories than were residents of other countries.

The data base represented in this brief overview of research findings is limited, in part because of a dearth of empirical studies of momentous personal events. There frequently is no obvious way to verify idiosyncratic experiences of trauma, hearing the news, critical incidents, and insight. Because a detailed, objective record of what happened to individual people during a momentous event rarely exists, researchers have often relied on others present at the scene for memory validation; when these others are family members, stories may agree because they have been jointly recounted over the years. In the absence of verifying information, researchers have settled for an assessment of memory consistency, which in no way guarantees that the memory accurately represents the original event. An individual may consistently remember an event that was initially perceived and encoded inaccurately (Terr, 1990), or that was reconstructed shortly after its occurrence. Furthermore, these studies say relatively little about the accuracy of memories of extreme emotional trauma.

Despite these qualifications, research supports a conclusion that fits nicely with commonly held conceptions of human memory: memories of personal life episodes are generally true to the original experiences, although specific details may be omitted or misremembered, and substantial distortions occasionally do occur. Schacter (1996) put it well: "On balance, however, our memory systems do a remarkably good job of preserving the general contours of our pasts and of recording correctly many of the important things that have happened to us. We could not have evolved as a species otherwise" (p. 308). In a court of law, inaccuracy of even minute details can have profound consequences, and a blanket assumption of memory accuracy or authenticity would be ill-advised. But in most everyday situations absolute accuracy is not required. It is not important to know for certain whether Lenore Terr saw a newsreel about the bombing of Hiroshima precisely on a Saturday. Accuracy of memory for date of occurrence could be critical if a crime had been committed, but the influence of the memory on Terr's life is little affected by the veridicality of precise temporal information. In instances such as this, reported events are similar enough to original circumstances to allow for meaningful analyses of memory function.

Peripheral Details versus Central Themes

The definition of personal event memories includes detailed images of concomitant circumstances. Yet personal details often appear to be irrelevant to the core meaning of a recollection: "In most instances of daily remembering, it is meanings and not surface details that we must recall" (Neisser, 1982b, p. 16). The view that autobiographical memory preserves core truths even as details are distorted or lost is captured by a scene in the film *The Night of the Shooting Stars* (De Negri, 1982). A mother recounts to her tiny infant her childhood memories of the Fascist reign in Italy. In closing, she offers this qualification: "My story ends here, my love. I don't know if things happened exactly like that. I was only six then. But the story is true." Research studies support a similar conclusion: that the central themes of momentous events usually are faithfully recorded in memory, even though details may be lost or distorted. Why, then, are minute details so often represented in autobiographical memory? What comparative adaptive advantages are afforded by remembering peripheral details?

One view holds that specific details, although interesting or amusing when telling the story, are largely irrelevant or even injurious to a basic function of memory, which is to record the past in a way that usefully informs future behaviors. Ross (1991) discussed Titchener's view that "image accuracy that is too precise is deleterious to the formation of organized memories" (p. 18). According to Titchener, "It is, in reality, because the image breaks up, because the nervous impressions are telescoped, short-circuited, interchanged, suppressed, that memory, as we have memory, is at all possible"; were our memories to contain exact copies of earlier perceptions, "our mental life would, so far as we can imagine it, be an inextricable confusion of photographically accurate records" (Ross, p. 18).

Several research studies have demonstrated how remembering details can interfere with assessing more central themes. Murphy and Balzer (1986) had college students view videotapes of graduate students presenting lectures and then rate the teachers on a number of dimensions, such as grasp of material or organization and clarity. Some videotapes were rated immediately after viewing, and some were rated the following day. A group of "expert raters"—in this case, graduate students—also evaluated the performance of the teachers after multiple viewings. When college students' ratings were made after a delay rather than immediately, they agreed more closely with the graduate students' expert ratings. The loss of specific details from memory appeared to enhance the global validity of performance evaluations: "We argue that under certain conditions, raters may depend on their general impressions of ratees rather than on their memory for specific details, and that these schematic evaluations may preserve a greater proportion of valid information, as compared with irrelevant detail, than is available immediately after observing ratee behavior" (p. 39).

Garner, Gillingham, and White (1989) had adults read a passage about insects and then recall "just the really important information."

Half of the participants read a passage that contained "seductive de-tails"—interesting details that were irrelevant to the main themes of the text—whereas other participants read a text without seductive details. Readers exposed to seductive details were far less likely to include main ideas in their recalls: "It appears that, even for very skilled adult readers, seductive details can disrupt macroprocessing enough to cause readers to miss what a passage is about, globally speaking" (p. 49).

The idea that remembered details can be misleading rather than re-vealing casts a new light on Brown and Kulik's (1977) speculative evolu-tionary model. Brown and Kulik proposed that memory of personal details accompanying consequential and emotional events would have high survival value for primitive humans. For example, if a member of the group was attacked by a dangerous carnivore, remembering where the injury occurred, what activity brought on the attack, and other details such as lighting, smells, and sounds could be essential in identi-fying and avoiding similarly dangerous situations in the future.

Although vividly remembering life-threatening encounters would ap-pear to have obvious survival value, it could be disastrous if life-and-death reactions to potentially dangerous situations were made primarily on the basis of minute details. Suppose that a life-threatening animal attack occurred at twilight, when the victim was resting by a waterhole, and was preceded by alarmed bird calls. A detailed memory would pro-vide a valuable record of potential danger, but it would be maladaptive to link fear and avoidance exclusively to the *exact* circumstances at that moment. Because idiosyncratic details will vary from encounter to en-counter, future avoidance of parallel dangers could not be based on exact pattern matching. Nor could it involve an extended, deliberate, purposeful analysis of minutiae. At times of high emotion, concomitant details may be automatically recorded in memory alongside more gen-eral structural characteristics; but it would not have been adaptive for our ancestors to focus narrowly on minute details to the exclusion of more global characteristics of life-threatening encounters.

To understand the special functional significance of remembering personal details in the lives of modern humans, we must look beyond survival pressures that acted upon early humans. Unlike the model pro-posed for our ancestors, in which life-or-death choices were made auto-matically on the basis of memory representations of prior experiences, modern functions of remembering and recounting personal circum-stances—to sharpen communicative intent, to provide a mental frame of reference and point of comparison for future decisions and actions, and to modulate emotional reactivity (Pillemer, 1992b)—frequently (but not always) involve the use of language, conscious awareness, and deliberation. It is in this modern linguistic and cognitive context that the purposes of remembering peripheral details are especially apparent.

Memories of apparently trivial details can fulfill important psychological functions which are distinct from the deliberate transmission of central messages. In prelinguistic cultures it would have been difficult to share with others the subtle nuances of remembered episodes. Once events could be represented linguistically, humans were capable of exchanging detailed event descriptions, and memory sharing came to serve culturally important functions in its own right, apart from the transmission of information essential for day-to-day survival. Sharing minute details of past experiences transmits meaning over and above the explicit message of an interaction (Pillemer, 1992b). Linguist Deborah Tannen (1990), for example, described the "power of details" in conversation, and the ways in which the act of sharing remembered minutiae can signal intimacy, caring, or romantic intent. (Communicative functions of sharing detailed recollections are analyzed in Chapter 5.)

A functional analysis of memories of peripheral details provides one explanation for their susceptibility to distortion, which is greater than that of memories of central themes. Survival in the modern world depends on the accurate representation of the core characteristics and meanings of critical episodes, but the social, emotional, and directive functions served by remembering minutiae often do not depend on absolute veridicality. Different life situations have varying social and emotional demands, and the form and content of memory sharing may be shaded accordingly. Loftus and Kaufman (1992, p. 216) commented on this possibility: "When we repeatedly recount the flashbulb, we do so in an everchanging environment. Our specific listeners change, and thus the type of information we include also changes. Our needs to impress people, or to gain their empathy, or to reduce tension is not the same from one occasion of retelling to the next. As the story changes, does the memory change with it?"

Although Brown and Kulik (1977) emphasized the survival value of remembering personal circumstances during momentous events, modern purposes served by detailed remembering and recounting stretch far beyond basic survival pressures. Contemporary functions served by remembering specific episodes in expansive detail, and by sharing the memories with others, are explored throughout this book.

Chapter 3

*

Memory
Directives

*T*o FUNCTION effectively in new and changing life situations, people must make predictions about future events; they must construct successful plans of action; and they must access relevant past information at the moment it is most useful. This is where memory is essential. According to Schank (1990), "intelligence is really about understanding what has happened well enough to be able to predict when it might happen again. . . Comprehending events around you depends upon having a memory of prior events available for helping in the interpretation of new events" (p. 1).

Most cognitive psychologists locate the predictive and directive functions of memory in abstract knowledge structures, such as scripts, schemas, rules, or plans. The knowledge is represented in semantic rather than in episodic memory, and it is general and broadly applicable rather than specific and idiosyncratic. Scripts are "conceptual representations of stereotyped event sequences" (Abelson, 1981, p. 715) which provide general, all-purpose predictions or guidelines for what usually happens in familiar situations, such as eating in a restaurant (reading the menu, placing an order, eating, paying), meeting someone for the first time (exchanging greetings, shaking hands), or attending a college class (sitting attentively, taking notes). In contrast, autobiographical memory, with its representations of particular instances, is seen as having "its own value independent of the general memory function of prediction and preparation for future events" (Nelson, 1988, p. 267).

The emphasis in cognitive psychology on abstract knowledge structures has obscured the predictive and directive functions provided by vivid memories of specific episodes. Schank (1980) asked, "Why should scripts be the only kind of past experience that aid processing by making predictions and filling in causal chain inferences?. . . A person who has experienced something only once might well expect his or her second time around to conform to the initial experience" (pp. 42–43).

Similarly, Tulving (1983) argued that, in addition to scripts, memories of singular events can aid prediction and guide subsequent behavior: "if you have been to many dinners at 'old' Oxford colleges you may have a well-formulated script that 'contains' all sorts of relevant information about such dinners. The script permits you to answer relevant questions—for example, do they say grace before dinner?—as well as behave appropriately when you find yourself in the situation. On the other hand, if you have only been to one such dinner, you may still be able to answer many of the same questions on the basis of your recollection of the particular event" (p. 64).

A recollection of a student participant in a questionnaire study of memories of the first year in college (Pillemer et al., 1996) illustrates how a particular episode can provide general guidelines for future behavior:

> I remember coming home from the freshman scavenger hunt. The group of . . . students I was with . . . didn't have enough money to buy Senate Bus tickets in Boston to get home—We tried to take the commuter rail, but it didn't run on Saturdays. . . We got on the [subway] and off at Woodland and walked home—all 6 some-odd miles. Three or 4 of us walked faster than the rest of the group, which had grown by meeting people on the train. The 3 or 4 fast walkers barely missed dinner at the dorms—The rest of the group got a ride from someone's grandparents who lived in Wellesley. I had popcorn and apples for dinner. Now I always check bus schedules.

The student did not have to suffer through a series of similar experiences in order to develop a "trip into Boston" script that included checking bus schedules—one memorable event was enough to inform her subsequent behavior.

Scholarly emphasis on scripts is not the only reason why directive functions of remembering specific episodes have been largely overlooked. It is also because traditional memory research is unlikely to reveal the prescriptive quality of personal event memories. In the typical laboratory experiment, the "meaning" of remembering for the participant is dictated from the outside. Recalling the target items—numbers, words, stories—is the stated purpose of the research. The memories have no other functional role in the life of the participant. It is not surprising, then, that laboratory studies rarely if ever have identified directive and predictive functions associated with remembering specific life episodes. In sharp contrast to the cognitive psychology laboratory, everyday situations rarely require that information be remembered just so that memory performance can be observed—memory for the sake of remembering. Remembered events are personally meaningful, and they can have an active and enduring influence that extends beyond the immediate local context.

In the pages that follow, six functional categories of personal event memories are identified: memorable messages, symbolic messages, originating events, anchoring events, turning points, and analogous events. The categories are not mutually exclusive; memorable and symbolic messages are general categories that subsume the other memory types, and all of the categories overlap to some extent. After the memory subtypes have been described, three overarching questions are addressed: Do momentous events, and accompanying personal event memories, have a causal influence on attitudes and behaviors? When in the life course are memory directives especially likely to take hold? How do the memories described in this chapter fit within the broader structure and organization of extended autobiographical narratives?

*

Memorable Messages

Spoken statements provide the clearest illustration of memory directives. People often make pronouncements, give orders, or offer advice in face-to-face conversation, and when the speaker is powerful, respected, or loved, the words may persist in memory for years. For example, historian Simon Schama's father had his 7-year old son memorize a speech from Shakespeare's *Henry V,* which the boy then recited in front of his school. Afterwards, his father explained: "You know why I have done this? Because the spoken word is the Jews' weapon. We can't really be soldiers; we must always rely on the spoken word" (Kaye, 1991, p. 51). The long-remembered statement offers a rule of conduct: as a Jew, always rely on the spoken word. Schama adopted his father's deep appreciation of the power and value of language.

As an undergraduate student at Harvard, child psychiatrist Robert Coles experienced an identity crisis and was unsure about what career path to pursue. Physician and poet William Carlos Williams pushed Coles towards medicine: "Try medicine, why don't you. Lots to keep you busy, and lots to make you think. The great thing is—you get to forget yourself a lot of the time" (Claffey, 1989, p. 72). Williams intervened repeatedly during Coles' medical training, encouraging him to stick with medical school and suggesting that he specialize in psychiatry.

When astromoner Cecilia Payne Gaposchkin was 12 years old, she moved to London with her family. Her teacher wrote her a farewell letter: "You will always be hampered," she said, "by your quick power of apprehension." Gaposchkin interpreted the statement as a directive: "She was one of the wisest people I have ever known. I cannot count how often those words have served as a warning against hastily jumping to conclusions . . ." (Gaposchkin, 1992, p. 253).

In their original study of "memorable messages," Knapp, Stohl, and Reardon (1981) asked adults to recall spoken statements from their pasts that "seemed to have a significant impact on their life" (p. 28). Most statements contained explicit or implied rules for behavior. Respondents claimed to remember the specific moment in which the statement was uttered, and most believed that their memory of the spoken words was exact. The speaker of the directive usually was of higher status than the recipient. The messages often were perceived as being relevant in multiple life situations, and most were seen as having a long-term positive effect on the person's life course.

Goldsmith and Pillemer (1988) obtained memories of spoken statements from college students. Unlike Knapp et al. (1981), we did not ask for messages that had had a significant impact; rather, the request was simply for the first spoken statement to come to mind. In addition, students were asked for memories of a statement made by a parent, teacher, sibling, and friend. The overall proportion of memories that contained explicit prescriptions for behavior was only 17%, but almost one-half of the first parental statements that came to mind were directives.

Other researchers have observed that spoken statements are commonly remembered. In psychotherapy, "many clients refer to statements made by their parents or teachers in the past. Actual contact with these significant others may not have occurred for many years, but their statements nevertheless play a central role in the present life of the clients" (Hermans, Kempen, and van Loon, 1992, p. 29). In a study of personal narratives produced by children between the ages of 4 and 9, Ely and McCabe (1993, Study 1) analyzed instances of remembered speech. Directive speech acts, defined as "utterances addressed to a hearer in order to motivate the hearer to perform some act" (p. 677), were reported more frequently than any other type of speech act. The strong early encouragement that children receive to attend to and remember parental advice and prohibitions may increase the attention paid to directives offered by powerful others in childhood, and throughout life.

Illustrations of memorable messages abound in everyday life. Two additional examples come from the personal lives of psychologists who are themselves leaders in the scientific study of episodic memory. Elizabeth Loftus was agonizing over the decision of whether to testify for the defense in the trial of accused war criminal John Demjanjuk, known as Ivan the Terrible. Taking the case would have compromised her Jewish heritage; turning it down would be inconsistent with her extensive prior work on uncovering faulty eyewitness identification. A close friend offered some guiding words: "Do you know what Emerson said about consistency? A foolish consistency is the hobgoblin of little minds." The rule statement helped Loftus resolve her dilemma: "'The hobgoblin of little minds,' I repeated. For two days that strange phrase became my litany. I latched onto it like a lifeline, allowing it to pull me out of the quicksand of my indecision" (Loftus and Ketcham, 1991, p. 232).

Endel Tulving had been struck by a specific comment made by a colleague about the tenure prospects of a young scholar. Although the scholar's work was promising, he "had not written his book yet." For Tulving, the observation applied to his own career as well: "At the time of our conversation, I had been in the psychological research business for a long time, had published a number of papers in various journals, had been promoted to full professor. . . But I, too, had not written my book yet. Trying to conceal my embarrassment, I changed the topic of conversation, but I never quite recovered from the emotional impact of the casual comment of my friend. From that day on I started thinking about writing 'my book'" (Tulving, 1983, p. vii).

This example illustrates how memorable messages become influential through a constructive process on the part of the recipient. The colleague was not speaking about Tulving's career. Nevertheless, Tulving imposed a personal meaning on the exchange, and his interpretation of the event as it applied to his own life created the prescription for behavior. The observation that a junior colleague had not written his book yet was actively transformed into the directive: "I must write *my* book." A similar constructive process undoubtedly underlies the formation of many or even most memorable messages. The recipient of the message purposefully thinks about what was said, why it was said, and what it means within the context of his or her life at that moment. The processing of meaning is inseparable from the memory itself: the interpretation becomes the message.

A specific spoken statement need not be connected to a momentous life decision in order to be memorable; even mundane prescriptions for behavior can persist indefinitely in episodic form. For example, when I park my car in a tight space, the impulse to straighten the wheels is interrupted by the remembered voice of a friend who many years ago admonished: "Leave it there!" It is good advice, because the turned wheels allow for an easier exit. Although this situation has recurred many times, the advice was never repeated, and it has remained connected, in part, to its episodic roots.

∗

Symbolic Messages

Many memorable messages contain an explicit directive or prescription for behavior, while others more closely resemble the example provided by Tulving, in which the directive—"I must write *my* book"—was inferred rather than received directly. Speakers may not have intended to provide a directive and they may be unaware that a "message" has been delivered, but their words are memorable nevertheless. The message is created through an active, constructive process on the part of the recipient.

A memory of college offered by a Wellesley alumna illustrates how a professor's casual statement can acquire symbolic meaning:

> My first Shakespeare class . . . would have to rank as one of my most influential experiences, since it started me on the life I'm following now (graduate school in Elizabethan literature). But the memory I have from that class is very small and tight. Oh well. Although I have good feelings and good memories about the entire class (1st semester of sophomore year) I remember the first day best. I was fascinated by the easy way [the professor] roamed through Shakespeare, by just the amount of knowledge he had. He seemed to know everything. In fact, after class, I asked him if he could identify a quote I had found about fencing, "Keep up your bright swords, for the dew will rust them." Immediately he said, "*Othello*, Act 1, Scene 2 I believe." Which turned out to be exactly right. I wanted to know a body of literature that well. I'm still working on it. (Pillemer et al., 1996, p. 330)

In a follow-up question about the event's influence on her life, the alumna interpreted the episode as a personal directive: "Well, it made me an English major with a concentration in Shakespeare and a desire to teach undergraduates." Yet the directive was not provided explicitly. The professor's response to her question symbolized a level of accomplishment which she took as a model for her own professional life.

A second example is provided by journalist Anna Louise Strong, who was a fervent publicist of the Soviet Union and China in the United States during the middle of the twentieth century:

> I discovered the world in the Child Welfare Exhibit of Kansas City in 1911. . . The very same week I discovered socialism . . . in Kansas City I came to socialism backward as an employer of labor. The architectural draftsman who helped draw plans for the booths and central court of our exhibit came to me in the midst of the crowds of the opening and asked how much longer we would need him. . . "Not that I want to leave but I ought to know. As far as I can see, there's nothing for me to do after Saturday." "No, there's nothing after Saturday," I answered. . . Joyously weary with the opening, I could not sleep. The words of the draftsman came back in their full meaning. I knew he had a wife and two small children and had been without a job for months. . . How did it chance that I, a girl in my twenties and in no way related to this man, had the power to refuse him the right to a living?   (Strong, 1992, pp. 615–616)

There is nothing explicit in the "words of the draftsman" that pointed Strong to socialism, but Strong's constructed meaning of the incident led in that direction. For Strong, the memory was a symbol of the failures of capitalism.

In some instances, symbolic messages inform rather than direct. The memory illustrates an underlying truth about oneself, other people, or the way the world works. The inferred message offers insight into questions such as "What is my worth as a person?" or "Whom can I trust and depend on?" A Wellesley undergraduate offered the following memory of her freshman year in college:

> One event that has stuck in my mind over the past few years is the experience of Flower Sunday. . . The one event that day that has always left me somewhat sad is that my Wellesley big sister did not give me flowers. If she was pressed for money or hadn't had the time to get some, etc. I would have understood. However instead she said or rather announced to me that she wasn't going to give me any because she didn't think they were worth it— needless to say I was the only first year on the hall without flowers. It left me feeling that I wasn't quite as good as the others.

The older student's announcement was not intended to be an explicit commentary on the rememberer's value as a person, but the recipient interpreted it in that fashion.

Several examples follow in which a brief symbolic interaction is a commentary on the relationship between parent and child. The first example was provided by a Wellesley undergraduate:

I remember very clearly having to say good-bye to my parents. Freshman year represented my first real break from home. I remember that it was very important to me to be able to show my parents that I could adjust well—to the academic environment and to dorm life. I was absolutely determined to do it well. I was scared and homesick already when it was time for my Mom and Dad to leave. I remember being a little surprised to see my Dad's eyes well up with tears as we said good-bye. In a way that was when I really realized how important to him I am.

Anna Howard Shaw, a prominent member of the woman's suffrage movement, long remembered her father's emotional reaction upon her arrival in the United States from England at age four:

On landing a grievous disappointment awaited us; my father did not meet us. He was . . . nursing his grief and preparing to return to England, for he had been told that [our ship] had been lost at sea with every soul on board. One of the missionaries who met the ship took us under his wing, and conducted us to a little hotel, where we remained until father had received his incredible news and rushed to New York. He could hardly believe that we were really restored to him; and even now, through the mists of more than half a century, I can still see the expression in his wet eyes as he picked me up and tossed me into the air.   (Shaw, 1992, pp. 475–476)

Author and feminist Gloria Steinem remembers "coming back from one of the Eagles' Club shows where I and other veterans of a local tap-dancing school made ten dollars a night for two shows, and finding my mother waiting with a flashlight and no coat in the dark cold of the bus stop, worried about my safety walking home" (Steinem, 1992, p. 662).

All three memories demonstrate parental love and care in encapsulated, episodic form. No authoritative statements were spoken, no explicit directives were given, but in each instance a powerful and long-lasting message was communicated, a symbolic demonstration of the bonds that existed between parent and child.

*

Originating Events

Another genre of personal event memories involves origins. People frequently trace the beginning of a life path, or the birth of a set of enduring beliefs or attitudes, to a single momentous event. Memories of originating events need not carry an explicit, rule-structured directive; they inspire rather than prescribe. The memories are a source of motivation and reorientation in the pursuit of life goals. Originating events are similar to McAdams's (1988) "episodes of continuity," in which "the past nuclear episode serves as an explanation or a foreshadowing of some aspect of one's present life situation" (p. 142). Although examples of originating events presented in this chapter focus mainly on academic or career paths, similar episodes undoubtedly mark other beginnings, such as the start of a lasting friendship or love affair. In these areas as well, people often can recount when, where, and how "it all began."

Originating events frequently take place in the formative childhood years. Psychologist Jerome Bruner was 9 years old when he saw a museum display of a human form accompanied by the chemicals that make up the human body. The sign read, "Man is nothing but these chemicals." "'I thought to myself, that misses all the mystery of how it works together,' Dr. Bruner said. That childhood experience was reflected again and again in his career of searching out the mysterious in the mind" (Goleman, 1987, p. C1).

Einstein was 4 or 5 years old when he was shown a compass: "That this needle behaved in such a determined way did not at all fit into the nature of events. . .I can still remember—or at least I believe I can remember—that this experience made a deep and lasting impression on me. Something deeply hidden had to be behind things" (Bernstein, 1983, p. 297).

Janet Scudder traced the origins of her artistic career to an early childhood event:

> "What do you think it was that made you decide to devote your life to art?" a friend once asked me. . . The question sent my thoughts wandering back through the past for an answer until they stopped before the tiny figure of myself when I was about six years old. I had been out in the garden playing with the flowers. The colors evidently stirred something latent in me for I can remember, as distinctly as though it happened yesterday, the feeling of intense excitement that swept over me and carried me into the house and up to my grandmother. . . "How did they ever get these beautiful colors?" I demanded breathlessly. . . She put out her hand and touched me and then the flowers—for she had been blind for many years—and very solemnly and impressively explained that colors were given flowers by God. "He painted them!" I gasped. She nodded, still very solemn. "How?" At this time she laid down her knitting and her voice came a bit uneasily. "Why do you ask that, my child?" "Because I want to paint some just like them. I've got to! I must!" I am sure that the creative instinct was born at that moment. . . (Scudder, 1992, p. 349)

Originating events occur in adulthood as well as in childhood. At the age of 24, prominent physician Anne Walter Fearn took a trip to California that changed her life:

> On the train I was attracted by a lovely looking woman and although I never spoke to her I overheard her brilliant conversation with others. I was told that she was a "woman physician." . . . I never learned the name of the woman who made such a deep impression on me, but I never forgot her. . . In San Francisco . . . I met the orthopedic surgeon Dr. Harry Sherman. To him I poured out the story of my chance encounter and my enthusiasm for this unknown woman doctor. He suggested that it might interest me to meet a few of the women doctors of San Francisco. . . A new world was opened to me.   (Fearn, 1992, p. 528)

Anthropologist Margaret Mead described an influential interaction with psychology professor R. S. Woodworth: "When I took his psychophysical methods . . . we all sat transfixed as he made new discoveries with his back to the class, talking delightedly to himself. Later he was to ask me a question which set my feet on a path from which they have never strayed: 'When does an Indian become an Indian?' Most of the behavioral science world still does not understand that a day-old baby is a perfect day-old sample of the culture within which it is born" (Mead, 1974, p. 311).

Physician and researcher Dorothy Reed Mendenhall's interest in biology blossomed during a particular college lecture: "Harris Wilder was the first great teacher I had ever had. I well remember my feeling after his first lecture in general biology. During the entire hour I sat spellbound. I was not conscious of my surroundings and was oblivious of the passage of time. At the end of the lecture I gasped, sat up, and said to myself, 'This is it, this makes sense—this is what I have been waiting for all these years'" (Mendenhall, 1992, p. 176).

Popular rhythm and blues vocalist Luther Vandross traced the origins of his musical career to first hearing singer Dionne Warwick's voice:

> I was 13; I'll never forget it. Murray the K was the DJ, and he used to give shows at a place called the Brooklyn Fox Theater on Easter and on Christmas. . . So I'm sitting there and I'm watching the show. . . And then on stage walks this woman—this girl; young woman—in a red, spaghetti-strap chiffon evening dress—cocktail length, meaning right above the knee or right at the knee. And she started singing. . . And, I mean, the tone of her voice pierced me like a fork. It was just incredible to me. And at that moment I know I decided that I wanted to be a singer.   (Toombs, 1995, p. 13)

Originating events are not unique to prominent individuals. A student participant in a pilot study of memories of an art history course at Wellesley College reported that her life was altered by the first class meeting:

> I remember that I sat in the front row in the center section on the left half somewhere, next to my friend. . . I don't remember the *exact* material, except that it was Egyptian art and was taught by [professor's name]. She was an *amazing* lecturer—super excited about the subject, talking non-stop, and racing back and forth across the stage. The time went very quickly. . . [The professor] had gotten me so excited about art history, that I left the auditorium absolutely positive that art history was my calling in life.

A participant in a questionnaire study of memories of the first year in college (Pillemer et al., 1996) also traced the origins of her academic plans to one class meeting:

> In my first Philosophy class . . . I remember a discussion on a moral dilemma concerning a woman and two children. The woman was taking care of a friend's child and her own child while at an outing by a lake. The children are out on a canoe which capsizes, both children are drowning. The dilemma was: which child should she save? . . . [The professor] was very eloquent on the subject, and it seemed like everyone in the class was talking. He . . . looked very much like a 'philosopher.' It was in ___ (a room which has windows on three sides) and the wind blew through the room. It was very much a sensory as well as intellectual experience and was the class which made me become a Philosophy Major.

Memories of originating events convey a sense of enduring influence and even causality. The initiating episode is seen as the original motivating force behind a momentous decision. But it is possible that the memory simply represents the first conscious acknowledgment of a gradually shifting life path. Yet another possibility is that originating events are identified and selected only retrospectively; a coherent and orderly life story is constructed in which past events are spuriously linked to known outcomes. The issue of causal influence will be explored at length later in this chapter.

*

Anchoring Events

An originating event is perceived as creating, or at least contributing to, a new life course. In contrast, an anchoring event serves as a touchstone for a continuing set of beliefs about the world. The broad relevance of an anchoring event may become apparent only retrospectively, as subsequent events validate its intellectual or emotional thrust. The remembered episode does not set a course as much as provide a lasting reminder of the way things are. It can validate current beliefs and feelings, it can offer reassurance at times of trouble or difficulty, and it can refocus thoughts and behaviors in accordance with the underlying lesson represented by the memory.

Two examples of anchoring events were provided by participants in our study (Pillemer et al., 1996):

> [A professor] said to us that the most talented people he'd ever known in his life he had seen come through his classrooms at Wellesley, and the obvious high esteem in which he held Wellesley students was an added boost to me. My self-esteem and self-awareness of my own abilities has not ever been low, but in moments since my Wellesley years when my own doubts, or the doubts of others as to my ability to do something have bothered me, I hear this man's words and know I can give it as good a try as *anyone* else could. (p. 331)

> I had a professor . . . in my senior year. . . One day in class he said "The most wasted resource in this country is female brain power." . . . He was not impressed with me or my work particularly. I remember telling myself that he was crazy when he made this remark. I hadn't been out of Wellesley and working for more than 6 months before I found for myself that what he had said was true. Wellesley was an ivory tower in terms of the regard in which women were held; but wider society was far less respectful, and the women in it held themselves in lower esteem. I guess this was an influential experience because I thought about it 1,000 times after I graduated. In fact, when I started writing this I remembered the thinking about the incident better than the incident itself. (p. 331)

The professor's praise of Wellesley students in the first memory became a sustained source of reassurance, particularly at moments of self-doubt; whereas the professor's statement in the second memory came to anchor a troubling belief about the world beyond Wellesley. Although the episodes themselves did not initiate new plans of action, subsequent events in the lives of the two women resonated strongly with their professors' messages, and the memories came to represent underlying truths about how the world works. The influence of the memories appears to have grown as their contemporary relevance was repeatedly demonstrated.

Not all anchoring events come neatly packaged as verbal pronouncements from powerful others. Reformer Jane Addams recounted an experience from a trip to Europe which illustrates how a belief system can be anchored by a symbolic memory image:

> "One of the most poignant of these experiences, which occurred during the first few months after our landing upon the other side of the Atlantic, was on a Saturday night, when I received an ineradicable impression of the wretchedness of East London, and also saw for the first time the overcrowded quarters of a great city at midnight. A small party of tourists were taken to the East End by a city missionary to witness the Saturday night sale of decaying vegetables and fruit . . . we saw two huge masses of ill-clad people clamoring around two hucksters' carts. They were bidding their farthings and ha'pennies for a vegetable held up by the auctioneer, which he at last scornfully flung, with a gibe for its cheapness, to the successful bidder. . . During the following two years on the continent . . . nothing . . . carried with it the same conviction of human wretchedness which was conveyed by this momentary glimpse of an East London street.   (Addams, 1992, pp. 511–512)

Addams's first-hand exposure to human suffering contributed to her strongly held beliefs: "I gradually reached the conviction . . . that the contemporary education of young women had developed too exclusively the power of acquiring knowledge and of merely receiving impressions; that somewhere in the process of 'being educated' they had lost that simple and almost automatic response to the human appeal, that old healthful reaction resulting in activity from the mere presence of suffering or of helplessness" (Addams, p. 512). The haunting and enduring first image of East London misery sustained her view of the world as troubled and in need of all that "educated women" could offer.

At the age of 4 years, Malcolm X had a terrifying experience of racial hatred and violence:

> My mother was pregnant again, this time with my youngest sister. Shortly after Yvonne was born came the nightmare night in 1929, my earliest vivid memory. I remember being suddenly snatched awake into a frightening confusion of pistol shots and shouting and smoke and flames. My father had shouted and shot at the two white men who had set the fire and were running away. Our home was burning down around us. We were lunging and bumping and tumbling all over each other trying to escape. My mother, with the baby in her arms, just made it into the yard before the house crashed in, showering sparks. I remember we were outside in the night in our underwear, crying and yelling our heads off. The white police and firemen came and stood around watching as the house burned down to the ground.   (Malcolm X, 1965, p. 3)

The memory of this formative episode anchored Malcolm X's political beliefs concerning race relations in the United States. He recounted the incident, and subsequent harassment experiences, when he spoke publicly (1964, pp. 3–4).

Jane Addams's and Malcolm X's memories anchor continuing beliefs about the condition of the world. Personal event memories can also anchor enduring feelings about the self. A personal acquaintance, now an adult, described an influential early adolescent experience:

> Timothy John had been my cat and he slept with me and he seemed important to me and he began running away. A lot of times I would have to go out in the cornfields by our house, searching for him, calling for him. It was in the summertime, it was dusty, and the corn leaves would scratch my arms and face as I ran through the rows calling and looking for him. Sometimes I would be crying. It happened that one Saturday morning he had been out all night and I woke up knowing that he wasn't home. I was sitting on the couch and I was reading a book from the library that had *Black Gold* in the title. It was about oil. I was about 12 at the time. I decided, "I'm not going to go out and look for him." I can hear my mother's and grandmother's words—"Oh, just let him go. He'll come back"—but never before could I just do that. But that day I could. It felt different to me to sit reading my book, knowing he was out, and not feel compelled to go look for him. I remember the feeling. It was a liberating feeling.

This feeling remained an active component of the speaker's sense of self. The early image of self-control in the face of loss was replayed when painful emotional separations were thrust upon her in adulthood.

*

Turning Points

Turning points are a prominent variant of originating events, in which a specific episode, or series of episodes, appears to alter or redirect the ongoing flow of the life course. McAdams (1988) observed that "nuclear episodes suggesting transformation in the life story are often seen by the individual reconstructing his or her past as turning points marking the end of one chapter and the beginning of another" (p. 144). A particular moment of changed perspective persists in memory; like an originating event, it provides continued inspiration and guidance with respect to new goals or plans. Changes in career aspirations, for example, are frequently tied in memory to a precise turning point. Psychologist Jerome Kagan described a shift in his academic interests during college:

My commitment to chemistry was also weakened by a psychology professor's idle comment in the introductory psychology course. He had posed a question I cannot remember, but to which I apparently gave a good answer. He asked me to stay and as we walked across the campus he said I had an apperceptive feeling for psychology and added, "You would probably be a good psychologist." The sentence rings as clearly now as it did that afternoon twenty-two years ago. I began to think about psychology more seriously. (Kagan, 1972, p. 140)

Anthropologist Margaret Mead experienced a similar turning point while at Barnard:

By the spring I was actively considering the possibility of entering anthropology, but I was already launched on my Master's essay in psychology. Then one day, when I was at lunch with Ruth Benedict and was discussing with her whether to go into sociology, as Ogburn wanted me to, or into psychology, as I had already planned to do, she said, "Professor Boas and I have nothing to offer but an opportunity to do work that matters." That settled it for me. Anthropology had to be done *now*. Other things could wait. . . (Mead, 1992, p. 298)

Psychologist Theodore Newcomb traced the redirection of his career path to a pinpointed occurrence:

My formal transfer to Teachers College . . . was "decided upon" at a single moment, during my second year in New York. Every Tuesday and Thursday at 9:00 I left Goodwin Watson's class in "Psychology of Character" for a required class in 'New Testament Exegesis' at the Seminary. At the end of the latter class, on a certain Tuesday, the professor, who had just devoted the entire hour to lecturing on the Greek word for "straightway" . . . announced that he would need the full hour on Thursday, also, to lecture on that word. The contrast with the "Psychology of Character" . . . was too much for me. I "decided" at that moment that I would not complete the theological degree. . . (Newcomb, 1974, p. 370)

Margaret Bourke-White's career as a photographer took a dramatic turn for the better when she went to New York to get an "unbiased opinion" of her work from architect Benjamin Moskowitz:

The tall dark man . . . was plainly a commuter on his way to the train. As I outlined my problem, he was unobtrusively though steadily edging his way toward the elevator. I did not realize he had not taken in a word when he pushed the down button, but I was chilled by the lack of response. If the elevator had arrived immediately, I am sure that the next morning would have found me on the doorstep of the Museum of Natural History, but as we waited, the silence became so embarrassing that I opened my big portfolio. Mr. Moskowitz glanced at the picture on the top. . . "Let's go back into the office and look at these," said the unpredictable Mr. Moskowitz. He let his train go, stood up the photographs against the dark wood paneling of the conference room and called in the other members of the firm to look them over. After the kind of golden hour one remembers for a lifetime, I left with the assurance . . . that I could "walk into any architect's office in the country with that portfolio and get work." Everything was touched with magic now.   (Bourke-White, 1992, pp. 429–430)

Some turning points are prompted by negative feedback. A Wellesley College alumna recounted a painful encounter with a professor:

In my sophomore year, I took an English literature course. I loved the course material, enjoyed writing papers, and felt pretty good about it until . . . I wrote an essay on my interpretation of a poem. I felt I had great insight into a special meaning within the verse. When the paper was returned, the teacher told me I didn't have any understanding of the material and she hoped I wasn't going to be an English major. I remember her pinched face and small, tight mouth as she said these things to me. I thought no way do I want to be like her. So I changed my major from English to Sociology.   (Pillemer et al., 1996, p. 333).

Turning points are represented in the collective memory of groups of people as well as in the personal recollections of single individuals; the communal memory continues to inform and inspire group members in their newly redirected pursuits. After a series of disappointing performances in the league playoff series, in 1989 and 1990 the Detroit Pistons became champions of the National Basketball Association. The Piston team members, their coach, and the media identified one fleeting moment of a particular basketball game played years earlier as the turning point from habitual losers to champions:

How were they to know that this moment of immeasurable regret and sorrow would turn out to be so beneficial? Three years later, the Detroit Pistons will admit without hesitation that what happened to them on the night of May 26, 1987, helped mold them into what they are today. . . *That night.* Everyone connected with the Detroit organization remembers what *that night* was. It is hardly necessary to embellish any references to *that night* by saying, "Yeah, remember the time we were leading Boston by 1 with a couple of seconds to go and we thought the game was over and then [opposing player] Bird stole the ball?" . . . The sequence will never be forgotten.   (Ryan, 1990, pp. 81, 88)

In an instant, Boston star player Larry Bird had turned a certain Detroit victory into agonizing defeat by stealing the ball and throwing it to a teammate who scored the winning basket.

The Detroit team viewed this incident as pivotal, not only for the 1987 playoff series, but also for their eventual development into a championship team. Comments made by coaches and players three years later reflected its continuing influence: "How often do we think about it? Try last night, just prior to going out on the floor." "[That game] cemented our mental toughness. . . It taught us how to persevere mentally." "Ever since [that game] in Boston we've learned that you never give up. If we're down 10 points with two minutes to go, we always believe we've got a chance to win the game." "It's become a positive thing for us. We now react to that situation with a certain set we should have used that night." (Ryan, 1990, pp. 81, 88). Long after *that game* was completed, the searing memory of defeat continued to offer inspiration and an improved perspective on how to win.

Some momentous public events instigate change on an individual level and also function as turning points at the societal level. Basketball star Magic Johnson stunned the world with his 1991 announcement that he had contracted the AIDS virus. For individual admirers, the news was shocking and memorable, and it appeared to alter the way that some viewed the AIDS epidemic. The victim did not match the usual stereotypes of AIDS patients; he was an immensely popular, talented athlete at the prime of his career. For some people, the tragedy provided a powerful personal directive: "I heard about AIDS but I didn't know much about it. Then when I heard what had happened to Magic Johnson. I asked an older guy and he explained. It sounds scary and I know I'll do whatever it takes to never get it" (Ribadeneira, 1991, pp. 1, 53).

On a societal level, Johnson's announcement offered the possibility of a dramatic turnabout in public attitudes towards AIDS: "No, tragedies like this do not happen to heroes. Our heroes, and especially our children's heroes. Yet it has happened to basketball superstar Earvin (Magic) Johnson. And America will not—indeed, cannot—ever be quite the same. We have wrestled with the AIDS plague before, but never quite like this. Not in this context, anyway. And not with the sense of shock that greeted yesterday's news" (Kahn, 1991, p. 1). According to author and AIDS expert Randy Shilts, "This is a turning point in the history of AIDS. This is a crucial moment, and in terms of prevention, he has already done wonders" (Bennett, 1991, p. 1).

*

Analogous Events

One way that memories of past episodes inform current beliefs and actions is by analogy: the lessons from an earlier, structurally similar experience are applied to present circumstances. According to Schank (1990), "figuring out how to behave in a new situation is most certainly helped by being reminded of an old situation that is like the new situation. The old situation then becomes a guide to follow or even a guide to what not to do" (p. 24). The power of analogies based upon specific prior events has been documented in psychological domains as diverse as the acquisition of a cognitive skill (Ross, 1984), the analysis of momentous historical moments (Erikson, 1975), or the study of reminders in everyday life (Schank, 1980).

Because present events are rarely identical to prior episodes, memories must inform current activities through analogy rather than exact pattern matching. Psychologist George Miller recounted a memorable early childhood event which provided a model for his subsequent experiences as a teacher and scientist:

> One day when I was seven or eight years old I was walking home. . . In the dirt between the sidewalk and the curb I found a small wheel that had come off some other child's toy. I cleaned it enough to see that it was an unusually nice wheel; red, with a small rubber tire. As I walked along slowly, alone, examining the wheel, it occurred to me that if I had another just like it, all I would need would be an axle and it could roll along. And if I had another pair, I could make something. I could mount them under a block of wood and make a car . . . When I reached my front walk at home I was trying to remember where I had seen a small can of paint. As I started up the walk, I looked in my hand and saw nothing there but the single wheel. Surprise etched the experience into memory. In the 60 years since, that boy, staring dumbly at his toy wheel, has revisited me many times. Soaring imagination mocked by hard reality—who has not experienced the discrepancy? . . . The tendency to see what something could be more clearly than what it is has sustained me as a teacher. . . (Miller, 1989, p. 414)

A memory recounted by a Wellesley College alumna demonstrates even more directly the analogical function of remembering specific episodes and learning from them:

> A second influential experience that I can recall involved an Art History paper. I wrote about a sculpture from a picture I had, rather than going to the museum to view it as we had been instructed. When I received the paper back it had no grade, but instead a note which said "see me." Upon meeting with the instructor I was informed that the piece about which I wrote was currently being restored. Since I had not followed instructions and written about a piece I had seen, I was required to write another paper. In addition to being extremely embarrassed, I learned a valuable lesson about not taking shortcuts. (Pillemer et al., 1996, p. 331)

The alumna reported that the memory comes to mind "when the temptation to take a shortcut is present."

Sometimes analogical remembering involves an episode that happened to someone else: "By storing information about the problems of others, even if they are fictional characters, we can learn from their actions. When our own circumstances match those of people we have heard about, we can conclude that we need to modify our behavior so as to learn from the commonality of experience" (Schank, 1990, p. 22). Hillary Clinton, a 1969 graduate of Wellesley College, remembered a story told to her by a Dean of the College. The story provided a symbolic model of how a "Wellesley woman" should respond under trying circumstances:

> I'll never forget being in that old red building by the lake. . . Dean Frisch sat with several of us for a cup of coffee and told a story that stuck in my mind. Years and years before, she said, she had gotten caught in a blizzard on a bus in Montana. Everyone was herded into a bus station. Her eye was caught by a young mother with two small children. Dean Frisch watched the young woman coping so well in this terrible blizzard, awful conditions, nothing to eat, and suddenly knew, she said, that she had gone to Wellesley. She introduced herself and sure enough, the young woman *had* gone to Wellesley!. . . Dean Frisch said, "You can *always* tell a *Wellesley* woman.". . . And from then on we'd say to each other, "Would *you* be picked out as a Wellesley woman by Dean Frisch in a deserted bus station in the middle of a blizzard somewhere in northern Montana?" (Campion, 1994, p. 10)

To be useful, memories of analogous events must be triggered by present circumstances. Reminding is based on event similarity, but similarity is a labile concept (Srull and Wyer, 1990, pp. 177–178). Past and present experiences can be similar with respect to surface details, or only with respect to the most abstract relationships between people and events. Several years ago, my then toddler daughter's beloved blanket was in the wash when I dropped her off at a babysitter's house. I reassured her that when I came to pick her up the blanket would be in the car. Later, when I was tempted not to bother with the blanket, I remembered a time when a senior colleague had asked me to order a book for him and, not taking the request seriously, I had neglected to do so. When my colleague learned that I had not obtained a copy for him, he was clearly annoyed. The lesson? Bring the blanket. Yet the concrete circumstances, including the people and types of objects involved, were quite dissimilar.

The analogy is even more abstract in a second personal example. I was reinserting a contact lense after a swim. As I held the lens in one hand, I dropped the plastic cap of the wetting solution with the other hand. My automatic reaction was to reach for the cap with the hand that held the lens, but I was able to stop in time. This mundane event triggered a childhood memory. At about age ten, I was fishing off a pier. As I attempted to place a large fish on a stringer, it jumped. I reached for the fish with the hand that held the stringer, and my whole morning's catch fell into the lake. The encapsulated moral—do not let go of something valuable to save something of lesser value—applies to both episodes, but they are related only at the most general level of structural consistency.

Analogous events play an important role in collective as well as individual remembering (Pillemer, 1992b). In the business world, employees have access not only to explicit job-related guidelines and reward systems provided by the company for which they work; they also experience an implicit "corporate culture" as it is expressed in informal conversation and unofficial activities. Past happenings within the corporation provide valuable analogues to current situations: "Employees also take note of all critical incidents that stem from management action—such as the time that so-and-so was reprimanded for doing a good job when not asked to do it beforehand or the time that another worker was fired for publicly disagreeing with the company's position. Incidents such as these become an enduring part of the company folklore, indicating what the corporation really wants. . . They are the unwritten rules of the game" (Kilmann, 1985, p. 64).

A second example involves the financial markets. John Kenneth Galbraith (1990) described "recurrent episodes of speculation," including the tulip bulb craze and subsequent financial bust in seventeenth-century Holland and events leading to the United States stock market crash of 1929. Galbraith observed that these episodes share common features, "the things that signal their certain return, and have thus the considerable practical value of aiding understanding and prediction" (pp. 1–2). Collective memory of disastrous prior episodes dampens the speculation that inevitably leads to financial ruin, but only up to a point: "the financial memory should be assumed to last, at a maximum, no more than 20 years. This is normally the time it takes for the recollection of one disaster to be erased and for some variant on previous dementia to come forward to capture the financial mind" (p. 87). Collective memories can be valuable, but only if they are triggered by analogous present circumstances, and if they become an active part of current decision-making.

*

Retrospective Causality

Autobiographers frequently draw implicit or explicit causal connections between specific early episodes and the subsequent direction of the life course. Mackavey, Malley, and Stewart (1991) conducted a content analysis of short autobiographies written by 49 distinguished psychologists. A memory was defined as an "autobiographically consequential experience" (ACE) if "it described an event, person, or set of circumstances in the individual's life that was remembered as having affected the unfolding of the life story in a personally significant way . . . the memory must also have established a causal connection between the event or experience and the consequence" (p. 53). ACEs were a common component of the 49 written autobiographies: a total of 250 ACEs were identified, 31% of which involved a pinpointed life episode. Because the coding scheme required that a causal connection be explicit in the narrative, some consequential events undoubtedly were excluded from the analysis (p. 53).

The popular view that singular episodes can exert a causal influence on the life course is artfully expressed by Dickens in *Great Expectations*. Pip, the narrator, has just returned from his first, momentous visit to Miss Havisham's house: "That was a memorable day to me, for it made great changes in me. But it is the same with any life. Imagine one selected day struck out of it, and think how different its course would have been. Pause you who read this, and think for a moment of the long chain of iron or gold, of thorns or flowers, that would have never have bound you, but for the formation of the first link on one memorable day" (1956, p. 68).

Hard-nosed experimentalists and humanists alike question the validity of causally linking current activities to specific prior episodes. Erikson (1969, 1975) cautioned against what he termed the "originological fallacy," which "deals with the present as almost pre-empted by its own origins" (1975, p. 160). Mack (1971) broadened the attack on subjectivity in historical analysis to include the "critical period fallacy," in which a key life period of unusual developmental significance is identified only a posteriori, and "eventism," in which a life episode is viewed as "*the* turning point" from which "all subsequent events and work are derived" (p. 156). Connelly and Clandinin (1990) discussed the "illusion of causality," in which "a sequence of events looked at backward has the appearance of causal necessity" (p. 7). In gender studies, Crawford et al. (1992) warned against "the coherence which biography brings; the coherence of the reinterpretation of past events as antecedents of what follows, that is, of what we 'know' to be the consequences" (p. 47).

People are especially likely to search for underlying causes when a current event has negative and unexpected consequences (Wong and Weiner, 1981). Young children's experiences with trauma provide dramatic illustrations of highly motivated, and seemingly illogical, causal attributions. "The traumatized child asks himself two questions—'Why?' and then, 'Why me?' In his afterthought he rakes through the past, and in so doing he often defies the rules of simultaneity and sequence" (Terr, 1990, p. 159). In their efforts to answer the "Why me?" question, children invent "omens" that could have served as a warning, and they mentally re-order event sequences to render the trauma predictable and understandable. For example, some children who had been hostages in the Chowchilla bus kidnapping "retroactively put things that followed a traumatic event into places that precede it" (Terr, p. 160). One 7-year-old girl received a crank phone call after the kidnapping; she subsequently "remembered" that a phone call preceded the abduction. This reconstructive error offered some psychological consolation to the terrified young victim: she "could now accept partial responsibility for being kidnapped. She had been warned. But Leslie could also feel a little less helpless than she originally had felt" (Terr, p. 160).

Post hoc attributions of causality also appear in children's explanations of their parents' decision to divorce. Wallerstein (1980) identified a subgroup of children from broken families whose parents had divorced for "reasons unrelated to marital unhappiness, and who thus could not understand what had disrupted their families" (p. 232). Wallerstein observed unusual and faulty reasoning about the underlying causes of divorce. For example, one 13-year-old "offered the bizarre explanation that his father had been baking bread and that his mother had burned it and this had precipitated the divorce" (p. 232). In reality, the mother had suddenly and unexpectedly wanted a divorce following a tragic accident. The child's constructed causal episode—burning the bread—

may appear illogical, but it provides an answer, inadequate though it may be, to Terr's "Why?" and "Why me?" questions.

Public tragedies are also commonly followed by a collective search for causal precursors. In 1993, Boston professional basketball player Reggie Lewis received conflicting diagnoses about the seriousness of his heart condition. Then, during an informal workout, Lewis suddenly and shockingly collapsed and died. Media coverage of the tragedy reflected not only deeply felt expressions of grief and mourning, but also a preoccupation with pinpointing the cause. The questions "Why?" and "Why Reggie?" were asked repeatedly. In an article titled "The pall will linger for as long as the questions remain," *Boston Globe* columnist Michael Madden observed: "So, as the tears flowed . . . the question kept haunting back. Why?" (1993, p. 51). In a companion piece titled "Exact cause may prove elusive," columnist Will McDonough bemoaned that "sadly, we may never know the exact cause of his death. Just because an autopsy is done by the state medical examiner doesn't guarantee there is going to be a definite answer" (1993, p. 49). If a Boston hero, young and vigorous, could die so suddenly, then all people are susceptible to similarly tragic ends. But if an exact cause could be pinpointed, feelings of control and predictability would return.

Financial disasters, such as the stock market crash of 1929, also provoke a furious search for causal explanations. According to Galbraith (1990), "the least important questions are the ones most emphasized: What triggered the crash? Were there some special factors that made it so dramatic or drastic? Who should be punished?" (p. 107). Galbraith located the cause of the disastrous speculative episode "within the market itself" (p. 107), but he observed that this explanation is unacceptable to most financiers. Instead, "it is necessary to search for external influences . . . In the absence of these factors, the market presumably would have remained high and gone on up or declined gently without inflicting pain" (p. 107). Once a precise "cause" of the disaster is identified and externalized, business activity can return to normal, eventually leading to the next speculative episode and subsequent downturn.

Scholars concur that people are susceptible to the originological fallacy—when reconstructing a life history from their present perspective, they falsely attribute causal power to specific antecedents of current events. Does this observation pose a damaging challenge to the idea that specific past episodes exert a guiding influence on the life course? Not necessarily. Acknowledging that causal attributions can be erroneous in no way excludes the possibility that some such attributions are valid. In addition, a salient episode can be persistently influential without predetermining a life: "there is an important difference between claiming that childhood experience is *the* cause of later events versus arguing that it is a partial or contributing cause of individual behavior" (Runyan, 1982, p. 210).

Another way to think about the psychological impact of momentous events requires a shift in focus: the *memory* rather than the event itself is viewed as the persistent, enduring causal agent (Pillemer, 1992b; Pillemer et al., 1996). From this perspective, a personal event memory is much more than a passive record; it is an active agent of direction, guidance, and deepened understanding. The psychological reality of the event for the rememberer, including the constructed meaning it holds within the context of an autobiography, takes on a life of its own apart from the objective, historical truth, however that elusive quality of objectivity is defined.

Through its repeated activation in memory, a momentous event, or more properly, the belief system attached to the memory of the event, ultimately becomes causal; to use an evocative term suggested to me by Jerome Bruner, a momentous event is *retrospectively causal*. The recurring memory intrudes into consciousness and applies its guiding force. The comment made to Endel Tulving by a colleague—that a young scholar "had not written his book yet"—prompted Tulving to think about writing "his book," but the effect persisted; Tulving "never quite recovered from the emotional impact of the casual comment of [his] friend" (1983, p. vii). The statement made by Cecilia Gaposchkin's teacher—"You will always be hampered by your quick power of apprehension"—came to mind frequently over the course of Gaposchkin's life: "I cannot count how often those words have served as a warning against hastily jumping to conclusions" (1992, p. 253). The Wellesley alumna whose professor commented that "the most wasted resource in this country is female brain power" said she "thought about it 1,000 times" after graduation. The alumna who wrote an art history paper about a sculpture that she had not seen, and was found out by her professor reported that the memory comes to mind "when the temptation to take a short-cut is present" (Pillemer et al., 1996, p. 331).

In these examples, the psychological impact of a specific event resides in its continuing presence in memory and thought, especially at times of decision-making. Its enduring influence is tied to the persistence and persuasiveness of the belief system that was constructed at the time of occurrence and elaborated in the months and years that followed.

*

Critical Junctures

The examples illustrating how momentous events can endure as vivid memories and as active life influences also demonstrate how idiosyncratic such events are. Lenore Terr was profoundly affected by viewing the Hiroshima newsreel as a child, but the theater was full of people for whom the viewing was not a defining moment. One Wellesley student's interest in the Vietnam war also was born in a movie theater: "I remember going to see the movie *Platoon*, and being completely devastated by it. I cried my eyes out. After that, I got very interested in the Vietnam conflict and read a lot of books on it. I wanted to learn as much as possible about what it was like to serve there. It was this movie that got me going." Yet countless other college students viewed the same movie without experiencing it as a directive.

Momentous events often appear to involve an element of chance: the person happened to be in the right place at the right time when a life-altering statement was heard or a novel solution to a dilemma was unexpectedly discovered. Bandura (1982) developed a psychological model of the life course that emphasized the importance of chance encounters: "some of the most important determinants of life paths often arise through the most trivial of circumstances. Although the separate chains of events in a chance encounter have their own causal determinants, their intersection occurs fortuitously rather than through deliberate plan" (p. 749).

These two factors—idiosyncratic responsiveness to potentially influential events, and the role of chance in providing such events—undermine scientific attempts to foresee and predict life-altering occurrences. Yet although it may not be possible to pinpoint exactly which events will prove to be momentous in a person's life, there may be identifiable circumstances under which a person is especially susceptible to the influence of specific episodes (Pillemer et al., 1996). According to Bandura (1982), "A science of psychology does not have much to say about the occurrence of fortuitous intersects. . . However, psychological knowledge can provide the basis for predicting the nature, scope, and strength of the impact they will have on human lives" (p. 749).

The directive influence of specific episodes ought to be strongest when scripts governing how to think and behave are violated or missing (Pillemer, 1992b). Schank (1980) theorized that specific memories are laid down and retrieved when mental processing fails: "when we have failed to predict accurately what will happen next is when we are most in need of a specific memory to help us through the rough spots. To do this, our index of memories must be in terms of their relationship to processing prediction failures" (p. 41). Similarly, when people encounter new situations, well-established scripts to guide behavior do not exist, and the information contained in specific episodes assumes heightened importance.

When scripts are violated or unavailable, people are especially attentive to immediate environmental cues. For example, Knapp et al. (1981) observed that receptivity to memorable messages spoken by significant others is especially high during life crises, when the recipient is floundering and actively seeking help. These informative specific instances are recorded as vivid memories, which may be reactivated at future moments when general scripts again prove to be inadequate.

When people undergo a dramatic physical and emotional change or upheaval, specific cues existing in the environment assume a critical role. One such change is the transition to college, the primary focus of the discussion that follows (Pillemer et al., 1986; Pillemer et al., 1988; Pillemer, Krensky, Kleinman, Goldsmith, and White, 1991; Pillemer et al., 1996; Stewart, Sokol, Healy, Chester, and Weinstock-Savoy, 1982; Wapner, 1981; Wapner, Ciottone, Hornstein, McNeil, and Pacheco, 1983). Wapner et al. (1983) summarized the importance of this transition: "For the person entering college, the change in setting represents a shift from the familiar to the unfamiliar, from a setting where living and schooling is separate to a setting where for the most part living and schooling have merged. An array of strangers are present who may have drastically different values. The individual must become self-reliant. Marked changes in status may be experienced" (p. 124). Hatcher (1994) asked college students to identify the event "that defined for them the passage from childhood to adulthood" (p. 169); the event chosen most frequently was leaving home for college.

If students are especially attentive to, and influenced by, specific events occurring during the transition to college, then personal event memories should be overrepresented at the point of transition. A series of questionnaire studies confirmed this prediction. Pillemer et al. (1986)

asked Wellesley and Harvard undergraduates to report the first memories to come to mind of their freshman year and to indicate when in
the school year the reported events had occurred. Most of the memories described specific, one-moment-in-time events (such as a particular
conversation with a roommate) rather than general feelings or repeated
happenings (such as an overall evaluation of the roommate as a conversational partner). The temporal distribution of memories across the 9-
month academic year showed a marked peak at the beginning of college, with about 30% of all freshman year memories dated in September.
A follow-up study indicated that memory clustering was not the result
of participants using a retrieval strategy in which they began their memory search at the beginning of the designated time interval and thus
"found" more memories there. Students were asked to report memories
of events that occurred between February of senior year in high school
and October of freshman year in college. The distribution of memories
again showed a sharp peak in September of freshman year, and a smaller
peak in June, another landmark transition point—high school gradu-

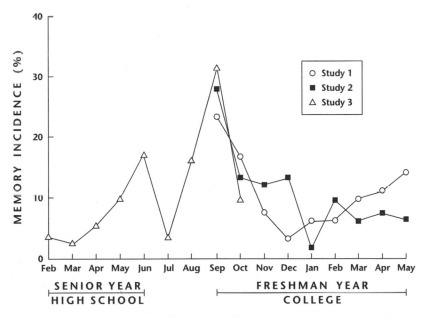

Figure 1. Temporal distributions of memories of senior year in high school and
freshman year in college. Respondents were Harvard (Study 1) and Wellesley
(Studies 2 and 3) undergraduates. Source: Pillemer, Rhinehart, and White, 1986.
Copyright © John & Sons Limited. Reproduced with permission.

ation. A questionnaire study of freshman year memories reported by Wellesley alumnae who had graduated from college 2, 12, or 22 years earlier also demonstrated a marked temporal clustering of remembered events, with about 40% of memories dated in September (Pillemer et al., 1988).

Additional studies examined the temporal distribution of college memories when students and alumnae were explicitly asked to describe influential experiences rather than the first memories to come to mind (Pillemer et al., 1996). For current Wellesley students, influential freshman year events were again overrepresented at the point of transition, with more than 30% of memories dated in September. When Wellesley alumnae who had graduated 1, 11, or 21 years earlier described influential events that had occurred at any time during their 4 years of college, memories clustered at both major transition points: beginning of freshman year and, to a lesser extent, end of senior year. One-quarter of all datable memories, representing all 4 college years, occurred during the first 3 months of freshman year in college. Figures 1 through 4 show the

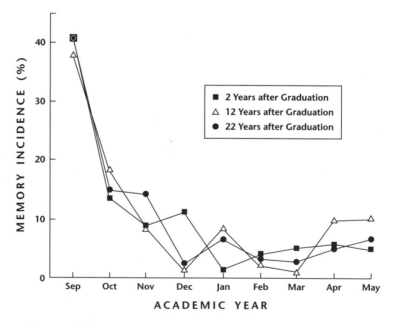

Figure 2. Temporal distributions of freshman year memories reported by three groups of Wellesley alumnae. Source: Pillemer, Goldsmith, Panter, and White, 1988. Copyright © by the American Psychological Association.

pronounced and consistent clustering of college memories at transition points. Other researchers also have found that memories tend to cluster at the beginning or end of school terms (Kurbat, Shevell, and Rips, in press; Robinson, 1986).

The beginning weeks and months of college appear to mark a critical period during which students attend closely to particular episodes. One common focus is adapting to a new academic regimen. A Wellesley undergraduate recounted this freshman year encounter with a professor: "I remember taking a philosophy course and feeling incredible pressure to get all my reading done. (Of course, I never did.) Then, the professor told me, the most important thing I should learn from college is what *not* to read. Basically, what you could get away with not doing and still do well. A *valuable* lesson to say the least."

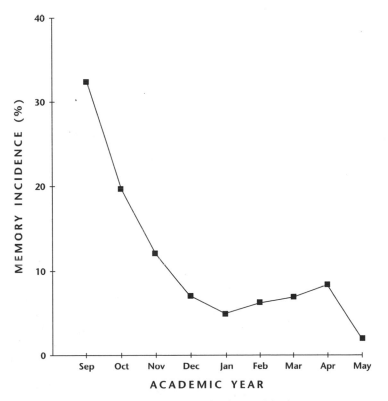

Figure 3. Temporal distribution of memories of influential freshman year experiences reported by Wellesley undergraduates. Source: Pillemer, Picariello, Law, and Reichman, 1996.

Another first year student was enlightened by a more experienced peer: "I remember getting back my first chemistry exam and getting a C on it. I was crushed, I had never done so poorly. I rode my bike back from class to the dorm that day and passed two friends who were sophomores. They asked what was wrong and I told them. One said, 'Don't worry, you'll get used to it.'"

Sometimes a beginning student takes academic feedback more seriously than the professor intended: "My first writing assignment—freshman year—a description. I described the autumn foliage. The comment I got back—'too kodachrome'—puzzled me. The colors *were* kodachrome, to me. There must be something wrong with the way I saw them. Perhaps I remember this because it was part of the process of jettisoning hope and trust and opting for survival which characterized my first months there" (Pillemer et al., 1996, p. 334).

In other instances, early criticism served as a motivator. A graduate of the University of Chicago playfully recounted an incident in which a professor's harsh comments were inspirational:

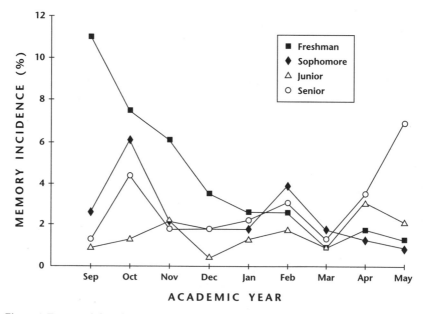

Figure 4. Temporal distributions of memories of influential college experiences for each year in college separately. Respondents were Wellesley alumnae. Source: Pillemer, Picariello, Law, and Reichman, 1996.

when I was a tenderhearted, soft-shelled first-year transfer student . . . I was scarred for life with this notation from Mr. Redfield in the margin of one of my papers. . . "This is a hideous barbarism." I had called the dynamic inter-play of three themes a "trialectic," having ignorantly thought dialectic meant two theses in the process of synthesis. . . My consciousness was seared, but I was inspired. I took three years of Greek, including a reading seminar on *The Symposium* with Mr. Redfield, and majored in general studies in the humani-ties. I set out to lose my barbarity and become a member of the class of educated persons. . . Mr. Redfield's austerity did inspire.   (Rasley, 1993, p. 6)

Memories of the transition to college also frequently involve social comparisons, including concerns with being accepted or fitting in. The memories capture the oftentimes painful process of learning the rules in a new social milieu:

I remember my first day at Wellesley. . . I was trying to settle in a bit and decided to put up my memo board on the door. I peeled off the paper to the adhesive on the back and stuck the board *firmly* on the door. Just then, a woman . . . walked by and said, "You're not allowed to tape anything to the doors." I was *so* embarrassed. I had to yank the board off the door, bending it in the process because the adhesive was so strong. I worked on getting the residue adhesive off whenever there wasn't anyone in the hall. Whenever someone came by, I'd hide in my room! I was *so* miserable and embarrassed. I later saw, as I walked around my new dorm, that there were signs *everywhere* telling us that because the dorm had just been renovated, not to tape things to doors and door frames!

I remember being so embarrassed calling a fraternity for me and my friends, so we could get one of the guys to pick us up [for] a party. The guy on the phone told us he'd be there at nine o'clock. . . It was 8:45 when we went down and eagerly waited wondering what the 1st fraternity party we were going to go to would be like. . . We piled into the van as the driver and another guy made small talk with all of us. When we got to the fraternity, we got out of the van and didn't go directly into the house. The guys seemed annoyed by this, but we didn't care. We didn't want to go into the party so early and we hoped that nobody had seen us get off the van. We went for pizza and then went to the party and met slimy men who seemed as though they just wanted sex. So we left. The lesson for that night was—"Don't ever ride the 'Meat Truck'."

At times, a student's initial fears about social acceptance are un-justified:

My birthday being October, I was very distressed freshman year that none of my new friends would have a party, etc. for me. I was used to big celebrations and was seriously bummed that I wouldn't have much fun here. I didn't expect a party because I was a new friend and figured no one would really care. On my birthday . . . my friends bought me a cake and hid in my closet in order to surprise me. I was so happy. This was significant because I actually felt accepted here and realized that maybe I was a special person. I was rather low on self-esteem at the time and it was a tremendous help to know others cared. This one event helped shake my "woe is me attitude" a great deal.

Other memories capture the students' early efforts to acquire strategies for coping in the new environment, by attending closely to comments and behaviors of students who seem to be functioning effectively:

I remember sitting in the chapel during freshman orientation week and listening to several people talk on the freshman experience. I remember one person in particular, I think that it was the student college president, saying how she was sure, when she came to Wellesley as a freshman, that she wasn't going to experience much homesickness, but that as her parents drove away, sure enough she felt scared and lonely. I think I was wearing a pair of pink slacks that day and I was sitting off to the left as you face the organ's front. (Pillemer et al., 1986, p. 120)

It must have been reassuring to learn that even future student college presidents are scared and lonely when they arrive on campus.

The special salience of transitional educational events is apparent for teachers as well as for students. New teachers, who have yet to accumulate a storehouse of knowledge about classroom processes, are particularly attentive to directives they derive from pinpointed classroom episodes. "Novices . . . often struggle to make sense of classroom events, and in this struggle, their knowledge is shaped in fundamental ways, that is, their stories are formed. A focus on events, therefore, is likely to capture a fundamental process going on as novices learn to teach" (Carter, 1993, p. 7).

Meier (1986) provided a personal example that illustrates the guiding influence of a particular classroom event on a novice teacher:

When I was a student teacher, I asked one of my students to read her paper out loud for the class to hear. As she started to read, I moved across the room to close the door. Afterwards, my supervisor told me that when I ask a student to read out loud, I should listen attentively. Otherwise, turning my back and moving away may give the student and the class the unconscious message that I do not value what is being read. Ever since this small incident I never move away when I ask a student to read aloud. (pp. 299–300)

The evidence for critical periods, during which specific episodes are especially likely to be perceived as momentous and to be recorded as vivid memories, focuses here on the college experience. Other periods of novelty and flux, such as the transition to married life and parenthood, an abrupt career change, or a move to a dramatically different living situation are also likely to be marked by heightened susceptibility to the influence of particular episodes. Mackavey et al.'s (1991) analysis of autobiographically consequential experiences reported by prominent psychologists, described earlier, supported this idea: specific influential events often were linked to life transitions.

The idea that particular life episodes are especially salient and influential during certain critical periods challenges the dominant view in cognitive psychology (outlined in Chapter 1) that acquiring general knowledge about the world is far more important for successful human adaptation than is specific experience. Neisser (1985) is surely correct in asserting that "many of the important things in human experience are ongoing situations rather than single events" (p. 274), but even singular instances, when they occur during periods of change, flux, or novelty, can be remembered with clarity and repeatedly activated in memory. Pinpointed episodes happening during the first days or weeks of college set a general tone for adaptation to college life; a student's early success or failure is determined in part by the quality of particular experience.

The salience of distinctive moments occurring within an extended time interval has been demonstrated also in a dramatically different psychological domain. Kahneman, Fredrickson, Schreiber, and Redelmeier (1993) examined people's reactions to physical pain. Participants' hands were immersed in bitterly cold water for varying durations and with fluctuating temperatures, and the subjects provided ongoing ratings of their discomfort. The "worst" and "final" moments of an extended pain experience accurately predicted participants' retrospective overall evaluations. Kahneman et al. concluded that "the cognitive system may represent extended experiences in terms of transitions and singular moments. . . We do not claim that other information is necessarily lost, only that it is often not used" (p. 404). Similarly, transitional and peak moments occurring within extended life periods may be especially influential because of their heightened salience in memory.

*

Memory Landmarks

Understanding of current situations is enhanced, and guidelines for behavior are unearthed, by recalling relevant prior episodes of learning.

Personal event memories also support a directive function that operates at a higher, meta-cognitive level. Memorable episodes provide an organizational skeleton for the production of extended autobiographical memory narratives; they guide or "direct" the reconstruction and retelling of life histories. Narrative representations of a person's life are built around highly salient and memorable episodic nodes.

Constructing a coherent, temporally ordered life history depends on having access not only to the meaning of momentous past events, but also to the imagistic components of personal event memories. As the narrative unfolds, the rememberer mentally moves from scene to concrete scene; general descriptions of "how things were" are punctuated with specific descriptions of particular instances. The extended narrative is anchored by concrete, perceptual landmarks. Moving from landmark to landmark, the temporally ordered life story unfolds.

Oral traditions provide a useful, if incomplete, analogy to the process of composing an individual life history. Epic poems and ballads are made up of "concrete, easy-to-image words and ideas. . . It is difficult to find an abstraction in these genres that is not personified or in some other way represented by a concrete person, object, or action" (Rubin, 1995a, p. 60). The location of action frequently shifts, invoking the use of spatial memory systems (Rubin, 1995a). Reconstructing a ballad or epic tale from memory is a process of connecting a series of concrete images.

A life history is constructed by connecting time periods surrounding momentous events into a coherent story. In the introduction to his autobiography, noted educator Malcolm Knowles described this process: "I thought for a while about what I have wanted to say but have not yet said, and what came into my mind were highly personal experiences that influenced the shaping of my life. . . There emerged a series of episodes that seemed more or less isolated as I recalled them but that gradually, with some rearrangement, became loosely connected. So what I have ended up with is a series of snapshots of a life in the process of becoming something: in this case, an adult educator" (1989, pp. xvii–xviii).

In many published autobiographies the narrative flow is structured around a temporally ordered series of concrete episodes. For example, prominent physician Anne Walter Fearn's (1992) story of her life is anchored by specific memories of originating events, critical incidents, and turning points: leaving her father at a young age to escape a plague of yellow fever; overhearing a conversation on a train that encouraged her to pursue a career in medicine; taking her final exams in medical school; volunteering to practice medicine in China; arriving in Soochow, where she was to work; meeting her husband; giving birth to their child, and the child's tragic early death; her husband's illness and death; and returning to China from the United States later in life. Each of these experiences is represented as a vivid memory containing a detailed description of location, dialogue, and so forth. For example, her momentous decision to work in China was recorded as follows:

> . . . one noon shortly before commencement, when we were all gathered in the college mess hall, Dr. Margaret Polk . . . mentioned that if she had had my unusual advantages in hospital work she wouldn't mind going to China. . . "I'll go in your place for a year, M. P.," I said, "while you take another year's work in the hospitals." The twenty or thirty fledgling doctors seated around the table thought that it was a grand idea and chipped in with suggestions. By the time the meal was over a plan had been evolved down to the most minute detail. "I'll pay your expenses to China," said M. P., growing enthusiastic, "and the Woman's Board of Foreign Missions can pay your salary for a year." "All right," I said, "but I won't go as a missionary. I'm not even a church member. I'm a physician."   (Fearn, 1992, p. 530)

Fearn's moment of decision to practice medicine in China is stored in concrete images, but the verbal depiction is polished as well. The reader has the feeling that this story has been recounted before. The sharing of personal event memories, so common an activity in Western cultures, appears to be an important step in narrative creation. When we tell other people where we were when a momentous event occurred or an important decision was made, and when we rehearse the story privately, we cement the personal location cues to the memory and enhance its retrievability. If the location or other salient details of an event cannot be visualized, imagery cannot be used as an aid to recall.

Engaging histories have the same underlying episodic structure as do personal autobiographies. A compelling history of the French Revolution, ancient Greece, or World War II does not focus solely on the general stream of experience; the historical narrative is composed of a network of interconnected episodes. Collective as well as individual histories are built around concrete nodes of specific experience—originating events, turning points, anchoring events, and critical incidents. The events provide a temporally ordered backbone for narrative expression. For example, the history of the civil rights movement in the United

States is well captured by the book *Eyes on the Prize* (Williams, 1987) and the companion public television series. The history moves from episode to episode: the 1954 *Brown v. Board of Education* Supreme Court decision; the murder of Emmett Till in 1955; Rosa Parks's refusal to give up her bus seat to a white passenger; the Montgomery, Alabama, bus boycott; the 1963 march on Washington, where Dr. Martin Luther King delivered his famous "I have a dream" speech; the 1965 riots in Watts. Details of these events stand out: the tense moment when the uncle of Emmett Till pointed to this nephew's abductors in a Mississippi courtroom and said, "Thar he" (p. 53); or Coretta Scott King's recollection of her husband's leadership role in the Montgomery bus boycott: "He came home very excited about the fact that he had to give the keynote speech that night . . ." (Vecchione, 1986).

An underlying episodic structure is more prominent in some autobiographies and histories than in others. Individual and group differences may influence the extent to which pinpointed episodes rather than more general descriptions of experience are represented in life histories and in conversations about the past. These differences notwithstanding, it is difficult to conceive of engaging human storytelling or penetrating historical analysis without a temporal organization based on a sequence of concrete episodes.

Chapter 4

*

Image,
Narrative, and the
Development
of Self

*P*UBLIC EXPRESSION of personal event memories depends on the spoken or written word. A person recounting a memory must translate the initial perceptual and sensory registration of a momentous event into a shared, narrative representation. Upon reading Lenore Terr's (1990) childhood memory of seeing a newsreel of the bombing of Hiroshima (presented at the beginning of Chapter 2) we vicariously relive Terr's horror as she describes seeing the shadow of a person who was "vaporized" by the intensity of the blast. The image retains its immediacy: "That shadow still lives today in my mind" (p. ix). Yet readers do not have direct access to Terr's sensory experiences, and they must rely on her verbal depiction of what she saw, heard, and felt.

Terr's account reflects at least two levels of representation: it blends perceptual imagery with narration, inference, and interpretation. Empirical studies described earlier show that memories of momentous events almost always have an imagistic core. Terr was consciously aware of perceptual imagery distinct from the words that she used to describe it: "I remember how Hiroshima looked on the screen I can see it now as I write" (1990, p. ix). Sensory memories can also be expressed implicitly and nonconsciously rather than explicitly and consciously. Terr repeatedly experienced what might be called emotional memory: "From the moment I saw that newsreel, if a light was turned on in the middle of the night or if a sudden noise awoke me from sleep, my heart would start pounding at once even before I awoke. I would breathe in gasps, sweat, and say to myself, 'This is it. The bomb'" (p. ix).

In this chapter I present evidence for the idea of separate but interacting imagistic and narrative memory systems. The dual memory model is then used to construct an explanation for childhood amnesia. The final section explores how narrative memory evolves during the preschool years, and how parent-child conversations about the past foster the development of an autobiographical sense of self.

∗

Dualistic Memory Representations

Cognitive, clinical, and developmental psychologists have characterized autobiographical memory as consisting of at least two basic levels of representation. The first is sensory, perceptual, affective, and automatic; the second is verbal and purposeful. Many theoretical accounts identify the imagistic level as a more primitive system, developing earlier both ontogenetically and phylogenetically. Although particulars of the various models differ and specific qualities of the two levels are not always described explicitly, core characteristics of the two systems are strikingly similar across disparate research domains.

The terms "levels" and "systems" are used interchangeably to describe imagistic and narrative memory. This need not imply that distinctive memory functions are performed by different brain systems, or that memory necessarily consists of structurally distinct subsystems, although recent neuropsychological research is consistent with the existence of multiple memory systems. For present purposes, the distinction is simply heuristic; conceptualizing personal event memory as consisting of two basic levels of representation helps to organize diverse clinical observations and research findings.

Image versus Narrative

In their original flashbulb memory paper, Brown and Kulik (1977) embraced a duality of image and narrative. They proposed that flashbulb memories are "fixed for a very long time, and conceivably permanently. . . However, our guess is that the *memory* is not a narrative and not even in verbal form, but represented in other, perhaps imaginal, ways" (p. 85). The core imagistic memory is "not directly accessible" (p. 87). The verbal narrative is constructed or created from the underlying imagistic trace.

White and Pillemer's (1979; Pillemer and White, 1989) developmental account of autobiographical memory is based on a similar memory duality. One memory system is "present from birth and operational throughout life. . . The memories are expressed through images, behaviors, or emotions" (1989, p. 326). A second memory system "emerges during the preschool years. . . Event representations entering the higher-order system are actively thought about or mentally processed and thus are encoded in narrative form. . . Memories in the higher-order system can be accessed and recounted in response to social demands" (p. 326). As in Brown and Kulik's model, the narrative system does not replace the imagistic system; rather, they coexist throughout life. Whereas imagistic memories are activated by situational and affective cues, narrative memories are addressible through conscious, purposeful recall, and they can be called up in situations remote from the original learning context. Outputs of the imagistic system are brought into the narrative system when they are actively thought about or shared with others.

Terr's (1988, 1990) work with child victims of trauma suggested a developmental model in which perceptual-behavioral memory precedes and is distinct from verbal memory. Terr observed that individuals who had been traumatized before about 3 years of age could not describe their experiences in words, but the traumas were nevertheless represented in play, fears, and dreams. She speculated that "traumatic occurrences are first recorded as visualizations, or even, by the youngest infants, as feeling sensations. These perceptual registrations occur long before any remembrances can be recorded in words" (1990, p. 182). Terr's clinical observations led her to postulate "two different kinds of memory—one a primitive kind operational from the earliest moments of conscious life (perceptual-behavioral memory), and the other, a more developed form that does not become fully operational until some time around twenty-eight to thirty-six months (verbal memory)" (1990, p. 182).

Other clinical observations of trauma support the idea of dualism of sensory and narrative memory. Langer (1991), for example, discussed Auschwitz survivor Charlotte Delbo's distinction between "thinking memory" and "sense memory" (p. 7). Translating sensory images into words poses a formidable challenge: "The problem is compounded by the limited power of words to release the specific kinds of physical distress haunting the caverns of deep memory" (p. 8). Herman (1992, p. 177) described the necessary shift from image to words in the treatment of trauma victims: "Out of the fragmented components of frozen imagery and sensation, patient and therapist slowly reassemble an organized, detailed, verbal account, oriented in time and historical context." Spence's (1982) more general discussion of remembering in psychotherapy focused on the necessary but difficult step of translating the primary data of experience—images—into a narrative depiction: "It is sometimes assumed that because psychoanalysis is first and foremost a 'talking cure,' words are the natural unit of meaning. It would be more accurate to say that words allow us to make contact with the data of experience; these are largely visual data that are accessible only to the patient. It is through language that they become accessible to the analyst" (pp. 58–59).

Epstein's (1994) sweeping theoretical integration of psychodynamic and cognitive perspectives suggested a dichotomy between two basic modes of operation—experiential and rational—that is similar to the imagistic-verbal dualism in several respects. The primitive, experiential mode "represents events primarily concretely and imagistically," whereas the advanced, rational mode "is a deliberative, effortful, abstract system that operates primarily in the medium of language" (p. 715). Epstein speculated that the experiential system preceded the rational system in evolution, with the rational system appearing quite recently.

Within cognitive psychology, Johnson and Multhaup's (1992) Multiple-Entry, Modular memory system (MEM) consists of two basic components: a perceptual memory system "for engaging in and recording perceptual activities," and a reflective memory system "for engaging in and recording selfgenerated activities" (p. 34). Perceptual activities include seeing, hearing, and other forms of sensory experience, whereas reflective activities include purposeful cognitive processes such as planning and speculating. The perceptual system develops earlier in life than the reflective system, although "learning, of course, continues throughout life in all subsystems" (p. 38).

Implicit versus Explicit Memory

The primary distinction between imagistic and narrative representational systems focuses on memory form and content: imagistic memory records basic perceptual and sensory experiences and feeling states, whereas narrative memory records the output of higher-order, verbal translations of direct perceptual experience. A second dimension involves levels of conscious awareness. Perceptual representations may or may not reach consciousness, depending upon whether they are actively and consciously attended to, thought about, or talked about.

Experimental research has focused extensively on the distinction between nonconscious and conscious memory processes, what has come to be called implicit and explicit memory (Roediger, 1990; Schacter, 1987), or unaware and aware uses of memory (Jacoby, 1988). In a typical implicit memory experiment, subjects are first shown words, drawings, or other visual or auditory stimuli. After a time delay of minutes, days, or months, they are presented with incomplete perceptual representations of the original stimuli and asked to name or otherwise identify them. For example, in an experiment involving words, the initial stimuli might include the word *umbrella*. After 24 hours the subject would be presented with the incomplete word *u—r—a*, and would be asked to complete the fragment. Implicit memory is demonstrated if subjects who had prior experimental exposure to the word "umbrella" complete the word fragment more successfully, or more quickly, than subjects without prior exposure. An important aspect of implicit memory is that it is nonconscious (Tulving and Schacter, 1990). A subject may rapidly complete the word fragment without being aware that he or she viewed the word on a separate occasion one day earlier.

Implicit memory, like the imagistic memory systems described earlier, is based in perception: "the argument is for two memory systems, one encoding a structural description of perceptual input, the other representing the event itself, in its episodic context" (Tobias, Kihlstrom, and Schacter, 1992, p. 85). Tulving and Schacter (1990; Schacter, 1994) described a perceptual representation system (PRS) underlying implicit memory that can function apart from explicit memory. The PRS is an early developing system that is involved in the identification of specific perceptual objects. Access to the stored information is inflexible, or "hyperspecific"; expression of implicit memory is tied to specific cues. Once an implicit memory is expressed, however, it is potentially accessible to explicit memory (Schacter, 1987, 1994). Products of implicit memory may be "selected" for representation in episodic memory: "the outputs of the PRS subsystems can serve as inputs to episodic memory . . . a key function of the episodic system is to bind together perceptual with other kinds of information (e.g., semantic, contextual) and thereby allow subsequent recall or recognition of multiattribute events" (Schacter, 1994, p. 257).

Although empirical support for the distinction between implicit and explicit memory has come largely from experimental studies of visual or auditory memory, cognitive psychologists have broadened the scope of their analysis to include memories of emotional events. Schacter observed that Freud's patients showed implicit but not explicit memory for early traumas: "Although these patients could not explicitly remember the traumatic events, their memories of them were expressed indirectly (implicitly) in various ways (1987, p. 504). Tobias et al. (1992) provided an example of a woman whose lifelong phobia of running water was traced to a childhood episode when she had been trapped under a waterfall; the authors commented that "this dissociation between the person's emotional response and his or her conscious recollection is analogous to the dissociation between implicit and explicit memory observed in the laboratory" (p. 70).

In earlier work, Magna Arnold (1969, p. 173) introduced the related concept "affective memory," defined as "a reliving of past likes and dislikes as soon as the same situation recurs." The emotional reaction is "experienced as a 'here-and-now' feeling rather than a memory." LeDoux (1992) also described emotion as a form of memory in the context of modern psychophysiological research and theory: "Memories for the affective significance of experiences are mediated by different brain circuits than conscious memories. . . Affective memories can be but are not necessarily memories in the sense of conscious recollections. However, they are memories in the sense that they represent information storage in the nervous system and in the sense that they can have powerful influences on future information processing and behavior" (pp. 270–271). The two memory systems function side by side throughout life: "explicit memory and implicit emotional memory systems are working at the same time, each forming their own special brand of memories" (LeDoux, 1996, p. 182).

*

Multiple Memory Systems:
An Evolutionary Perspective

Systematic research and clinical observations point to two distinct modes of memory. The first mode automatically records perceptual, imagistic, sensory, and affective experience. It can operate outside of conscious awareness, implicitly rather than explicitly. The perceptual-affective memory system is intact early in infancy. The second mode records the output of purposeful, conscious, narrative mental activity, and it evolves during early childhood. The two levels of representation often interact, as when a memory image is the focus of conscious attention and is subsequently described in words.

The two levels of representation differ along a number of dimensions: image versus narrative, automatic versus purposeful, implicit versus explicit. It would surely be premature to make a strong case for a global neuropsychological division in the brain corresponding to these two loosely connected sets of attributes. Nevertheless, research in cognitive neuropsychology increasingly supports the existence of multiple memory systems: "Memory was traditionally thought to be a unitary faculty of the mind. Recently, however, many researchers have adopted the hypothesis that memory consists of a number of systems and subsystems with different operating characteristics. The problem of what these systems and their properties are, and how they are related to one another, now occupies the center stage in research on memory" (Tulving and Schacter, 1990, p. 301). McKee and Squire (1993) were even more assertive about the existence of multiple underlying memory systems: "One of the important insights about memory to emerge recently is that memory is not a single entity but comprises several abilities mediated by distinct brain systems. The major distinction is between a form of memory (termed declarative or explicit) that provides the basis for conscious recollections about previous encounters and various forms of nonconscious memory that support skill and habit learning, simple conditioning, and priming" (p. 397). The separate systems described by these authors—implicit versus explicit memory or conscious versus nonconscious memory—capture some of the qualities of the imagistic and narrative modes described in this chapter.

Other researchers are more cautious about drawing a direct connection between observed performance on memory tasks and underlying brain structures (Jacoby, 1988; Roediger, 1990). One issue is that the number of hypothesized systems needed to explain the influx of new data could skyrocket in the near future. Roediger estimated that "some 20 to 25 different memory systems might be implicated just on the basis of dissociations discovered by cognitive neuropsychologists in studying brain-damaged patients" (p. 1053). Johnson and Multhaup (1992) offered a sensible intermediate perspective: "Memory serves an extraordinary range of functions. . . . It is possible that a single, undifferentiated cognitive system accomplishes all of this, but it seems unlikely. On the other hand, it seems even more unlikely that different specialized cognitive/memory subsystems evolved to handle each of these functions. A more likely possibility is that several subsystems evolved and work together in different combinations and degrees to flexibly meet the many cognitive demands we face" (pp. 33–34). This model of interacting memory subsystems working together "in different combinations and degrees" fits nicely with the levels of representation presented in this chapter.

Evolutionary analysis offers a useful, if inconclusive, way to investigate the existence of separate memory systems (Sherry and Schacter, 1987). In a speculative and far-reaching book, Merlin Donald (1991) proposed an evolutionary theory of human cognition that is consistent with the image-narrative duality. According to Donald, primate evolution produced increasingly efficient forms of mental representation. The "cognitive culture" of apes is *episodic:* "Their lives are lived entirely in the present, as a series of concrete episodes, and the highest element in their system of memory representation seems to be at the level of event representation. . . Such memories are rich in specific perceptual content. . . The important feature of this type of memory is its concrete, perceptual nature and its retention of specific episodic details" (pp. 149–150). Animals remember events, but they cannot "re-present a situation to reflect on it, either individually or collectively" (p. 160).

In Donald's hypothesized intermediate evolutionary stage, our ancestors possessed *mimetic* representational abilities: "Mimetic skill or mimesis rests on the ability to produce conscious, self-initiated representational acts that are intentional but not linguistic" (p. 168). Past events are reenacted through signs, gestures, tone of voice changes, and gross body movements, as in ritual dance. Mimetic cognition is governed primarily by the visuomotor system, is "guided by perceptual metaphor" (p. 226), and is limited to "modeling event perceptions" or "representing the outputs of the archaic episodic mind" (p. 188).

The appearance of *mythic* culture marked the birth of the modern mind: "The myth is the prototypical, fundamental, integrative mind tool. It tries to integrate a variety of events in a temporal and causal framework" (p. 215). The appearance of language offered "a wholly new system for representing reality" (p. 259). Through language, myth linked together disparate episodes into larger systems of shared meaning. Language operated on and refined the products of more primitive representational systems: "Symbolic invention on a grand scale allowed the inherent structure of episodic events to be articulated . . . events could be mentally restructured, interrelated, and reshaped in the mind's eye. The human mind had come full circle, starting as the concrete, environmentally bound representational apparatus of episodic culture and eventually becoming a device capable of imposing an interpretation of the world from above" (p. 268).

Donald argued that later developing cognitive systems do not replace earlier systems. Rather, the three modes of representation are functionally, but not necessarily anatomically, distinct, with the more evolved forms of representation coming to dominate the activities of the corresponding cultural epoch. (Donald proposes an additional transition to *theoretic* culture, in which "external symbolic storage" plays a central role. External memory is the "*exact* external analogue of internal, or biological memory, namely, a storage and retrieval system that allows humans to accumulate experience and knowledge" [p. 309]. External memory includes written records, computers, and other devices for recording information. Because the present discussion focuses on internal memory representations, external memory devices are not central to the analysis.) The perceptually based early systems operate in parallel, and in interaction, with the language-based system: "the episodic mind would have become encapsulated, gradually surrounded by more powerful methods of representing reality, while it continued to produce its traditional outputs" (p. 271). The evolution of episodic, mimetic, and mythic culture each "involved the construction of an entirely novel, relatively self-contained representational adaptation. . . The result is, quite literally, a system of parallel representational channels of mind that can process the world concurrently" (p. 357). The temporary locus of mental representation can shift from channel to channel, depending on situational demands.

Donald's evolutionary model supports a conception of personal event memories in which narrative representations exist alongside imagistic, perception-based, core representations. The narrative system has access to at least some of the products of the imagistic system, and therein one observes the difficult process of translating perceptual images into story-like narratives. The subjective experience of remembering is consistent with the notion of parallel systems. When one tries to remember past episodes, visual, auditory, and other stored sensory images are "searched for" by the narrative processor; they are "perceived" in much the same way as are external stimuli; and they are "talked about" as if they were objects of thought, separate from consciousness itself.

Evolutionary analyses point suggestively to an early developing, imagistic form of memory whose core function is to represent events. With the appearance of language, words could be used to describe past experiences for the purpose of avoiding danger and promoting basic survival, and this may indeed have been the initial focus of verbal sharing. But the same narrative memory system that served initially as an efficient tool for representing concrete events may also underlie a variety of modern, specialized memory activities. According to Rubin (1995a, p. 98), "the general view held by most students of the brain is that new functions evolve from older ones, leaving the brain as a collection of leftover parts cannibalized for new purposes rather than as a planned, organized whole." Similarly, Sherry and Schacter (1987) observed that "traits and structures can have many effects on the environment in addition to the function for which they have been shaped by natural selection . . . memory systems that evolve initially as solutions to one environmental problem may come to serve many other functions" (pp. 448–449).

The evolution of narrative memory set the stage for a diverse array of functionally distinct forms of memorial expression. Memory images can be consciously inspected and interpreted with respect to their relevance to present situations; they can be purposefully recalled or consciously avoided in the service of emotional needs; they can be transformed into stories, the sharing of which serves a wide variety of interpersonal and societal functions; and the form of narrative renditions of events can be manipulated in order to sharpen communicative intent.

*

Childhood Amnesia

Further support for the distinction between an early developing imagistic memory system and a later developing narrative memory system comes from studies of childhood memories. Infantile or childhood amnesia, identified about 100 years ago by Freud, builds on the observation that most adults can recall few if any specific episodes from the first years of life: "What I have in mind is the peculiar amnesia which, in

the case of most people, though by no means all, hides the earliest beginnings of their childhood up to their sixth or eighth year" (Freud,
1905/1953, p. 174). Freud believed that early memories are actively
blockaded from adult consciousness by a wall of repression. Forgetting
is motivated by the sexual and aggressive quality of infantile thoughts
and behaviors: "It is impossible to avoid a suspicion that the beginnings of sexual life which are included in that period have provided
the motive for its being forgotten—that this forgetting, in fact, is an
outcome of repression" (Freud, 1916–1917/1963, p. 326). All childhood
events fall victim to amnesia because any memories of this forgotten
period could by association trigger the release of troubling images and
feelings.

The idea that memories of early childhood are held at bay by massive
repression is the conventional view of psychoanalytic theory, but it is
not the only model that Freud considered. In addition to the "blockade"
model of childhood amnesia, Freud alluded to an alternative "selective
reconstruction" model (Pillemer and White, 1989; White and Pillemer,
1979). Within this alternative conception, early memories are inaccessible to adult consciousness because of a disjunction between a lower and
a higher level of cognitive information processing. Early memory images elude consciousness because they are discordant with adults' purposeful recollective efforts. Modern theoretical accounts of childhood
amnesia within developmental and cognitive psychology favor the selective reconstruction perspective—that is, they attribute the paucity of
early memories to developmental changes in cognitive and social functioning rather than to a psychodynamically motivated blockading of
childhood experience.

Scientific interest in childhood amnesia has increased dramatically in
the last decade. In 1972 Campbell and Spear commented on the lack of
systematic research on the forgetting of early childhood experiences:
"the entire phenomenon of infantile amnesia appears to have been repressed by the scientific community rather than investigated systematically" (p. 216). When White and I synthesized research and theory on
childhood amnesia in 1979, we found almost no mention of this psychoanalytic construct in the then-current developmental or cognitive
psychological literature. Now research on childhood amnesia appears
regularly in leading psychological journals. Much of this renewed interest can be attributed to the scientific allure of selective reconstruction:

if childhood amnesia is the result of age-related changes in cognition rather than repression, then it provides a dramatic forum for demonstrating the breadth and explanatory power of contemporary developmental research and theory.

Earliest Memories

Although Freud's initial observations about childhood amnesia were based on case examples, systematic studies of adult long-term memory have convincingly demonstrated an underrepresentation of early childhood events. When adults are asked to report and date their earliest memory, the average age of the memories is strikingly consistent. Early studies by Dudycha and Dudycha (1933a, 1933b, 1941) and by Waldfogel (1948) pinpointed the age of the earliest memory at about 3 1/2 years, notably earlier than Freud's age cut-off of 6 to 8 years. Contemporary studies also have produced a consistent picture. Among college students, Kihlstrom and Harackiewicz (1982) found a mean age of 3.24 years; Mullen (1994) reported a mean age of 3.4 years; and Howes et al. (1993) found a mean age of 3.07 years for females and 3.4 years for males.

Studies of the age of the earliest memory are limited by the fact that participants provided their own age estimates. The pattern of results is similar when people are asked to recount events with a known date of occurrence. Sheingold and Tenney (1982) found that few adults who had been under age 3 at the time of a sibling birth could recall the event, but most adults who had been 4 years of age or older could recall at least some information. Similarly, when children who had experienced an emergency preschool evacuation at age 3 or 4 were asked to recall the event 7 years later, only those preadolescents who had been 4 years old at the time of the evacuation showed convincing evidence of long-term memory (Pillemer, Picariello, and Pruett, 1994). In the clinical domain, Terr (1988) observed that traumatic events that occurred before about age 3 were unlikely to be recalled verbally, whereas traumas that occurred after age 3 could be described in words. Winograd and Killinger (1983) elicited memories of the 1963 assassination of President John Kennedy from high school and college students who had been between 1 and 7 years old at the time of the shooting. Few participants who were under age 3 recalled how they learned about the assassination, but by age 5 a majority of participants reported memories. Usher and Neisser (1993) obtained college students' memories of four salient childhood events: hospitalizations, sibling births, deaths of family members, and family moves. Some students were able to describe characteristics of events that had occurred as early as the third year of life, but memories were rarely reported if the events occurred before the second birthday. In addition, both Usher and Neisser and Winograd and Killinger reported an increase in the complexity of memory content with increasing age at the time of the event: people who had been older at the time of the events not only were more likely to report a memory, they also remembered the events in greater detail.

A third strategy for investigating childhood amnesia is to collect large numbers of childhood memories from adults and then graph memory incidence as a function of age when the remembered events occurred. Waldfogel (1948) conducted the classic study in which college students reported an average of 50 memories of events occurring before age 8. A graph of the number of memories reported by college students as a function of their estimated age at the time of the remembered experiences showed few memories before age 3 and a rapid increase in the number of memories between the ages of 2 and 5. Wetzler and Sweeney (1986) reanalyzed data from a study conducted by Rubin (1982, Study 1) in which college students provided the first memory to come to mind in response to 125 word cues. Memories of events occurring before age 3 were underrepresented compared to later memories, and the decrement was greater than expected as a result of simple memory decay over time. More recently, Rubin and Schulkind (1997) used the word-cueing procedure with college students and older adults and confirmed the paucity of memories before age 3 and the rapid increase in memories during the later preschool years (see Figure 5).

Although research studies of childhood amnesia present a consistent data pattern, age 3 should not be taken as an absolute or universal cutoff for readily accessible memories. In most studies memories are found both below and above the mean age of approximately 3 years. In addition, there are gender and cultural variations in the reported age of the earliest memory (described in Chapter 6). Finally, researchers have elicited early memories using impersonal questionnaires or word cues. The possibility exists that people may report earlier memories in more naturalistic contexts.

Developmental Explanations

Studies of long-term memory in older children and adults portray a consistent pattern: childhood events that occurred before age 2 or 3 are unlikely to be remembered, and the incidence and complexity of memories increases with increasing age at the time of occurrence. This pattern does not support the idea that all early memories are kept out of consciousness by a wall of repression. Rather, there is a tantalizing parallelism between adult memory studies and studies of preschool children's cognition: both point to ages 2 to 5 as a critical period for memory development. Early on, Waldfogel (1948) interpreted the distribution of early childhood memories produced by adults as favoring a developmental rather than a psychodynamic explanation: "When the memories were plotted according to the age of their origin, it was found that there was an increment from year to year which took the form of an ogive and seemed to parallel the growth of language and memory during childhood. This suggested, first, that memory for childhood events

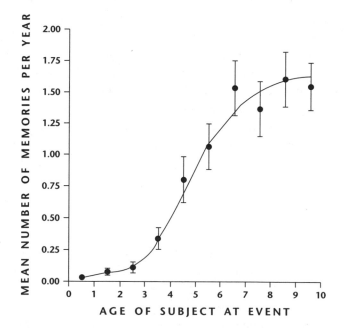

Figure 5. Distribution of word-cued autobiographical memories for the first ten years of life. Source: Rubin and Schulkind, 1997. Copyright © by the American Psychological Association.

might be related to the level of mental development at the time of their occurrence; and, second, that factors besides repression determine the extent and content of childhood recollections" (p. 32).

Which aspects of early mental development are directly implicated in childhood amnesia? Hypothesized psychological factors include language development (Nelson, 1993; Terr, 1988), socially induced changes in the categories of thought (Neisser, 1967; Schachtel, 1947), developmental changes in cognitive processing and understanding (White and Pillemer, 1979; Pillemer and White, 1989; Pillemer et al., 1994), developmental changes in perception (Hayne and Rovee-Collier, 1995), development of a cognitive sense of self (Howe and Courage, 1993), development of an interpersonal or autobiographical self (Fivush, 1988; Nelson, 1993); and development of a representational theory of mind (Perner and Ruffman, 1995). Hypothesized brain mechanisms include hippocampal development (LeDoux, 1996) and neurocortical maturation (McKee and Squire, 1993). Most authors agree that the various explanations are not mutually exclusive, and that a full explanation of childhood amnesia rests on the joint influence of interacting underlying causes.

These accounts of childhood amnesia identify cognitive or social abilities emerging in toddlerhood that provide the foundation for the production of fully conscious, self-referenced narrative memories. By implication, adults cannot retrieve events from the first years of life because early episodes were experienced prior to the emergence of the requisite abilities for purposeful, narrative memory. For example, events that are experienced prelinguistically are not stored in a form that is compatible with voluntary verbal address, and events that occurred prior to the development of a sense of self are not woven into a coherent life history.

Although childhood amnesia has been attributed to lack of the cognitive qualities deemed necessary for a fully functioning autobiographical memory system, it would be a mistake to underestimate the memory capacity of preschool children. Childhood amnesia is not the result of an *absence* of sophisticated memory abilities in young children. On the contrary, recent experimental studies have documented surprisingly advanced forms of memory in infants (Howe and Courage, 1993). Nevertheless, the ways that memories are expressed do change in important ways during the preschool years, and these changes appear to be implicated in the lifting of childhood amnesia.

Prior to the establishment of language as a truly representational medium, infant memory consists of imagistic, affective, and behavioral representations. When memory is assessed nonverbally using a deferred imitation paradigm, even young infants show long-term episodic memory (Bauer and Wewerka, 1997; Meltzoff, 1995). For example, Meltzoff presented 14- and 16-month-old infants with single demonstrations of novel activities. In one of them the experimenter touched the top of a box with his forehead, causing the box to light up. Four months later, infants who had seen the demonstrations were far more likely to act out the unusual behaviors than were control infants. The fact that infants used their foreheads to light up the box suggested that they carried forward an image of the experimenter's specific behaviors rather than a general rule of the form, "press the box and it will light up."

Studies by Myers and colleagues (discussed in Chapter 1) identified behavioral memory for specific infancy events after delays of years (Myers, Clifton, and Clarkson, 1987; Perris et al., 1990). Perris et al. showed that a single experience in a psychology laboratory at 6 1/2 months of age was represented in the behavior of 2 1/2-year-old children, even though the toddlers for the most part could not answer verbal memory questions. At time 1, infants participated in a study of auditory localization where they reached for noise-making objects in the light and dark. At time 2, preschoolers who had participated in the experiment 2 years earlier were more likely to reach accurately for a sounding object than were control children who had not previously experienced the auditory task. The single prior experience in the darkened lab was also reflected in emotional memory: children who participated in the original experiment were more likely than control children to remain in the research room without protest after being "plunged into total darkness" (p. 1803): "There is little question that our dark trials were slightly aversive . . . there is equally clear indication that this was less true for the children who 2 years earlier, at 6.5 months of age, had experienced the dark situation" (p. 1804). Perris et al. stressed the potential importance for long-term memory of reinstating the original learning context; infant memory was demonstrated "under conditions preserving virtually every single aspect of an unusual and distinctive laboratory environment and procedure" (p. 1805).

Perris et al.'s demonstration of long-term emotional memory for a single laboratory experience in infancy is consistent with clinical research on trauma. Terr (1988) observed that children's memories of traumas experienced before age 3 were clearly represented behaviorally (in play) and emotionally (in trauma-specific fears), but children were rarely able to describe the trauma in words. Terr attributed lasting behavioral effects to perceptual memory: "Behavioral memory follows from visual memory, not from verbal memory. . . Associations to visual memories trigger behavioral repetitions, and the behaviors, in turn, set off more behaviors and more pictures" (1988, p. 103). Peterson and Rideout (1997) provided a case illustration in which a 16-month old boy was rushed to an emergency room after falling and cutting his head. The child was wrapped and bound while he was being sutured, and he protested so vehemently that he burst blood vessels in his neck, back and chest. At 34 months of age, he had no verbal recall of the trauma, but behavioral manifestations persisted; for example, he hated public places and refused to be wrapped in a smock to get his hair cut.

Studies of infant and toddler memory suggest that an imagistic and behavioral memory system is in place early in life, and that the system does not depend on conscious, verbal mediation. Additional support for an intact early implicit memory system is provided by laboratory studies that show age-related improvements on explicit memory tasks but not on implicit memory tasks (Roediger, 1990). This is not to say that implicit memory is immune to forgetting; implicit memory performance after lengthy delays is far from perfect (Lie and Newcombe, 1995), but memory is still discernible as long as the delayed test reinstates detailed aspects of the original learning context. Some early memory images are persistent enough to influence feelings and behaviors after months or years.

The rapid growth of language during the preschool years fosters the evolution of narrative memory. Children increasingly engage in explicit, conscious, purposeful, verbal memory activities. The emergence of a narrative memory system marks the end of childhood amnesia and the beginning of an autobiographical sense of self.

∗

Adult-Child Memory Talk and the Genesis of Autobiography

Although the waning of childhood amnesia has multiple interacting causes, language development and subsequent parent-child talk about salient personal events must be pivotal. Even researchers representing other theoretical perspectives acknowledge the centrality of language development for autobiographical memory (Hayne and Rovee-Collier, 1995; Perner and Ruffman, 1995). According to what has been called the "social interaction model" of autobiographical memory development (Nelson, 1993), the narrative memory system does not appear, fully formed, with the appearance of rudimentary language skills. Rather, the child actively constructs a socially accessible autobiographical memory system and a corresponding narrative sense of self through guided memory talk with adults.

Children begin to talk about the past at about 2 years of age (Hudson, 1990, 1993; McCabe and Peterson, 1991; Miller, Potts, Fung, Hoogstra, and Mintz, 1990). Language develops rapidly during the third year of life, and the toddler is increasingly able to describe present and past events in words. The use of verbal descriptions frees up memory from its strong dependence on cues provided by the physical environment; memories can be talked about in contexts that are quite remote from the original situations in which the remembered events took place. Yet memory talk does far more than simply provide a new representational medium for the expression of memories. Language is the tool with which adults model and teach the child what autobiographical memory is: its canonical structure, its functions in everday discourse, and its enduring value for the individual, the family, and the larger community.

According to the social interaction model, children and adults actively co-construct a set of memory activities that the child then internalizes (Fivush, 1991; Fivush and Reese, 1992; Hudson, 1990, 1993; McCabe and Peterson, 1991; Miller et al., 1990; Nelson, 1988, 1993; Pillemer and White, 1989). With respect to narrative expressions of memory, the 2-year-old is a virtual tabula rasa. For example, McCabe and Peterson analyzed toddler-parent memory talk in the home and concluded that the child's memory performance was almost entirely dependent on adult guidance: "We did not find any 'natural storytellers' at age 2. We only found parents who differed in the extent to which they tried to get their children's stories and in the manner in which they went about such collaboration" (1991, p. 250). Viewing personal event memory as a product of social construction represents a major step away from the traditional view of memory as an evolving internal process.

Parent-child dialogue influences three related aspects of the child's emerging autobiographical memory system: (1) memory structure and content, including information about what makes a memory narrative coherent, interesting, and understandable to others; (2) meta-memory functions, including input about why remembering and memory sharing are critically important activities; and (3) the development of a stable sense of self, anchored by a temporally ordered life history composed in part of accessible personal event memories. Each of these products of memory talk will be considered in turn.

Although young toddlers can talk about the past, parent-child memory talk is strikingly one-sided. Parents provide the structure or scaffolding for such conversations. Consider the following interaction between a 26-month-old child and her mother (Hudson, 1993, p. 16):

M: Do you remember when we went to the dentist?
C: (nods)
M: Did you sit up in the big chair?
C: (nods)
M: Who'd you bring with you?
C: Um, Guy.
M: Did he sit in the chair with you?
C: (nods)
M: Do you remember the girl's name that cleaned your teeth, what's her name?
C: Um.
M: Do you remember what her name was?
C: Whisper to me.
M: Do you want Mommy to whisper to you?
C: (whispers in mother's ear) Phyllis.

As children progress through the preschool years, from ages 2 to 5, their memory narratives become increasingly lengthy and complex, and their constructions become less dependent on direct questions and cues provided by adults (Fivush, Haden, and Adam, 1995; see Pillemer and White, 1989 for a review). By engaging the child in memory talk, the parent indicates the desired form and content of autobiographical memory. For example, parents' memory questions often focus on the canonical categories for a good story, including who, what, where, when, and why, and in time the child comes to internalize these categories and thereby structure her own memories in the canonical format (Eisenberg, 1985; Fivush and Hamond, 1990; Fivush and Reese, 1992; Pillemer and White, 1989; Tessler and Nelson, 1994).

In addition to guiding the child's internalization of the proper structure for a memory narrative, parents also indicate what is acceptable memory content: "the caregiver communicates, perhaps directly and insistently, perhaps subtly and unobtrusively, his or her own version of the child's experience. The caregiver may do this by asking questions or making comments that direct the child toward those aspects of the experience that he or she regards as important" (Miller et al., 1990, pp. 299–300). Miller et al. described a conversation between a mother and her 35-month-old son, held in the presence of a researcher. The mother was trying to direct her child's depiction of a visit to a fire station towards "interesting or novel aspects of the experience"; she asked questions such as "What about the noise the truck made?" "Did you see the fire hose?" "Was it a dog in the fire station?" The child, meanwhile, had his own set of interests and communicative agenda, which focused primarily on the objectionable topic (from the mother's point of view) of the firehouse toilets. The mother tried desperately to shift the topic of conversation: "And besides toilets, Calvin! What else did you see?. . . That's enough of that . . . I'm sick of the bathrooms and the toilets. . . That's not important!" The mother's questions and interruptions carried information about what topics are suitable for memory sharing: "By intervening in these ways, the mother carved out for the child the reportable or publicly claimable parts of the experience" (Miller et al., 1990, p. 300).

Parents not only provide a scaffold for the structure and content of children's memory narratives, they also implicitly and explicitly direct their child's attention to the underlying functional significance of memory sharing. Children must learn that memory sharing is considered important and desirable (Eisenberg, 1985). Several authors have identified social functions that joint remembering serves. Nelson (1993) makes a bold claim for social interaction as both the mechanism by which memory skills are learned and also the ultimate purpose of autobiographical memory: "the functional significance of autobiographical memory is that of sharing memory with other people, a function that language makes possible. . . I suggest further that this social function of memory underlies all of our story-telling, history-making narrative activities, and ultimately all of our accumulated knowledge systems" (p. 12). The idea that autobiographical memory is primarily a social instrument was expressed by Janet in 1928:

Janet asks why narrative memory with its predilection for inaccuracy has become the dominant form of human memory. . . The essential goal of retention and remembering is not limited to recounting actions; rather, it is to bring hearers to an experience of the sentiments they themselves would have had if they had been present at the events. Event narration is primarily a social function. The beginning of narrative memory formation can be dated from the occasion when the young child utters what Janet terms the classic phrase of infancy: "I will tell it to Mama." (Ross, 1991, p. 148)

By engaging in memory talk, young children develop an accessible store of personal event memories. Events did not just happen; they happened to a particular child within the enduring context of his or her life. The events happened to the *self*.

Several authors have located the origins of a sense of self in adult-child dialogues about the personal past (for example, Fivush, 1988). Miller et al. (1992) argued that a concept of self is a by-product of narrative activities: "It is assumed that children come to understand who they are not only by reworking and transforming their experience in solitary contexts but by virtue of hearing how significant others portray and respond to them in conversational contexts . . . conversational partners furnish children with models for the interpretation of self and other" (p. 48). Bruner (1987) eloquently made the case for the self as an achievement of narrative construction: "eventually the culturally shaped cognitive and linguistic processes that guide the self-telling of life narratives achieve the power to structure perceptual experience, to organize memory, to segment and purpose-build the very 'events' of a life. In the end, we *become* the autobiographical narratives by which we 'tell about' our lives" (p. 15). Tessler and Nelson (1994) also depicted the self as a reflection of the contents of autobiographical memory: "the relation between autobiographical memory and a sense of self is a dynamic, interactive process in which self and memory organize, construct, and give meaning to each other in a way so intimate that we can truly say that we are what we remember and that our memories are ourselves" (p. 321).

Parent-child conversations about family photographs compellingly illustrate the ways in which memory talk fosters the emergence of self in relation to other people. Edwards and Middleton (1988, pp. 18–19) reported the following conversation between a mother and her 6-year-old daughter Rebecca about a photo in which another young girl is pictured:

C: Mummy Rebecca and? (pointing to girl in picture with herself.)

M: Natisha. A little girl . . . I think that was her name.

C: Natisha.

M: Do you remember playing with her?

C: Natisha. Natisha. Is she my friend?

M: Yes.

C: Did she know Paul? [her brother]

M: Erm well yes but she you two played games together. She was a French girl and although you didn't speak each other's language you still got on well.

[Rebecca's father enters the room]

C: Dad here's me with my friend at France.

F: Oh yes. What's her name?

C: Natisha.

In the process of reconstructing the story, the child's selfhood was expanded to include a friendship with a little girl in France. When addressing her father, the girl in the photograph is no longer an unrecognizable stranger, she is "my friend Natisha."

In other examples, the parent actively makes connections between the child's past and present selves. A mother and her 4-year-old son Paul discussed a photograph of the family having a meal together:

C: Where where am I? There is my seat.

M: Mm. You're not quite in that photograph. Here look (pointing to another picture of Paul sulking) you'd got the grumps that day.

C: Why?

M: I think you was tired in that photograph.

C: Well I couldn't eat all that.

M: What are they?

C: Strawberries and cream.

M: Mm.

C: I didn't like the cream.

M: Did you not?

C: No no.

M: It was fresh cream. Don't you like fresh cream?

C: No.

M: You like ice cream though don't you?

C: Mm.

M: What's Daddy enjoying?

C: He. . .

M: He's got a big grin on his face hasn't he? Look at his salad. . . It was a sea food meal.

C: Yeh the cran meal thing. You remember?

M: Yes when I had the crab.

C: Did I eat mine all up?

M: Erm, no I don't think you liked it did you?
C: No.

As Edwards and Middleton point out, Paul's mother does not discuss the past event in isolation; she also highlights enduring qualities of Paul and his relationship to family members. Paul likes ice cream but not fresh cream, his parents like crab but he does not, when Paul is tired he gets grumpy. The co-construction of Paul's past experiences provides the episodic foundation for his evolving sense of who he is.

Discourse Styles in Adult-Child Memory Talk

Although parent-child conversations about the past occur in all families, marked individual differences are evident in the structure and content of memory talk; these differences help to determine the type of rememberer the child will become. Fivush and her colleagues identified a distinction between high-elaborative and low-elaborative (or repetitive) parents (Fivush, 1991; Fivush and Fromhoff, 1988; Fivush and Reese, 1992; Reese and Fivush, 1993; Reese, Haden, and Fivush, 1993; also see Hudson, 1993). High-elaborative parents engage in lengthy conversations about the past, they provide narrative structure for their children's memories, they ask elaborative questions, and they embellish and add details to the co-constructed narratives. In contrast, low-elaborative parents provide less narrative structure and fewer embellishments, and they often repeat their questions.

The following two mother-child conversations illustrate the low-elaborative style:

M: Do you remember last Christmas?
C: Last Christmas.
M: What did you get for Christmas? Do you remember?
C: What?
M: You can't remember anything. How about a dump truck. Do you remember the dump truck?
C: Yeah.
M: What else did you get?
C: What did I get.
M: Do you remember going to the circus?
(Fivush and Fromhoff, 1988, p. 346).

M: Do you remember when we were down in Florida?
C: Yeah.
M: And we were dyeing Easter eggs?

C: Uh huh.

M: What did we do?

C: Hm. Like what?

M: Like remember, well how did we dye the Easter eggs?

C: Oh. Got some little paint something, goes like that.

M: And can you explain more to me what we did?

C: Oh. The Easter bunny came. . .

M: But I mean about dyeing the eggs, remember that day we were all dyeing the eggs?

C: Yes.

M: How did we do it?

C: What's this for?

M: A tape recorder. Can you tell me how we did that?

C: That, what is that stuff called?

M: What?

C: What we painted the eggs?

M: Dye?

C: No. The little . . . what is that for?

M: It's just a tape recorder, don't worry. I want to know about, how did we do it? Do you remember how we did it and what we did? (Reese et al., 1993, pp. 422–423)

In these examples, low-elaborative mothers probed for the correct answer to a memory question. They did not engage in the process of memory co-construction as a primarily social activity. In the first instance, the mother changed the topic in response to her child's memory failure; in the second instance, the child strayed from the topic when it became apparent that his performance was unsatisfactory.

The following two examples were provided by high-elaborative mothers:

M: Do you remember what Auntie Elizabeth brought you that day when you saw brother for the very first time? Do you remember what she brought you?

C: Yeah.

M: Your most favorite thing in the whole world? Your favorite friend? Who is it?

C: Baby Dillon (her brother).

M: Baby Dillon. Is that who your most favorite friend is?

C: Yeah.

M: That's real special. I was talking about something that's furry and brown and real soft.

C: Yeah.

M: It was the first time you got your. . .?

C: Yeah.

M: Who do you sleep with every night?
C: Teddy bear.
M: That's right.
    (Fivush and Fromhoff, 1988, p. 346)

M: Do you remember something really, really, really special that you and I
    got to do?
C: Uh uh.
M: Got on the train. . .
C: Yeah.
M: We went to the Omni. . .
C: Un huh. And we saw Sesame Street Live.
M: Right. Where were our seats?
C: Um, I forget.
M: Way up high. How high?
C: In the balcony.
M: So high all the way over the. . .? Do you remember? The stage?
C: Yeah.
M: What did we see?
C: We saw Big Bird. We saw, um, the Honkers, we saw Ernie and Bert, we
    saw Grover.
M: What was the stage set up like?
C: I don't know.
M: It had a bell on top. . .
C: Oh, school.
M: Yeah, yeah. . . Do you remember what some of the kids in the audience
    got to do?
C: Uh uh.
M: Go up on the stage.
C: I wish I had got to.
M: Well yeah, but we were up so high, we got to see Big Bird puttin' his head
    on and stuff like that, remember?
C: Yeah.
M: When we could see before anybody else could see 'cause we could see
    over the top of the stage.
C: Hm.
    (Reese et al., 1993, p. 424)

These high-elaborative mothers varied their questions, provided elaborate memory cues, and actively engaged in the memory process even when their children were producing very little information. In fact, it is precisely when children are participating in the conversation but are not recalling any new information that the difference between high- and low-elaborative mothers is most evident: high-elaborative mothers "embellish on the event in order to perpetuate the memory narrative" (Reese et al., 1993, p. 418).

Although all parents use aspects of both high- and low-elaborative styles, many show a dominant or preferred style (Fivush and Reese, 1992). High-elaborative mothers communicate to their children the idea that remembering is a valued and enjoyable social activity, whereas low-elaborative mothers communicate the view that memory is a storehouse of knowledge or facts: "The message they may be giving their children is that the interpersonal aspect of these conversations is not as important as the issue of accuracy in memory" (Fivush and Reese, 1992, p. 9).

Tessler and Nelson (1994) proposed a related distinction between narrative and paradigmatic memory styles, based upon a dichotomy introduced by Bruner (1986). Narrative parents make frequent references to autobiographical information and their verbal style is dynamic, playful, interpretive, imaginative, and connected. Paradigmatic parents make frequent references to the child's knowledge base rather than to autobiographical episodes, and their verbal style emphasizes explanation, specification, and concrete distinctions.

McCabe and Peterson's (1991) typology included topic-switching, repetitive, and topic-extension, narrative styles. Like low-elaborative mothers, parents who frequently switch topics or ask direct questions and simply repeat back their children's responses do not engage in extended narrative co-constructions with their children. In contrast, topic-extending parents closely resemble high-elaborative parents; they willingly engage in prolonged conversations about past events with their children and persist in the face of the children's limited conversational skills and even resistance. McCabe and Peterson indentifed a fourth style, confrontational topic-extension, in which a parent who is actively participating in memory talk interjects abrupt correctives. The adult seems as concerned with teaching the child how to produce a correct narrative as she is in engaging the child. The benefits of such teaching may be offset by the dampening effect repeated correctives have on the child's spontaneous memory construction and elaboration. For example, a 40-month-old boy responded to the parental question, "What did you see in our harbor?" followed by the cue "We saw a big pile of something," with an elaborate description: "We saw a big pile of something. It was, it was a pile of salt and it was for the street to get to make the cars rusty." His mother corrected, "Well they don't actually get it in just to make the cars rusty. That's not the purpose." When the boy's father followed up with the question, "It's on the roads to melt the?" the child responded, "I don't know," ending the elaboration he began moments earlier (pp. 244–245).

Does the form of parent-child conversations about the past influence children's autobiographical memory? Researchers have recorded parent-child conversations about specific personal events, coded the quality of memory talk, and examined whether children's memory performance at a later time is predicted by memory styles demonstrated months or years earlier (Fivush, 1991; Hudson, 1993; McCabe and Peterson, 1991; Reese et al., 1993; Tessler and Nelson, 1994). Several main findings are apparent. First, children's own memory style reflected the style used by their parents. Second, events that were discussed with parents were more likely to be recalled at a later time period. Third, parental style at time 1 predicted children's recall at time 2, with children of parents who utilized the high-elaborative, narrative, and topic-extending styles producing more specific and elaborate memory narratives.

Reese et al. (1993) examined mother-child conversations about salient one-time events the two had experienced together. Conversations were recorded at four different time periods, when the children were 40, 46, 58, and 70 months of age. At each time point, children with high-elaborative mothers provided more memory information. A clear relationship between mothers' conversational styles at 40 months and children's memory at later time points also was apparent: "The more elaborative mothers are at the 40-month time point, the more memory responses children are providing 1 1/2 and 2 1/2 years later . . . maternal elaborations early in the preschool period facilitate children's later memory responding" (p. 419). Importantly, the amount of information children remembered early on did not predict their later memory performance; rather, memory style appeared to be the key factor in promoting rich narrative production years later: "what mothers do early in development is important for getting their children 'into the system.' High-elaborative mothers engage in rich, embellished discussions of the past with their young children, even though their children are not yet able to participate fully in these conversations. In this way, children of high-elaborative mothers learn both the forms and the values of reminiscing" (Reese et al., 1993, pp. 426–427).

Tessler and Nelson (1994) had mother-child pairs engage in planned activities and recorded their conversations. In a first study, mothers and their 3-year-old children visited a museum of natural history. Consistent with other studies, when mother-child conversations in the museum were analyzed, children's conversational styles closely resembled their mothers' styles. One week later, children were interviewed without their mothers present. No child recalled objects from the museum that had not been talked about with his or her mother during the visit: "in every case the sole objects recalled were those that had been the focus of joint conversation by mother and child" (p. 311).

In a second study, mothers and their 4-year-old children took photographs of 12 self-selected neighborhood situations or activities; their conversations during the picture-taking session were recorded. One week later, children were interviewed alone about the activity, and they were shown a picture book containing their photographs and asked questions about them. Three weeks later, the picture book was again presented to the children and the children were queried about it. As in the first study, children's conversational styles paralleled their mothers' styles. Children only recalled information that had been talked about earlier, and children of narrative mothers recalled more information about the pictures than did children of paradigmatic mothers. Children's memory styles appeared to be well established: when the experimenter asked questions in a style that differed from the mothers' style, children "reformatted" them in a manner consistent with the style to which they were accustomed. For example, narrative children might reply to an impersonal, knowledge-based question about a picture of a bank, such as "What do people do in a bank?", with a specific autobiographical episode: "My sister threw my piggy bank on the floor and it broke" (p. 317).

Parent-child communication also appears to enhance memory for highly negative events. Goodman, Quas, Batterman-Faunce, Riddlesberger, and Kuhn (1994) interviewed 3- to 10-year-old children who had undergone a painful medical procedure involving urethral catherization between 6 and 27 days earlier. Mothers also described conversations that they had had with their children about the procedure. Children whose mothers did relatively little supporting, talking, and explaining were especially likely to give inaccurate memory responses; the results "implicate parental communication and emotional support as important influences on accurate memory for stressful events experienced in childhood" (p. 289).

The socialization of children's event memory is evident in these empirical studies; memory talk appears to have a persistent effect on both what children remember and how they remember. Schank and Abelson

(1995, pp. 33–34) made the strong (one could argue overly strong) claim that storytelling *is* memory: "We remember by telling stories. Storytelling is not something we just happen to do. It is something we virtually have to do if we want to remember anything at all. . . It is in the storytelling process that the memory gets formed. . . To put this another way, the stories we create are the memories we have. Telling is remembering." Developmental research supports the essential connection between talking about an event and remembering it later on. It also indicates that stories about the past do not conform to one uniform model. Styles of talking about the past vary considerably, and these variations are related to the way in which children structure the foundation events in their evolving autobiography.

While the social interaction hypothesis has already received empirical support, more refined analyses of the relationship between parent-child conversational styles and children's memory could present an even more compelling case. Nelson (1993, p. 12) asserted that "the initial functional significance of autobiographical memory is that of sharing memory with other people. Memories become valued in their own right—not because they predict the future and guide present action, but because they are sharable with others and thus serve a social solidarity function." In most of the research studies described in this chapter, the experimenter-defined purpose of remembering was simply to discuss past events. But in many everyday situations memories are not recounted simply for the sake of sharing them with others; rather, autobiographical memory talk serves one of several, more precise interpersonal functions (Pillemer, 1992b). Even the dichotomy between high- and low-elaborative parents suggested different functional purposes for memory; some mothers appeared to emphasize accurate event representation, whereas other mothers focused on interpersonal connection. Children of high-elaborative parents may become highly skilled raconteurs, but this need not imply that they have an advantage in other functional domains of memory.

Parents frequently engage in extended memory talk in order to guide their children's behavior, rather than to promote reminiscence for its own sake. Miller et al. (1990, p. 302) observed that working-class parents often demand accuracy in their children's memories: "They are saying, in effect, that the only defensible claims to personal experience are those that meet a criterion of literal truth." Adhering to the rigors of accurate reporting no doubt interferes with memory for its own sake, but it insures that the lessons learned from past experience will be true to fact.

In immigrant Chinese families, parent-child discourse about the past frequently focuses on rule violations, and how to avoid trouble in the future. A 3-year-old boy and his mother discussed a recent experience at the zoo:

> C: Yes, in the zoo I, that slide, I didn't let the other kids play.
> M: Yes. It was your fault, wasn't it?
> C: Yes.
> M: Papa was mad at you.
> C: Yes.
> M: Papa said, "How come you didn't listen to me?"
>   (Miller et al., 1990, p. 301)

Rather than drawing the child into an extended dialogue about the event, the mother takes the opportunity to illustrate what can go wrong and to reinforce the directive: "Obey your parents!"

In middle-class Caucasian families, memory conversations also commonly focus on prescriptions for behavior. Miller et al. (1990, p. 303) provided an example in which a mother recounted an episode from her own childhood in order to underscore the admonition that her 31-month-old child not climb on a chair:

> M: You know what, Billy? When I was a little girl, one time I was playing in the kitchen and you know what happened? I toppled over and I cut my mouth, and I had to go to the doctor and he had to fix it, yeah. So you have to be very, very careful.
> C: Uh huh. One day I'm topple over.
> M: But you don't wanna topple over because you could fall. . .

In this instance, the mother's narrative was not intended to draw her son into joint reminiscence, but rather to teach an important lesson about how to avoid danger.

These memories carry guidelines for present and future behavior, and as such they are early precursors of mature forms of memory directives—including memorable messages, symbolic messages, and analogous events. Early memory directives can be quite mundane, as when a parent reminds the child of past transgressions as a way to gain compliance. For example, a parent may say: "Remember the last time we were in this restaurant? What did you order? Did you finish it?" The parent models the process of inspecting past events for the purpose of informing a current decision. In another example, a father helped his daughter look for a book, and he modeled using memory to guide their search:

F: We had it last night. I saw it on the bed.

C: I can't find it.

F: We had it last night. Right here.

C: It must be under the bed.

F: Here it is . . . under *Doctor DeSoto*. Remember, we read this last night right before bed so we put it on top.

In each of these instances, the communicative goal focuses on specific learning or prescriptions for behavior rather than social bonding per se. In other cases, the primary function of memory sharing may be to alter an emotional state, as when a parent engages the child in detailed conversation about a pleasant past experience to shift the focus away from an undesirable present situation. Or the child may be encouraged to recount an unpleasant experience in order to promote emotional healing and deeper understanding. Outside of experimental settings in which a researcher sets memory sharing itself as the explicit agenda, there exist other targeted purposes or functions of memory talk, including but not limited to social bonding. This observation in no way undermines the idea that autobiographical memory is a product of social construction; rather, it indicates that particular uses grow out of particular kinds of memory talk between parents and children. Parents' implicit or explicit communicative goals influence which functions will assume center stage in the child's own memory operations.

Cognitive Constraints on Narrative Memory

Narrative memory does not burst upon the scene when the toddler first acquires language. Rather, early adult-child memory talk is one-sided, with parents providing virtually all of the narrative structure and much of the dialogue. Parents persistently engage their children in conversations about the past in the face of limited narrative skills, inattention, and even tortured resistance on the child's part. These early episodes of joint remembering lay the groundwork for the child's later self-generated recall efforts. The parent's questions implicitly outline what is memorable about an event and how to communicate the memory to others. In time, autobiographical memory becomes increasingly child- rather than parent-directed, and the child has at her disposal a growing cache of personal event memories and the necessary verbal skills for sharing them with others.

Although narrative skills open the door to autobiography, verbal processing alone does not insure that early memories will persist into later childhood and adulthood. Toddlers' sparse verbal accounts do not share the story-like qualities of mature narratives. Proposed cognitive constraints on narrative memory include the ability to use language as a truly representational system (Nelson, 1993); the representational ability to encode events as having been experienced by the self (Perner and Ruffman, 1995); the ability to comprehend and integrate extended event sequences (Barsalou, 1988); and the ability to understand the temporal and causal structure of unfamiliar and complex events and thereby to produce temporally and causally coherent narrative depictions (Pillemer, 1992a; Pillemer et al., 1994; Pillemer and White, 1989).

Establishing a convincing link between children's evolving cognitive abilities and adults' recall of their distant past requires longitudinal studies. Is an older child's or adult's memory for a salient early episode constrained by the quality of his or her narrative formulation of the event as a young child? Peterson and Rideout (1997) interviewed 1-to-3 year old children shortly after they received emergency hospital treatment for physical injuries. Children were reinterviewed 6, 12, and 18–24 months later. The influence of narrative skills on recall was apparent. Children who were under age 2 during the initial interview usually could not give a verbal memory, and they did not provide coherent narrative accounts during later interviews. In contrast, slightly older children who were able to describe their traumas in words during the first interview often could recount major aspects of their ordeals 2 years later.

Memory talk by itself does not guarantee that momentous childhood events will be remembered for many years. The child's initial level of understanding also predicts memory performance. Pillemer et al. (1994; also see Pillemer, 1992a) interviewed children about an emergency preschool evacuation following a fire alarm. Children were interviewed twice: 2 weeks and again 7 years after the event. At time 1, children who attended an older classroom (mean age: 4 1/2 years) were compared to children in a younger classroom (mean age: 3 1/2 years). Although all of the preschoolers were able to answer some memory questions at time 1, the memory narratives produced by the older children were more coherent and showed a better understanding of the temporal and causal sequence of events. Almost one-half (44%) of the older children but only 8% of the younger children spontaneously mentioned the actual cause of the fire alarm—burning popcorn—and 75% of older children but only 33% of younger children described a sense of urgency in evacuating the building. In response to the direct question, "Where were you when you heard the fire alarm?" almost all of the older preschoolers placed themselves inside the school building, as an adult would have done. Surprisingly, a majority of the younger preschoolers placed themselves outside in the playground, where they had gathered after the evacuation. The following excerpts illustrate this qualitative age difference in performance:

> I *(interviewer)*: Where were you when you heard that loud noise? Do you remember that?
> C *(4½ years old)*: I was at the blue corner making something.
> I: You were at the blue corner making something. So, do you remember what you were making?
> C: Yeah.
> I: What was it?
> C: A necklace.
> I: A necklace. Ah, that's very nice. When you heard that loud noise, though, what did you think that it was?
> C: The fire alarm.
> I: You knew it was the fire alarm. Oh, that's good. How did you feel when you heard that loud noise?
> C: Very kind of frowned.
> I: Frowned.
> C: Yeah.
> I: Were you scared? Or were you. . .
> C: No, just frowned.
> I: Just frowned. How did other people feel, do you remember how other people felt?
> C: No.
> I: Do you remember how Mary [teacher] felt or how the other children felt?
> C: No.
> I: No? What did you do after you heard that big noise?
> C: We went back in.
>
> I: Where were you when you heard that fire alarm?
> C *(3½ years old)*: We were sitting on the sandbox.
> I: On the sandbox. Uh huh. And what were you doing there?
> C: We were singing songs.
> I: You were singing songs. When you heard that loud noise, what did you think it was?
> C: The alarm clock.
> I: The alarm clock. Uh huh. And how did you feel when you heard that loud noise?

> C: I feeled sort of scared . . . but I don't feel scared . . . just
> feeled sort of scared.
> I: Sort of scared. How did other people feel . . . do you
> remember how Dorothy [teacher]. . .
> C: They feeled happy.
> I: They all felt happy? Why did they feel happy?
> C: They just did because they thought that noise was great.
> I: It was great, they thought the noise was great? What did
> you do after you heard the noise?
> C: After I heard the noise I just . . . um . . . my mommy . . .
> my mommy came and bringed me home.

This 3 1/2-year-old's memory for location and activity was not wrong in a technical sense, because the alarm could still be heard from the safety of the playground, and the children did in fact sing songs there. But the consistent age differences in location, alongside age differences in identifying burning popcorn as the cause and ascribing a sense of urgency to the evacuation, indicated that the 4 1/2-year-olds had a superior grasp of temporal sequence and causality. Research in a number of domains has pinpointed ages 3 to 5 as a critical period for the development of causal and temporal understanding (Pillemer, 1992a).

At time 2, 7 years later, the children (now preadolescents) returned to the school building and were interviewed about preschool experiences, including the fire alarm. Interviews were conducted by a researcher who was unaware of the children's memory performance at time 1. Only those preadolescents who had been in the older preschool group at the time of the fire alarm showed convincing evidence of long-term memory. Almost one-third of older participants were able to give a story-like narrative account in which causality was established, 57% provided at least a fragmentary narrative memory, and 86% selected their correct classroom location in response to a forced-choice question. In contrast, none of the younger participants gave an intact narrative, only 18% produced even a fragmentary verbal response, and their identification of classroom location was no better than chance.

The temporally and causally coherent narrative memories produced by the older preschoolers were potentially identifiable years later as an emergency building evacuation in response to a fire alarm, whereas the more limited narrative memories produced by younger preschoolers were not tied as clearly to adult-like conceptions of fire alarms and were not purposefully retrievable in response to a direct verbal probe. The same cognitive-developmental explanation may apply to other events for which childhood amnesia has been demonstrated. How could an adult remember the Kennedy assassination, the birth of a sibling, or the death of a relative, if the target event was poorly understood in childhood and was encoded in a way that is incompatible with an adult's conception of the event? With respect to the Kennedy assassination, the young toddler might encode parents' unusual and extreme expressions of sadness and the disruption of normal routines as adults monitored the news on television; but because a toddler has no conception of presidents and little knowledge of shooting or death, the primitive memory images could not be linked directly to the abstract world event and they are unlikely to be triggered in adulthood by the verbal cue "assassination of President Kennedy."

Repression as a Failure of Translation

Developmental research points to the selective reconstruction model rather than the standard psychoanalytic blockade model as the key to understanding not only childhood amnesia but also repression. Events that are experienced before about age 2—prior to the establishment of narrative memory—are encoded imagistically. When the child begins to engage in conversations about the past, events are also encoded narratively; but if the young child's understanding of the episodes is limited, and if the child has not yet internalized mature models of narrative structure, the verbal memories may not resemble an adult's conception of what transpired. Deliberate attempts to recall the event years later may fail because the imagistic or childlike memory representation is incompatible with the adult's purposeful reconstructive efforts.

Attributing childhood amnesia to a failure of translation from an imagistic, behavioral, or affective level of representation to a narrative representation is consistent with contemporary cognitive and clinical models, described earlier in this chapter, that distinguish between an early developing perceptual memory system and a later developing verbal memory system. Mandler (1990, p. 326) observed that "childhood amnesia usually involves preverbal memories, and these must be the most difficult of all to cue after one has reached the age at which one's thought processes become saturated with language." Mandler's own earliest memory was "entirely visual"; it was not until late adolescence that she accidentally "learned from an adult who had been there what exactly had happened" and identified her age at the time (18 months).

In the case of memories of complex and unexpected events, such as an emergency preschool evacuation or a presidential assassination, a translation problem may exist even after the child has acquired language. For participants in Pillemer et al.'s (1994) fire alarm study, a preschool memory of sitting in an unusually orderly fashion on the playground, on a cold day, without a coat on, singing songs, may be "discovered" later in life only when it is reconstrued from an adult's perspective: "That must have been a fire alarm!"

Spence (1982, p. 61) defined the transformation of childhood images into mature narratives as a central task of psychoanalysis. "What has been called the 'recovery' of childhood memories may refer to the patient's new-found ability to capture a complex image in words and present it, fully fledged, in language that for the first time conveys its true complexity in a way that we can understand." Memories do not suddenly reappear; rather, they become increasingly intelligible: "the memory was available from the beginning of treatment in more or less fixed form . . . what changes is not the memory but the patient's ability to describe it."

The reasons that an early trauma, such as a sexual assault, may not be remembered will include the child's incomplete understanding of the event and the absence of willing and nurturant adult conversational partners. Crawford et al. (1992) gave the example of a woman's buried memory of improper sexual contact that had occurred when she was 11 years old. According to Crawford et al., the memory probe "Were you ever sexually assaulted as a child?" could be ineffective because the original event was not encoded in this way: "We can be fairly sure, then, that this person would not have produced the above memory or any other memory in response to the request to provide a memory of child sexual assault. . . But the memory was not repressed in the sense that it was difficult to retrieve. It was just difficult if not impossible to retrieve by classifying it under the heading of 'child sexual assault.' It became intelligible in those terms only when retrieved using quite a different trigger . . . and only after many years" (p. 164).

Crawford et al. (1992) proposed a general clinical model of repression that fits nicely with cognitive models of selective reconstruction:

> From this analysis, we consider repression in the following terms. An event occurs. It is problematic. It has some immediate strong affect (most likely negative). The actor tries to construct a meaning, but is unable to do so because the social building blocks for doing so are not available. It cannot be

constructed in a meaningful way and in addition it does not fit with the person's definition of self. It never does become part of the construction of self because it has not been worked on (reflected on) and neither were there available tools for doing so. It is not erased, it stays there (possibly in the unconscious) until such time as something else triggers it. It is possibly triggered by a future episode that reawakens the affect (emotional response) or the unintelligibility. (p. 164)

This analysis has implications for the current debate about the possible recovery of "repressed" memories after a period of years (Loftus, 1993). According to the theory of selective reconstruction, early memories of trauma will be elusive when childhood events were not discussed or thought about in a way that would render them understandable within a fully evolved narrative conception of self. Direct verbal cues such as "Were you ever sexually abused as a child?" will be successful only if the memory is immediately recognizable as sexual abuse from an adult's viewpoint, or if a relevant sensory image is later recategorized as such. Some women whose initial answers to this question are negative may "discover" a memory of abuse at a later time, "in a social context where child sexual assault has been defined, talked about, written about" (Crawford et al., 1992, p. 164). From this perspective, memory "recovery" after very long time periods is possible, but the main culprit to overcome is inadequate cognitive understanding and narrative assimilation rather than the blockading energy of repression. The recovered memory reflects not only perceptual images of the original occurrence, but also the reconstructive and reinterpretive efforts that brought them into current focus.

Selective reconstruction does not rule out the possibility that memories of severe trauma may be actively avoided or even blockaded from consciousness, but motivated forgetting is an unlikely cause of childhood amnesia. Rather, the ubiquitous absence of early childhood memories reflects a disjunction between more primitive memory representations at encoding and higher levels of cognitive organization during recall. Failure to remember is overcome only when early memory traces, triggered by strong feelings or distinctive physical contexts, are reconstrued from an adult's perspective and linked to the overarching self narrative.

Chapter 5

*

The
Living Past
in Everyday
and Clinical Contexts

*A*LMOST 50 years after witnessing his father's suicide, historian Jan Wiener returned to the place where the death occurred. The visit released a flood of vivid memories. In 1941, father and 20-year-old son had fled the Nazi onslaught in their native Czechoslovakia, but it caught up with them in Yugoslavia. Over a game of chess, they discussed death:

We were sitting facing each other, the chessboard between us, our hands locked. I raised my eyes and looked into his face: the long grey hair combed back, the light blue eyes with the green specks and that bold hooked nose. "What choices do we have?" I asked, finally. "To die our own way or theirs. We are trapped and I cannot run any more." I looked out the window into the falling dusk. This is not happening, I thought. My father is supposed to know a way out. "Tonight," my father said in a low voice, "I will take my life." I had been prepared for these words, and yet they came as a blow because he said them softly. "What about me?" I asked. . . "Jan," he said, "you would do best if you did the same. There is no chance. I am not afraid of death. I am afraid of humiliation." "How will you do it?" I whispered. "Poison. It is completely painless. You fall asleep." After a long dark silence he asked, "What is your decision?". . . Finally I said, "I want to try to get away.". . . We went to my father's bedroom. He opened a drawer and took out 10 gold pieces. They were on a string. Father put them around my neck. He gave me the little money he had. "Try to get to Ljubljana and go to the Bolaffios' house," he said, referring to friends of our family. "They might help you. Tell them what has happened." He smiled faintly. "Dying is easy. Leaving you is difficult. I love you, son." We were standing, holding each other. Breaking the embrace, my father said, "Let's finish the game." And we sat down at the chessboard. I lost. "Promise me that you will wait until I am dead. If I am still breathing when you come into the room in the morning, wait. If the Nazis find me alive, they'll pump out my stomach and I would have lost the freedom to choose."

I went to my bedroom, undressed and tried to sleep. . . I ran to my father's room and opened the door. He was standing by a table, putting white powder on a wafer. He looked up and said firmly: "You must not disturb me any more! Take this"—he handed me two sleeping pills—"it will make you sleep. Good-bye, now. Goodbye." When I awoke early the next morning, I jumped out of bed and ran into father's room. . . His breathing became loud and slow. Then it faded away. I took my father's wedding ring and put it in my pocket. I bent down and kissed his forehead. I kissed his hand, took the other hand and gently folded them over his chest.   (Wiener, 1991, pp. 10, 30)

Wiener dramatically illustrates the narrative power of the episode. The vivid details are not necessary to communicate the main point of the story: that his father took his own life to avoid persecution by the Nazis. But the inclusion of particulars has an unmistakable impact. The embellished narrative commands sustained attention and interest. Were Wiener to recount the episode in conversation, interruptions or shifts of topic would be unlikely to occur. The explicit details also render the story persuasive, believable, and authoritative. Finally, the memory poignantly conveys Wiener's sorrow, and it elicits emotion and empathy in the reader far more effectively than would a straightforward statement of the form: "To avoid persecution by the Nazis, my father poisoned himself. I witnessed this event as a 20-year-old, just prior to my own escape."

Wiener's narrative is energized by a persistent connection to its underlying imagistic and emotional core. Wiener's description of minute details—he and not his father had lost their last chess match, his father handed him exactly two sleeping pills, his father stated his decision to kill himself in a soft voice—and his frequent use of verbatim quotes implies the continued existence of strong and vivid underlying visual and auditory memory representations. This was no disengaged, time-worn narrative that existed apart from its imagistic origins; rather, the vividness of his memories suggests that remembering involved mentally re-experiencing the past trauma. Wiener described the subjective experience of recall, triggered by his return to the house in which the suicide occurred, as engaged perceptual reliving: "A wave of remembering washed out the present, and I heard my father's voice" (p. 10). The perceptual images were accompanied by an upswell of involuntary emotional reactivity: "In the kitchen, there were the same wood-carved chair and unsteady table. My knees gave in and I sat down. I was trembling with the force of a memory I thought I had under control" (p. 10).

As this example suggests, the distinction between imagistic and narrative modes of representation is central to understanding not only the development of autobiography but also mature memory functions. Wiener's recollection and verbal description of unthinkable terror and loss derives its power in part from its intimate connection to sensory experience. Wiener does not simply call up a polished narrative account of the episode; he hears his father's voice, he sees the poison sprinkled on the wafer, and he bodily feels "the force of a memory." Similarly, the memory's communicative thrust—its hold on the listener's or reader's attention, its believability and authenticity, and its emotional impact—derives in part from its perceptual and affective intensity, the implied connection between what was experienced years ago and what is now said and relived.

This chapter examines the interactions between image and narrative in adult remembering and talk about the past. The impact of sharing personal event memories is enhanced when the speaker describes particular episodes rather than more general occurrences, and communicative power is greatest when the memories convey a connection to underlying sensory images. One salient communicative marker is the sudden and automatic verb tense shifts from the past into the present at the emotional highpoint of a memory narrative. Present tense shifts occur when especially vivid underlying imagistic and affective representations intrude into deliberate narrative processing. Other, more dramatic forms of mental reliving of past episodes can be observed primarily in clinical contexts. Finally, memory images influence thoughts, feelings, and behaviors implicitly as well as explicitly; to explain these unaware effects of specific memories, a speculative model of preconscious memory processing is presented.

*

Communicative Power of the Specific Episode

The social interaction model of memory development situates the genesis of autobiography in parent-child conversations about the past. Memory sharing continues to be a prominent part of spoken and written communication throughout the life course. It is a sophisticated process in which past events are not simply reported as they come to mind. Rather, memory sharing is governed by a system of rules or conventions, a grammar of memorial expression, that has become a topic of psychological analysis only recently (Pillemer, 1992b; Schank, 1990; Schank and Abelson, 1995).

Responses to a request for personal information, such as "How was the wedding?" or "How did your father die?" vary along a continuum from general and impersonal to specific and detailed. Jan Wiener could just answer, "My father died in the Holocaust," or he could give the extraordinarily gripping account presented at the beginning of this chapter. The type of memory response hinges in part on the context or "communicative frame" (Edwards and Middleton, 1986) in which the question is asked. It would not be surprising if Wiener chose to share intimate personal details with a loved one or a trusted psychotherapist, whereas a casual lunch companion or a medical examiner for an insurance company would be unnerved by a spontaneous outpouring of vivid detail and heartfelt emotion.

Spoken conversation is rule-governed (Grice, 1975; Myllyniemi, 1986). Grice's well-known conversational maxims include: "Do not make your contribution more informative than is required," "Be relevant," and "Be brief." In everyday conversation, recounting full-blown personal event memories frequently appears to violate the maxims of brevity and relevance. With respect to brevity, for example, Labov (1982, p. 227) observed that "when people tell narratives, they occupy a larger portion of social time and space than in most other conversational turns." Extended memory sharing frequently demands an explanation: "If during an encounter with a casual acquaintance the speaker repeatedly described personal memories, the listener would attempt to decipher the meaning of this unusual conversational style; a hidden agenda, perhaps, or a subtle indication of psychopathology" (Pillemer, 1992b, p. 243). Bruner (1990, p. 115) made a similar observation about the expectations of social science researchers who conduct interviews: "We expect answers like 'Meeting the financial strains' in response to 'What were the hardest times early in your marriage?' As interviewers, we typically interrupt our respondents when they break into stories, or in any case we do not code the stories: they do not fit our conventional categories."

Although recounting the details of specific past episodes is antithetical to the conventions of efficient discourse, memory sharing is a universal phenomenon nevertheless. Like self-disclosure (Archer, 1980; Jourard, 1979) and politeness (Brown, 1990), the way that we share memories depends on the relationship between conversational partners and the setting in which the interaction occurs. In general, detailed and extended memory talk will occur more frequently among intimates than among strangers, in private rather than in public, under circumstances where the communicative agenda is personal rather than professional, in psychotherapists' rather than dentists' offices. But specific communicative goals rather than general structural characteristics of relationships or settings matter most: a pediatric dentist may engage her patient in detailed conversation about last summer's vacation in order to shift attention from the unpleasant business at hand.

Tenney's (1989) analysis of phone conversations concerning the birth of a baby demonstrated the importance of communicative context in memory talk: details were presented, withheld, or elaborated depending on the psychological needs of the speaker and the perceived needs of the listener. For example, "one reporter went out of her way to spare her mother the details of her difficult labor, although she did not hesitate to describe her ordeal to a friend. Another reporter refrained from mentioning any problems to his grandmother until she began to reminisce about her own difficulties in labor" (p. 231). Even in psychology experiments, the frequency with which research participants will share personal event memories depends strongly on how the memories are elicited (Pillemer, 1992b).

Memory sharing is much more than a simple exchange of information about the past: "The *act* of sharing personal details with others communicates meaning over and above the particular informational content of the memories, and thereby helps the speaker achieve important interpersonal goals" (Pillemer, 1992b, p. 242). The decision to share a personal episode enhances communicative impact in predictable ways: increasing attention, authority, and memorability; promoting believability and persuasiveness; and fostering emotionality, intimacy, and empathy.

Attention, Authority, and Memorability

Successful communication requires that the speaker gain the attention and interest of the listener. It is impossible to make a memorable contribution to a conversation if no one is listening to what you have to say. Personal event memories, with their vivid sensory and emotional content and story-like structure, are more captivating than disengaged, general descriptions of past experience. Skilled teachers know how to capitalize on the power of the episode: "If you can begin with a story, an example, a startling statistic, a personal experience, or something that has significant attention-holding appeal, attention will be captured" (Weaver and Cotrell, 1987, p. 62). A speaker can generate interest and direct the conversational flow by recounting a relevant personal event memory: "Sometimes we speak solely to keep on being able to speak or simply to get the general topic of a story on the floor for discussion. For example, we might tell a story about a problem in a particular relationship if we wanted to discuss relationships in general" (Schank, 1990, p. 51).

Middleton and Buchanan (1994) illustrated the attention-getting qualities of the specific episode. Conversational participants were elderly members of a hospital-based reminiscence group in England. Sue, a woman in her seventies, first attempted to enter the conversation by offering general opinions about drinking: "I mean I've got nothing against drink. If people enjoy drink I—I think they're entitled to it, but it's not for me, apart from lemonade and shandy. I don't mind that." At this point, however, another conversation intruded. Sue regained the floor by sharing a personal event memory:

> I remember when my father was alive he used to like a bottle of stout . . . where we lived we had a fire grate with hobs I think they called them hobs . . . Dad used to drink it out the bottle and he used to stand it on the hob and he used to say it was *beautiful*. . . I used to go to church in those days and the parson we had a parson that used to visit and I said to me dad the parson—I said that the parson's coming . . . I said that you won't drink your stout while he's here will you? Ohh my dad was disgusted and he said I *will* drink me stout. He said you ought to be ashamed of yourself. And there it stood on the hob y'know and in walked the parson with his dog collar on. I didn't know what to do. And to make matters worse this *stout*. . . you could hear it bubbling like. . . And me father said "I don't I don't think going to church is doing my daughter much good." He said "She asked me not to have a bottle of stout 'cos you were coming." And [the parson] said "Well I've never heard such a thing in me life." He said "I like one meself occasionally." I never felt so bad after that.   (p. 2)

The anecdote explains her previously stated attitude toward drinking: "She both claims and shows in her narrated remembering that she went through an experience that was instrumental in her tolerating drinking in others whilst not being particularly partial to indulging herself" (Middleton and Buchanan, 1994). But telling a personal story replete with verbatim quotes and vivid details drew the group's attention far more effectively than her earlier impersonal comments.

The privilege of holding the floor comes in part from the speaker's demonstrated first-hand connection to relevant events. To claim entitlement or authority within a conversation, the speaker has the burden of producing a narrative that is rich in sensory and affective imagery—a narrative that indicates to the listener: "This really happened and I remember it."

Miller et al. (1990) analyzed a dialogue between 7-year-old Latoya and 33-month-old Justina in which the authority to speak also comes from demonstrated first-hand experience. The children were discussing why Justina and her mother had to vacate their apartment and move in with Latoya:

J: My toilet stool broke.
L: No! Up there in the bathroom, the ceiling fell down on the bathtub. So, you moved back with me. . . .
J: But! The toilet stool seat, the toilet stool seat. . .
L: Ain't nothin' happened to the toilet stool seat!
J: The toilet stool seat.
L: Naw! naw, naw.
J: Let, talk, about, Latoya! My toilet seat broke!
L: No, it didn't! I was there. I saw it. It's in the bathroom by the shower. OK. There was the toilet stool and the sink. And it was over there. OK.
J: And, and the bathtub. . .
L: And up in the ceiling it broke down.
J: It broke down and, so. . . The thing broke in the bathtub.
L: The *ceiling* broke in the bathtub.
J: The ceiling broke in the bathtub.

Miller et al. noted that Latoya's claim—"I was there. I saw it"—"explicitly establishes her entitlement to narrate the story" (p. 300), and Justina accepted Latoya's version of reality soon after. Entering a conversation with a personal event memory implicitly carries this same entitlement claim: "My account is privileged—I experienced this firsthand."

Personal stories are not only attention-getting and authoritative, they are memorable. Master teachers know the value of telling stories to get their message across. The power of psychoanalyst Bruno Bettelheim's teaching at the University of Chicago came in part from his ability to engage students through case studies and his own experiences in Nazi concentration camps. "Once, when Bettelheim was in the midst of one of his many remarkable stories, a student started to walk out. 'Stop! You can't leave while I'm telling a story. Before or after, yes. But not during a story. Stories are what you are going to remember from this class'" (Lazarus, 1990, p. 31). Schank (1990, p. 15) expressed a similar view: "People who fail to couch what they have to say in memorable stories will have their rules fall on deaf ears despite their best intentions and despite the best intentions of their listeners. A good teacher is not one who explains things correctly but one who couches explanations in a memorable (i.e., an interesting) format."

Stories about specific episodes are especially memorable because they focus on personal or unique aspects of experience, contain nonredundant information, and are not readily absorbed into existing general knowledge structures or scripts. Readers of Jan Wiener's story of his father's death already have scripted notions of the holocaust and of suicide, but they do not have existing mental representations corresponding to Wiener's detailed account. Furthermore, the stories are rich in sensory and affective details, which support durable imagistic memory representations. As Sue recounts the drinking story about her father and the parson, the listener is able to visualize the stout as it "stood on the hob," hear its bubbling sound, and feel the awkwardness caused by her father's annoyance. In story form, a memory has a coherent temporal and causal structure. If the recounted event is salient enough to be talked about or thought about by the listener, it will retain its organization in memory as an intact, rehearsable, recallable unit (Schank and Abelson, 1995). Finally, vivid details provide multiple opportunities for the listener to connect the story to her own particular life experiences: "We hear, in the stories of others, what we personally can relate to by virtue of having in some way heard or experienced that story before" (Schank, 1990, p. 83). These personal connections enhance the meaningfulness and affective intensity of the story and increase the likelihood that it will be revisited repeatedly in memory.

Persuasion and Belief

At the same time that recounting a detailed personal event memory gathers the attention and interest of conversational partners, it also enhances the believability or perceived truthfulness of the communication. As a result of the increase in truth value, a colorful memory is often more persuasive than a general or scripted account of past events. Bruce (1989, p. 50) identified persuasion as an "ultimate function of all story-telling memory mechanisms," and the detailed personal anecdote is compelling evidence: "Except perhaps in academic circles, a remembered episode is almost impossible to beat in an argument—it carries more persuasive weight than a wealth of scientific studies and can only be countered by the common rejoinder: 'But that reminds me of another occasion. . .'" (Larsen and Plunkett, 1987, p. 18). Similarly, Johnson (1988, p. 393) observed that "the conviction in the abstractions one is willing to assert is very likely increased by the availability of specific cases that 'fit'." Schank (1990, p. 10) put it succinctly: "We are more persuasive when we tell stories."

In order for a personal story to be persuasive, the remembered events must appear to be authentic: "people's attributions about the source of someone else's memories and beliefs determine how they will respond to them. If you say you made up an example that nicely illustrates a point, your argument is not as persuasive as if you say it is a real example. Even if you do not acknowledge that your example is made up, if I suspect that it is, I will probably give less weight to your argument" (Johnson, 1988, p. 391). Personal event memories are both believable and persuasive because their vividness implies a continued connection to underlying perceptual representations of the original episode. The memory is not simply a story concocted in response to present purposes; it appears to describe what "really happened."

Sometimes the connection between immediacy and persuasion is explicit in a memory narrative. Sports commentator Alex Wallau remembered a conversation with sportscaster Howard Cosell that occurred just before a boxing match between Muhammad Ali and Larry Holmes in 1980. Ali was near the end of an illustrious career:

> I'll never forget walking with Howard Cosell two or three days before the Holmes fight. There was an atmosphere in Las Vegas that gave Ali a chance. His physical skills had diminished; his reflexes were shot; his motor skills weren't the same. But there were intelligent ringwise boxing people who thought he might win. And I can take you to the exact spot in the parking lot at Caesar's Palace where Cosell said to me, "You know, Holmes is vulnerable to the right hand, and Ali has always been able to land the straight right. I think the old master is going to do it one more time." And I told him, "Howard, not only is Ali not going to win the fight; not only is he not going to win a round; he's not going to win ten seconds of any round." (Hauser, 1992).

Wallau's assertion that he could "take you to the exact spot in the parking lot at Caesar's Palace" is irrelevant to his specific prediction about the fight's outcome; nevertheless, it forcefully asserts that "I am absolutely certain that this conversation occurred," or "What I'm saying is true." Similarly, the verbatim quotations enhance the believability of the memory. Wallau could have described his successful prediction in general terms: "I knew that Holmes would dominate the fight against Ali, even though some of the most knowledgeable commentators felt otherwise"; but visualizing the exact location and reproducing the words that were spoken enhances the listener's trust in the accuracy of his account. The fact that Wallau foresaw Ali's downfall before the fight is important, and the memory locates his prediction temporally. Wallau did not reconstruct a belief in Holmes's superiority after the fact; he expressed his belief before a witness at an exact location in a Las Vegas parking lot days before the fight occurred.

A second example comes from United States Secretary of State George Shultz's 1987 testimony before congressional committees concerning covert military assistance to Iran. Shultz recounted an exchange with President Ronald Reagan:

> So I picked up the phone Sunday morning, and I called the President. I said, "Mr. President, I have something I should bring over here and tell you about right now." So he said, "Fine, come over." . . . I went up to the family quarters, and Al Keel, who was then Acting National Security Advisor, went with me at my request. And I told the President the items on this agenda, including such things as doing something about the Dawa prisoners, which made me sick to my stomach that anybody would talk about that as something we would consider doing. And the President was astonished, and I have never seen him so mad. He is a very genial pleasant man and doesn't—very easy going. But his jaws set and his eyes flashed and both of us, I think, felt the same way about it, and I think in that meeting I finally felt that the President deeply understands that something is radically wrong here.   (Select Committees on the Iran-Contra Investigation, 1988b, p. 5)

Shultz did much more than summarize the communicative exchange: he vividly described what was said, seen, and felt. Later in the questioning, when Shultz was asked about the President's prior knowledge, he responded: "I am positive from the way the President reacted to what I told him that he was totally surprised, astonished, furious, just no question about it. . . he reacted like he had been kicked in the belly" (p. 62). Senator Rudman, Vice Chairman of the Select Committee on Secret Military Assistance to Iran, treated Shultz's vivid account as compelling evidence: "Well, Mr. Secretary, based on your description, which I think even though you used terms like 'made you sick' and 'was the President looked like he got kicked in the stomach,' the fact is that may be even understated, as I understand it, the President's reaction. The President was outraged, am I correct?" [Shultz's response: "Yes."] (p. 63).

Shultz's detailed event descriptions are not atypical for the Iran-Contra hearings or for eyewitness testimony in general. Another key player in the Iran affair, Admiral Poindexter, began his description of a meeting with the President as follows: "I have a very vivid recollection of that meeting, and it was in the residence. The President pulled a footstool up to the coffee table and sat there very quietly, as is his nature, listening to all of the discussion up to that point. . . And the President listened to all this very carefully, and at the end of the discussion, at least the first round, he sat back and he said something to the effect. . . 'I don't feel we can leave any stone unturned in trying to get the hostages back'" (Select Committees on the Iran-Contra Investigation, 1988a, p. 25). Poindexter's observations that the President "pulled a footstool up to the coffee table" at the beginning of the meeting and "sat back" before he spoke are trivial details, unrelated to the content of the meeting, but they strengthen the sense that Poindexter's memory remains tied to its episodic roots, still sharp enough to be trustworthy.

Could Poindexter's side comment that Reagan "pulled a footstool up to the coffee table" actually influence people's judgments about the truthfulness of his memory? Bell and Loftus (1989) conducted controlled experimental studies of what they called "trivial persuasion in the courtroom" (p. 669). The presence of trivial detail in eyewitness accounts, such as seeing a store customer buy and then drop "a box of Milk Duds and a can of Diet Pepsi" rather than "a few store items," influenced mock jurors' decisions: when prosecution witnesses provided trivial details, jurors were more likely to select the guilty verdict. Bell and Loftus observed that "communicators should choose their words very carefully, because the minor details that a communicator reports might be as influential as information that has genuine significant value" (p. 670).

Detailed testimony is persuasive because the witness appears to have ready access to perceptual images laid down at the time of the crime. Scientific studies do in fact support a connection between memory vividness and authenticity: in general, truthful memories contain more sensory detail than suggested, imagined, or fabricated memories. Schooler, Gerhard, and Loftus (1986) showed people one of two versions of a traffic accident. Some people saw a yield sign, whereas other people did not actually see the sign but were led to believe that they saw it as a result of misleading postevent information. Participants' descriptions of the yield sign differed depending on whether they had really seen it: real memories were more likely to describe sensory or perceptual attributes of the sign, such as its color, size, or shape. Similarly, Johnson (1988) summarized research comparing memories for real versus imagined events as follows: "Compared with memories for imagined events, memories for perceived events have more sensory and contextual information" (p. 390). "Statement validity assessment," a controversial method for distinguishing between truthful and fabricated testimony, also focuses on the presence or absence of specific memory details in child victims' accounts: "it is assumed that persons who invent an account are unlikely to speak as if they are reexperiencing the episode, such as describing actual speech by one or more participants" (Raskin and Esplin, 1991, p. 280).

An association between sensory details and memory authenticity should not imply that vivid memories are invariably accurate. The original event may have been perceived inaccurately or embellishments may have been added to the memory after the fact. Neisser's (1981) analysis of John Dean's testimony before the Watergate Committee of the United States Senate in 1973 showed that although Dean's memories of interactions with President Nixon were highly detailed, they were by no means perfectly accurate. For example, Dean stated that "When I arrived at the Oval Office I found Haldeman and the President. The President asked me to sit down. Both men appeared to be in very good spirits and my reception was very warm and cordial. . . The President told me I had done a good job. . ." (Neisser, 1981, p. 9). Such details may inspire confidence in the overall truthfulness of the memory, but Neisser documented that Dean's account of what was actually said was off the mark: Nixon did not ask Dean to sit down, nor did he say that Dean had done a good job. Neisser showed, however, that Dean's memories were true on a deeper, symbolic level—although wrong on specifics, Dean had accurately captured the underlying spirit of the exchanges.

Bruce (1989) identified persuasion as a motivating force behind Dean's Watergate testimony: "Dean wanted to persuade the members of the Senate committee that Nixon was guilty and perhaps that he himself was not entirely dishonorable" (p. 50). The desire to persuade could push a speaker to elaborate beyond the limits of what is actually remembered: "We are not only trying to convince ourselves with our memory reconstructions. Recalling the past also serves a dialogic function. The rememberer's interlocutor (whether present in the flesh or in the abstract form of a reference group) exerts a subtle but steady pressure" (Bruner, 1990, p. 59). Labov and Waletzky (1967) observed that people provide embellished event descriptions in the service of persuasion. When a person who is asked if his life was ever in serious danger answers "Yes," his account of the event must justify the affirmative response. "He finds himself in a position where he must demonstrate to the listener that he really was in danger. The more vivid and real the danger appears, the more effective the narrative. If the narrative is weak and uninteresting, he will have made a false claim" (p. 34).

Skilled writers capitalize on the connection between vivid prose and credibility. Atlas (1991) analyzed a passage from Edmund Morris's book, *The Rise of Theodore Roosevelt,* which contained the following phrase: "a shiver of excitement strikes the line of people waiting four abreast outside Theodore Roosevelt's front gate. . . The shiver is accompanied by a murmur: 'The President's on his way downstairs.'" Atlas observed that "the truth is in the prose, the style, the quality of representation that compels us to believe. That 'shiver of excitement' is a little dubious, and Morris . . . is perhaps overly fond of the rhetorical flourish; but he has recreated a plausible and vivid moment, set the stage in a way that gives us the assurance of being in the hands of a truthful storyteller" (p. 43).

Politicians are acutely aware of the persuasive power of particular episodes. In his run for Governor of Massachusetts in 1990, John Silber adopted a campaign tactic successfully used by Ronald Reagan: make your point by recounting a specific anecdote (Wilkie, 1990). For example, Reagan had made frequent references to a "welfare queen" who fradulently obtained extra benefits. In a televised debate, Silber criticized a new sales tax as follows: "A gardener just mentioned to a friend of mine that instead of sending him a $350 bill he was going to send him four bills less than $100 apiece in order to avoid having to add the tax." To illustrate government over-regulation, Silber gave an example of a state inspector's visit to a nursing home. The inspector "came up one morning about 10, felt up all the toothbrushes and noted that the toothbrushes were wet" and thereby unsanitary. According to Silber, the nursing home operator, "being a commonsensical person, took her hairdryer and every morning after the people brushed their teeth, she just ran her hairdryer around the toothbrushes until they were dry." At the next inspection, Silber recounted, the inspector found dry toothbrushes and concluded that "these people haven't been brushing their teeth."

Although uncorroborated, this detailed story makes a point about intrusive governmental regulation far more effectively than yet another vague indictment of the system. The anecdote is memorable because it contains unique information, it is easy to visualize, it has a coherent storyline that can be retold or rehearsed as a unit, and it connects readily to voters' negative personal experiences with over-regulation.

An especially notorious and devastating use of a particular episode for political purposes involved the celebrated case of Willie Horton in the 1988 presidential race between George Bush and Massachusetts Governor Michael Dukakis. Horton, an African-American inmate in the Massachusetts prison system, received a weekend furlough through a program supported by Dukakis. Horton did not return, and he was subsequently found guilty of rape and assault. Republicans seized the opportunity: Lee Atwater, Bush's campaign strategist, "could hardly believe his good luck. The Willie Horton incident had everything he needed: a black rapist, a white victim, and a bleeding-heart Democrat to blame" (Oshinsky, 1991, pp. 26–27). This singular incident promoted the Republican view of Dukakis—"as an elite Eastern liberal, lacking in good sense and contemptuous of American values" (Oshinsky, p. 26)— far more effectively than any number of general pronouncements about the differences between the two political parties. The Willie Horton episode was concrete, salient, memorable, and dramatically illustrative of the deepest fears of many voters.

Emotion, Intimacy, and Empathy

When a speaker makes a point by sharing a personal memory rather than by stating a general belief or feeling, this specialized form of communication signals emotionality and intimacy. As a consequence, the listener may be more likely to respond empathically. Recounting specifics may be interpreted by others as a sign of emotionality because of an inferred connection between vivid memories and heightened affect. When people are asked to rate their memories of salient life events on a number of dimensions, memory vividness is related to the perceived strength of affective reactions: the stronger the emotions, the more vivid the memories (Pillemer et al., 1988; Reisberg, Heuer, McLean, and O'Shaughnessy, 1988). This commonly experienced connection between affect and memory informs our reactions to other people's memory sharing. When a speaker recounts a vivid memory, the listener infers that both the original event and the retelling were emotionally charged.

When a conversational partner breaks with the Gricean conventions of brevity and relevance and offers a detailed personal episode, the communicative intent often is to deepen the intimacy of the exchange (Pillemer, 1992b; Tannen, 1990). The recipient may respond in kind, thereby accepting the overture to personalize the communication; or he or she may continue to respond in general terms, thereby rebuffing the move towards intimacy. Some conversations portray a sort of intimacy "dance," in which conversational partners guardedly offer personal memories but pull back when the exchange becomes too intimate. Fenton Johnson's (1991, pp. 10, 12) description of a conversation that he had with his companion's father is an unusually poignant example. Johnson first visited the father after his companion had died of AIDS-related complications. His friend's parents are elderly German Jews and holocaust survivors, now living in California. Although the father "does not talk about his son with the women of his life," when alone with Johnson, another man who loved his son, he relates an early father-son experience:

> He tells of a day when his son, then 8 years old, wanted to go fishing. The quintessential urban Jew, my friend's father nonetheless bought poles and hooks and drove 50 miles to Laguna Beach. There they dropped their lines from a pier to discover the hooks dangled some 10 feet above the water. ("Thank God," he says. "Otherwise we might have caught something.") A passer-by scoffed. "What the Hell do you think you're trying to catch?" My friend's father shrugged, unperturbed. "Flying fish," he replied.

Johnson treated the sharing of this memory as a conversational overture to go deeper, and he responded with his "most vivid memory" of his lost companion, during their last visit to "the city of his [friend's] dreams," Paris. "On what would be his last night to walk about the city we sat in the courtyard of the Picasso Museum. There at dusk, under a deep sapphire sky, I turned to him and said, 'I'm so lucky,' and it was as if the time allotted to him to teach this lesson, the time for me to learn it, had been consumed, and there were nothing left but the facts of things to play out." This story crossed the boundaries of acceptable intimacy: "A long silence after this story—I have ventured beyond what I permit myself, what I am permitted. I change the subject, asking my friend's father to talk of the war years." The father then recounted "moments of affection, loyalty, even humor, until he talks of winters spent immobilized with pain and huddled in his wife's arms, their breaths freezing on the quilt as they sang together to pass the time, to stay warm." This story represented another uncomfortable boundary-crossing: "Another silence; now he has ventured too far. 'I have tried to forget these stories,' he says in his halting English." The pattern of memory sharing and holding back tracked the interpersonal boundaries between conversational participants.

According to Tannen (1990), exchange of personal details signals rapport, caring, romantic interest and involvement, whereas failure to engage in memory sharing signifies emotional detachment: "If interest in details is a sign of intimacy, a woman will resist such interest if it comes from someone she doesn't want to be intimate with. And everyone has had the experience of being told unwanted details—so many that they seem pointless, or demand longer or more intimate attention than one wants to give. . . . One way of resisting overinvolvement, for some people at least, is resisting telling details" (pp. 116–117).

Buehlman, Gottman, and Katz (1992) provided scientific support for a connection between detailed memory sharing, intimacy, and marital satisfaction. Married couples completed an oral history interview in which they answered open-ended questions about their relationship, including how they met, how they decided to get married, and what were good and bad times in the marriage. Memories were coded on a number of dimensions, including "expansiveness" or how expressive each spouse was during the interview. Three years later, couples completed questionnaires describing marital satisfaction and the incidence of separation and divorce. Although "most husbands and wives tend to be expansive during the interview, describing in detail memories and recollections about their relationship while at the same time disclosing their feelings about marriage" (Buehlman et al., p. 311), not all spouses provided detailed personal memories. According to study co-author John Gottman, "Ask one man how he met his wife and he'll just say 'at a dance' and won't elaborate, but someone else will tell a long story about the circumstances, describe the dress she was wearing and how he felt when he first saw her" (Davis, 1992, p. 81). Husbands' failure to be expansive in the first interview was a predictor of later separation and divorce.

Memory sharing is a sign of interpersonal connection and empathy even when the relationship between conversational partners is more casual. A woman whose adult son was tragically and unexpectedly killed in an accident reported that people would spontaneously provide detailed accounts of how they heard the news of her son's death. Personal memory talk seemed to carry the implicit message: "I shared this tragedy with you."

Beals (1991) identified a consistent pattern of empathic responsiveness to personal event memories shared electronically. She analyzed communications sent over a computer support network for novice teachers in which participants discussed problems, asked questions, and offered advice. Most of the messages focused on general topics, but occasionally they described pinpointed classroom episodes. For example, a teacher might discuss problems she was having with the school principal in general terms, or she might recount a particular moment of tension or humiliation. Beals found that specific memories were especially likely to elicit responses from other members of the network. One teacher included this elaborate description in a message entitled "bad day":

> My third class would not sit still for one minute it seemed and when I ended class (just a few seconds before the end of the period, or so I thought) it turned out that the clocks had been reset back five minutes, giving the class five minutes to go berserk. During this time I reminded one student about the quiz he was to make up that day only to be told that he could not come (for the third straight week) and he told me it was none of my business why. When I told him that that was his choice but that his quiz grade would be a zero if he did not show up, he swore at me and walked out of the class, refusing to stop when I called him. It was then that I noticed that while I was talking to him the rest of the class had left, even though the bell had not rung. I yelled down the hall, thoroughly exasperated, for them to come back—which most did, ever so slowly, but some had already left. I did not know whether to scream or cry. I had not felt like that since the first few weeks of student teaching.   (p. 36)

This episodic call for support triggered a number of empathic responses. Return messages included comments such as "Hang in there bob, its almost vacation. I know how you feel and i have a simple suggestion . . . just take a couple of minutes (or seconds) during the day and stop and look at yourself and think about what a good job you are doing" (p. 36). "Yo, Bob . . . I had lots of days like this, esp. lately during the close of the term. This past wednesday was the last day of the term, we had 12 inches of snow. . . To be frank, I didn't even try to teach, not math anyway. . . I devoted the entire day to reflection on the past semester, I asked them what they thought I had done wrong, what they thought they had done right and wrong over the year." "Bob, You have my sympathy and empathy. On occasion, I have found it helpful to drop back and tell myself that I cannot always take it so personally if something goes wrong." "As everyone else has said, you are hardly alone. I have found it helpful to bring up incidents with the other teachers. I have found, much to my relief, that some of the hardened veterans do not [fare] a whole lot [better than] we do on a daily basis" (p. 37).

Although Beals acknowledged that more extensive analyses of computer dialogues are necessary to confirm this pattern of results, her preliminary findings illustrate the communicative power of the specific episode even when participants are conversing at a distance. According to Beals, pinpointed episodes evoke frequent empathic responses because they vividly and effectively communicate the teacher's emotional needs: "The writers of general descriptions avoid detail, and thus keep their emotional distance. Providing specific details and evaluations of events peels back one's personal armor, so to speak, exposing what really matters to the teacher. This vulnerability demonstrated by the storyteller invokes the response (and support) of peers more frequently than do the safer, more distant descriptions" (p. 35).

Memory talk may come to be linked to intimacy and empathy during parent-child conversations about the past. These conversations encourage children to use their memories in particular ways. Children who receive loving approval when they recount their own personal memories, and also when they respond empathically to other people's memories, may adopt memory sharing as a preferred mode of emotional expression and connection.

An extended dialogue between a 28-month-old toddler and her parents, recorded on a personal home videotape, illustrates how memory sharing evolves through parental guidance and encouragement. The previous day, the child had cut her hand and received several stitches at the doctor's office. Her father had comforted her by telling her "Sarah stories," tales made up on the spot about a little girl named Sarah. The parents persistently prompted their daughter to talk about the event, despite her limited success in producing a coherent narrative:

    F (father): Do you remember that, honey?
      C (child): I remember that.
  M (mother): What did the doctor say?
        C: What doctor say.
        M: What did he say? Do you remember?

C: What he?

M: It was a she, actually. What did she say?

C: What'd she say.

M: She said: "I have something for you, Julianna. I have a. . .?" What did she give you?

C: What did she give you?

M: Remember?

C: What . . . ah . . . what. . . What doctors give me?

M: Yeah. Had balloons on it.

C: Had balloons?

Later on in the conversation, the topic resurfaces:

F: What did Daddy do, hon?

C: What Daddy do?

F: When your hand got hurt. What did Daddy do?

C: What Daddy. . .

F: What do you think he did?

C: What you think he did? [laughter]

C: What do you think he did?

F: Let's see. Did he. . .?

M: Did he cry? Did Daddy cry?

C: No.

M: Did Daddy . . . What did he do?

C: What.

M: Did he hold you on his lap?

C: Yes.

M: And did he tell you some stories? What kind of stories? Hm? Did he tell you stories?

C: Sarah. Just Sarah.

Later, when the child made a pretend phone call to her older sister, she was strongly encouraged to focus her fantasy conversation on the accident:

M: Tell her what happened to you yesterday. She might want to know that story, honey.

C: I . . . um . . . read story that called Sar run.

M: Mm. Hum! Tell her more, honey. She'd like to hear about it.

C: I . . . I finish block . . . he told a story for me that called um Sar run.

M: About Sarah?

C: Sarah?

M: Yeah. Daddy told you stories about Sarah?

C: Good-bye.

The parents repeatedly prompted their child to recount the previous day's trauma, with special emphasis on the security and comfort provided by her father. The tone of their encouragement strongly indicated that memory sharing is a desirable activity. For example, the child was told that her sister "might want to know that story . . . she'd like to hear about it." This toddler learned early on that it is not only acceptable to engage in detailed memory talk about emotionally salient events in her life, but that it is a way to gain the loving attention and support of others. In contrast, a child who is not encouraged to talk about an emotional episode but rather is implicitly praised for "toughing it out" could develop a dramatically different perspective on the meaning and value of memory sharing.

Although detailed memory sharing can enhance interpersonal connection, people vary in the extent to which they use memory talk as a strategy for deepening the intimacy of a conversational exchange. Tannen (1990), for example, speculated that "because women are concerned first and foremost with establishing intimacy, they value telling of details," whereas "men . . . find women's involvement in details irritating" (p. 115). Memory sharing varies systematically as a function of gender, culture, and personality, and these group differences are the focus of Chapter 6.

*

Present Tense Descriptions of Past Events

When a speaker makes a point by describing a specific memory rather than by succinctly providing information that is directly relevant to the issue at hand, the extraneous personal details carry a meta-communicative meaning that transcends the concrete content of the particular exchange. Vivid sensory details imply the existence of strong underlying perceptual and affective memory representations, which in turn imply intense emotional engagement on the part of the speaker.

Another verbal marker is especially interesting from a communications perspective: a sudden shift from past to present verb tense at the emotional highpoint of a memory narrative. Using the present tense to talk about the past violates standard conversational protocol. When people recount memories, they usually tell their stories in the past tense, using the present tense only when offering current commentary on the meaning of past episodes (Bruner, 1990). Present tense intrusions into stories about the past may provide special insight into the interaction between imagistic and narrative levels of representation in autobiographical memory (Pillemer, Desrochers, and Ebanks, 1998).

World War II veteran Howard Hoffman's autobiographical account of the war in Europe (Hoffman and Hoffman, 1990) contained both past and present tense descriptions. In one instance, Hoffman told about the beginning of the invasion of southern France: "I remember shortly after we landed we were in a large baronial-type farm that had a stable and horses, and a bunch of the guys had got horses and were riding horses. I don't remember seeing any civilians at this point. I remember it was a nice day, the day of the invasion. But anyhow I don't really recall very much combat in that region. In fact, none at all" (p. 89). During a later episode, Hoffman was in the thick of battle (present tense verbs are in italics):

> The next thing I knew, the lieutenant *says*, "All right. Now we're going to prepare for the attack." And I'*m* thinking, this *is* crazy. We *can*'t possibly be going to make an attack. In the meantime the 88s *are* over there to the right of us, and they *have*n't realized that the tank *has* been knocked out . . . this colonel *is* kind of walking up in front, getting everybody up there, getting ready to make this attack across this wheat field. . . Somebody spotted him, and all four of those 88s *come* around like this [gesturing] and *come* pointing at us, and then all of a sudden, boom! boom! boom! boom! boom! And those 88s *are* shooting directly at us. . . That'*s* the only time in the whole career that I've been in the army when I saw guys leave their rifles. Anything that wasn't nailed down they dropped and ran. . . I'*m* running though the woods with a radio on my back, wishing I didn't have it.   (p. 119).

The first memory, like many other episodes recounted by Hoffman, is told in the conventional past tense. The present tense descriptions in the second memory suggest that Hoffman is not simply retelling a story; he is mentally reliving some salient aspects of the horrifying episode. He shifts into the present tense while describing an emotionally momentous point in the memory itself—a moment in which his life was in grave danger.

Harvey (1986) analyzed several "danger of death" narratives collected by herself and by Labov and Waletzky (1967). The present tense was used "at the crucial point in these stories and at no other time" (p. 157). For example, a former naval officer remembered sitting in a small boat when it fell unexpectedly from a troup carrier into the water: "Then I remember falling . . . and there'*s* all kinds of debris around . . . and the debris was closing in . . . and there was. . . water around and I'*m* under water . . . there *is* ripping, crashing . . . say something hit me on the head as I'*m* . . . lurching about falling and then . . . there'*s* sort of things closing in on me, debris and then the debris *is* jo/it's wet so it's water and debris and foam bubbles and I'm under water" (pp. 158–159). Harvey concluded that "the use of the present tense is not to make the *audience* relive the event, but that the *narrator* is reliving an intensely personal experience with the use of the historical present as an unconscious signal or cue to the audience that this is the crucial part of the story—the reason why it is being told" (p. 156).

Of course, a narrator can deliberately recount personal stories in the present tense in order to enhance their vividness. Novelist John Updike described how present tense writing differs from use of the more conventional past tense: "Instead of writing 'she said and he said' it's 'he says and she says,' and not 'he jumped' at some past moment, but 'he jumps,' right now in front of you. Action takes on a wholly different, flickering quality; thought and feeling and event are brought much closer together" (1990, p. 1). Capps and Ochs (1995) observed that "use of the present tense, often called the historical present, brings temporally remote events into a present time vividness. . . This usage is characteristic of good storytellers who involve interlocutors in the story realm by dramatizing events as if they are taking place in the here-and-now" (p. 417). Similarly, contemporary adolescents in conversation with their peers intentionally use the present tense and direct quotations in their storytelling ("So my teacher goes, 'You need to finish your work,' and I'm like, 'It's already finished', and she says, 'OK'"), apparently in order to engage the listener.

The present tense accounts examined in this chapter do not appear to have been deliberately styled this way. Rather, the speakers spontaneously shift into the present tense at points of emotional intensity and vivid perceptual experience. One possible explanation is that underlying sensory representations directly influence the mode of narrative expression: the speaker momentarily relives the affective and perceptual states accompanying the narrated event, and this reliving prompts the temporary shift into the present tense.

Pillemer et al. (1998) presented a diverse collection of case examples in which present tense accounts marked emotional highpoints. Consistent with Harvey's (1986) analysis, memories often involved direct threats to the self. For example, Robert Krueger was U. S. Ambassador to Burundi in 1995 when he and his security officer Chris Riley were ambushed. Krueger shifted into the present tense as he recounted the event in a television interview:

We heard this, "Pop, pop, pop, pop, pop, pop, pop, pop, pop." All of a sudden, Chris *says*, "Jesus, it's gunfire!" And I *look* and I *see* the dirt kicking up all around us, and I *see* the windows shatter, the car in front of me, I *look* around and I *see* Larry Semme, the security officer in the—in the Toyota following me, in a Land Cruiser, with his long frame, and I *can see* the bullets hitting his car and the windows shatter there, and then I *see* his long frame lean out with a pistol, and he *returns* fire to up above, and meanwhile, Chris has said, "Back up Eddie." He *backs* up. We*'re* so close to the car in front of us that we *have* to back up to get around, and there*'s* so little room to get around that we *sideswipe* all the way down. The car that was that close in front of us had two dead and three wounded. The car behind me had 10 bullets through it. Ours—ours had only one.   (Koppel, 1996)

Astronauts who flew the Apollo 13 mission to the moon in 1970 were in deadly danger when their spacecraft malfunctioned. Years later, astronaut James Lovell described the moment in space when he discovered what had gone wrong:

I*'m* in the lunar module with a camera and I *tell* Jack, not once, not twice, but three times, I said, "Jack, we're jettisoning the service module, not the lunar module.". . . He *jettisons* the service module and I *pull* the command module and the lunar module together away and then *maneuver* a little bit to see if I *can* see the service module . . . it *comes* into view and as it *rotates* very slowly, one whole side of that panel was, was blown off.   (Buckner and Whittlesey, 1994).

As part of a clinical assessment, a female psychiatric patient in her twenties provided a more than 800-word description of her childhood experiences (Gee, 1991). She used the present tense for a past episode only once, when her safety was threatened while riding a horse: "Then finally we got to ride one day. And maybe this was about a week or 2 later and we got to ride some horses. And so we uh the first horse that I got on, he *starts* backing up on me and *gets* on his hind legs, you know. I*'m* scared out of my wits. I *don't* know what. I *don't* know what*'s* happening. It*'s* unbelievable. So I got off the horse and I got, I got off the horse and I brought him back to the barn because I was too scared to ride him" (p. 19).

Although verb tense shifts occur regularly at emotional highpoints in memory narratives, they are by no means limited to instances in which the speaker's life was in immediate danger (Pillemer et al., 1998). The present tense also is used to describe threats to other people. While on reconnaissance patrol with another soldier, Howard Hoffman interceded on behalf of a civilian:

He went up to the house and had me cover for him. I in the back, with my rifle or carbine, and he's up in the front. He went through the yard, and he was now on the back porch of this house. When I *look* down the street, I *see* coming down the street a girl. I thought to myself, what am I going to do? I better *warn* him since I *don't* want him to shoot the girl. So I *slap* on my rifle and he *looks* up at me like that and I *point* to the road, whereupon he *gets* his gun at ready and he *puts* his back up against the wall like he's going to leap out and start firing. I *slap* on my rifle again and *go* like this—shaking my head from right to left meaning "no"—and he *lifts* his hands in the air, indicating "What do you mean?" and finally I made the sign for a girl, which was kind of waving my hands in a sort of a figure eight or hourglass to indicate that it's a girl and not a German, at which point he nodded his head.   (Hoffman and Hoffman, 1990, pp. 96–97)

An eyewitness to an attempted bank robbery in Cambridge, Massachusetts, was interviewed by television reporters shortly after the event. Although the man could have been hit by a stray bullet, direct threats to life involved the culprits and a Brinks guard:

I heard a person saying "Stop! Robbery! Stop! Robbery!" And the next thing I *know* we *turn* around to see these people running down this way. And all of a sudden there's, someone's . . . they're firing return firing shooting back and forth at each other. . . Most of us got down on the ground. And the Brinks man *is* shooting in this direction and this man *is* standing facing him and he's got this outlandish disguise on—like frizzy hair like Groucho Marx, mustache, eyeglasses, fake like safety glasses. And they kept firing. There was about 15, 20, 30 shots going down.   (WBZ News, Boston, 1995, March 1)

Verb tense shifts are not limited to negative episodes; moments of intense positive excitement also are marked by present tense intrusions. Astronomer David Levy was interviewed by television journalist Charlie Rose about the collision between the comet Levy co-discovered and the planet Jupiter. Rose asked, "What's been, David, while I still have you, the most exciting moment for you after the discovery?" Levy replied: "The most exciting moment was Saturday night when we were getting ready for the NASA press conference. We were just practicing sitting down in the chair. Meantime, Hal Weaver from the space telescope, *comes* down, *walks* calmly over to Gene, *whispers* something to Gene. Gene just *leaps* out of his chair and said, 'You mean they saw the plume!' And the three of us were just absolutely as—flabbergasted" (Rose, 1994).

Isolated case examples are consistent with the idea that present tense retellings occur when the remembering process evokes strong feelings and sensory imagery, but analyses of extended oral histories are necessary to determine if present tense intrusions occur primarily at points of high emotion and vivid perceptual experience. Pillemer et al. (1998) analyzed the autobiographical account of Howard Hoffman, published in *Archives of Memory: A Soldier Recalls World War II* (Hoffman and Hoffman, 1990). Hoffman was interviewed twice, in 1978 and again in 1982, by his wife Alice Hoffman, an experienced oral historian. During both interviews he simply told about his wartime experiences, interrupted only occasionally by requests for clarification or more information. The first interview was published in full, covering 74 pages of text, but the entire second interview was not published because "it was nearly identical to the first recall document even though it was conducted four years later" (p. 7).

The first interview was coded for use of the present tense; 18 instances were identified in which at least one present tense verb was used to describe a personally experienced event or a closely related series of events. Most of these events (15 out of 18) involved a threat to Hoffman's life or to the lives of other people. The remaining 3 instances also appeared to be affectively charged: Hoffman hoping for a particular assignment when getting his orders, getting high by illicitly drinking ether while being treated for malaria, and walking in the dark over what turned out to be dead bodies. Although verb tense shifts were invariably coupled with emotionally salient events, intense emotions did not always produce a present tense account: Hoffman's autobiography also contained several exclusively past tense accounts of extremely stressful events.

Hoffman's recollections of World War II, like the diverse collection of case illustrations already presented, are consistent with the existence of distinct but interacting levels of representation in autobiographical memory: an underlying, imagistic, perceptually based system and a higher-order, verbal, narrative system. Present tense accounts may occur when intense affective and sensory representations momentarily intrude into ongoing, purposeful narrative processing. Attentional focus shifts fleetingly to the upswell of perceptual images and feelings, and these sensations are actively described in the present tense. For example, the eyewitness to the bank robbery quoted earlier did not passively recount the story of the ordeal; his eyes darted as if following the action visually, his hands waved, and he broke into the present tense as he mentally re-experienced visual and auditory aspects of the earlier trauma.

Because the ability to activate perceptual images varies across individuals (Kosslyn, 1994, pp. 395–404; Marks, 1983), present tense descriptions may be more commonly given by people who can readily visualize a past scene or hear a past sound than by people whose dominant modes of thought do not involve vivid imagery. Howard Hoffman's memories frequently captured perceptual aspects of his wartime experiences: he used the present tense to describe what was seen, heard, or felt. Alice Hoffman identified visual imagery as a prominent source of her husband's narrative memories: "Howard is a visual rememberer . . . he calls up a scene and then describes it" (pp. 144–145).

Hoffman's present tense accounts illustrate the active interplay between image and narrative. One time, he shifted to the present tense just at the point in the narrative when the Germans suddenly came into view: "I remember all of a sudden, we were kind of crawling over the crest of the hill and looking down the other side, and there on the other side of the hill *are* the Germans and there's a whole battalion of them, I guess" (p. 97). In another instance, Hoffman commented directly on the picture-like quality of his recollections: "I remember when we were back standing on the road itself, I can picture the scene, and standing there looking down at him, and he's already had some morphine so he's not feeling too bad, and thinking, I wish it was me" (p. 102). Hoffman described sharp auditory impressions as well as visual images: "all of a sudden, not more than fifty-sixty feet away, I *see* machine-gun fire, I *see* pistol fire, shooting, you know, it's just the edge of darkness, a bunch of Germans over there, shooting at us . . . there's still sporadic sounds coming from outside and shooting and explosions. . . I *can hear* on the radio, these guys *are* calling for mortar fire" (pp. 120–121).

Other examples also show that shifts into the present tense occur when a speaker is describing precisely what was seen or heard during a momentous event. Rivka, a holocaust survivor, described a climactic moment near the end of the war when her Nazi oppressors abandoned her in a forest. Tanks belonging to the liberating American army suddenly appeared:

On this night there was a dreadful downpour, with thunder and lightning. It was as though the heavens were opening up, and the Germans grabbed their dogs, who were barking, and ran away, leaving us on our own. . . I was lying on the ground. . . I put my ear to the ground and I *hear* things moving. The earth *is* reverberating. . . There was a terrifying flash of lightning and we *see* tanks with men. . . We *are* lying there and we *hear* speech, and what we hear *is* not German. A Dutch woman doctor lying next to me *says,* "I think I hear English." She lifts her head and I *push* it down. She *says,* "No, no, these are not Germans" . . . Someone ran to me and I was in such a state of ecstasy that I had froth on my lips and they thought I had epilepsy. A soldier *runs* up to me and wipes my mouth and he *says* in Yiddish, "Shush, ikh bin a Yid. There are Jewish soldiers here and I am a rabbi, an American." (Richmond, 1995, pp. 392–393)

Personal event memories told partly in the present tense have a live, intense, unrehearsed quality; perceptual memories have not been fully translated into conventional, polished narrative form. Howard Hoffman had rarely if ever recounted disturbing wartime memories: "In fact he felt some disdain for those who talked about the war, a sense that it was somehow unmanly to burden others with the true stories of the horrors of war. . . It was only after he decided to engage in this project that he told most of these stories. Hence it was as if he was telling those stories not told before. . ." (1990, p. 81). Similarly, Rivka, the Jewish woman who had been rescued in a forest by American soldiers, apparently had not recounted her story previously. At the end of her interview, she commented: "So much for a person to endure. I had to tell you about this. I have not told it to anyone before" (Richmond, 1995, p. 393).

The perceptually raw, relived character of present tense memories may diminish with repeated retellings. As the narrative level of representation becomes more fully developed, spontaneous reflections of underlying sensory images will become less prominent. Gradual changes in narrative structure may be evident in psychotherapy transcripts or legal proceedings, as patients or eyewitnesses repeatedly work up their perceptual images into stories. Psychological transformations accompanying therapeutic remembering in clinical contexts are described later in this chapter.

*

Intrusive Memory Images

The communicative power of recounting specific episodes emanates from the implied connection between imagistic and narrative levels of representation. Spontaneous use of the present tense suggests that the speaker is mentally reliving rather than passively recalling. Yet for the most part, purposeful narrative processing predominates in everyday conversations. Sensory images flicker at the edge of conscious aware-ness, informing rather than undermining prose renditions of past events, with present tense intrusions occurring automatically and with-out a noticeable loss of conscious control.

In contrast, some images of extraordinary trauma are not readily inte-grated into narrative depictions of self. The memories are experienced as intrusive, alien, uncontrollable, and even debilitating. In 1993, ten-nis star Monica Seles, the top-ranked player in the world, was viciously attacked by spectator Gunther Parche during a public tennis match in Hamburg. Parche ran onto the court and stabbed Seles in the back with a nine-inch boning knife. Although Seles recovered from the physical assault, she continued to be tormented by recurring images of the trauma: "Sometimes her dreams were vivid replays of the attack: She would see Parche's leering face, lunging down with the knife and trying again. She'd wake shivering after vague visions of a tennis court and a crowd, and the crowd shouting in fear. She couldn't get the sound of her own voice, howling as the knife came down, out of her mind. 'My scream is what stayed with me a long time,' Seles says. 'It was eating me alive. I'd go out on the court, I could be playing great tennis, and it would all start coming back'" (Price, 1995, p. 24).

Seles also was tormented by a memory of the moment in the hospital when a policewoman showed her the knife. Her description includes a dramatic interjection of the physical assault, reported in the present tense: "It had a greenish handle. Very long and sharp. The policewoman said, 'It's a boning kitchen knife.' [Parche] said when he was living with his aunt, he would cut sausages with it . . . and this lady from my agent's office was translating the German, and she said the word *sausages*. And he's cutting my back. . . And then they bring in my bloody shirt. . . That's when I lost it. I said, 'What is this?' And it hit me again" (Price, 1995, p. 24).

During Seles's recuperation, when she relaxed her training regimen and had time for reflection, images of danger intruded forcefully into consciousness and disrupted everyday functioning: "all these memories started coming back. . . All these fears came back, and it just went into this tailspin, spinning and spinning and the ball was getting bigger and bigger so that I couldn't sleep at all. I would be up all night in my room, just sitting. In the dark or light, I didn't feel comfortable leaving the house. Total depression. I was just reliving that moment. And the knife. . ." (Price, 1995, p. 25).

In contrast to more conventional forms of remembering examined earlier in this chapter, some images of extreme trauma are thrust nakedly into conscious awareness. Seles's memories of trauma appear to reflect several properties of the imagistic representational system. The memories are tied to concrete episodes; they represent perceptual, sensory, and affective experience (the sound of her own scream, the appearance of the knife, the special pronunciation of the word "sausages"); and they are activated involuntarily, outside of conscious control. Because the intrusive memories are affectively intense and perceptually vivid, Seles is forced to relive disturbing aspects of the original event. The dreaded sounds and visions are not part of a coherent narrative sense of self; they are seemingly imposed on Seles by a memory system that she cannot control.

Seles eventually was diagnosed as suffering from post-traumatic stress disorder (PTSD). Victims of unusually stressful events commonly develop symptoms that include mentally reliving the traumatic episode, avoiding situations associated with the trauma, and experiencing increased arousal. PTSD sufferers have "recurrent intrusive recollections of the event, and recurrent nightmares in which the event is re-experienced. Occasionally they re-experience the event during flashbacks, acting and feeling as if the event were recurring" (McNally, 1992, p. 231). Involuntary recollections of extreme trauma consist primarily of vivid sensory images and bodily feeling states. Herman (1992, p. 177) described the residues of trauma as "fragmented components of frozen imagery and sensation." Unwanted memories appear repeatedly, spontaneously, automatically, and involuntarily (Brewin, 1989; Harber and Pennebaker, 1992; Janoff-Bulman, 1992). These negative effects are "virtually universal among those who have experienced extreme, negative life events" (Janoff-Bulman, 1992, p. 104).

Memories reported by war veterans dramatically illustrate the involuntary reappearance of strong emotions and perceptual imagery. Harvey, Stein, and Scott (1996) interviewed United States combat veterans fifty years after D-Day. Veterans "spoke in detail of what they saw, heard, smelled, felt, and thought on this day that many described as singularly important in their lives" (p. 329). The stark and disconnected sensory quality of the recollections was evident: "Almost all of our respondents indicated that their memories of their experiences on D-Day were highly vivid and still unfold in slow-motion reels in their memories" (p. 330). The veterans reported having nightmares and daytime flashbacks: "Gruesome experiences . . . appeared to leave imprints on veterans' memories that they said they did not want to recall, but that on occasion. . . were forced back into their awareness" (p. 324). One veteran remembered the shocking death of a fellow soldier:

> I was enthusiastic about hitting the beach. But as we got nearer to the shore, German bullets began hitting the sides of the landing craft. . . I stepped off [the landing craft] into water up to my chest. I lost my balance and dropped my rifle . . . there were Navy men floating dead in the water. I took one of the bodies that was floating—and pushed it in front of me toward the shore. I figured I couldn't do anything to help the poor guy and his body would stop bullets. . . German machine guns opened up on us. . . The water was bloody. It was bright red. . . On my left, Sgt. Robinson got hit. He staggered, kneeled down and started to pray with his rosary beads. Then the machine guns cut him in half. I mean really cut him in half.   (p. 323)

Another soldier's memory was short and unthinkably horrific: "I was coming out of the water when this guy exploded right in front of me. There wasn't anything left of him except some of his skin, which splattered all over my arm. I remember dipping my arm in the water to wash it off" (p. 323). Visual and tactile images of unfathomable terror have persisted with dramatic intensity for 50 years.

Similar long-term effects of trauma—intrusive perceptual remembering, vivid reliving—have been observed in survivors of Cambodian concentration camps (Kinzie et al., 1984), earthquakes (Robb, 1989), and the holocaust (Langer, 1991). A holocaust survivor's memory of her arrival at Auschwitz is replete with concrete sensory imagery: "It was night, but it was light because there were flames and there were powerful searchlights in the square. The air stank. Some people in cars had died of thirst . . . We had no water. And as the doors opened, I breathed in air as if it would be water, and I choked. It stank. And eventually we saw these strange-looking creatures, striped pajamas, who got us into a marching line." The speaker interrupted her own narrative and commented on her subjective experience of reliving while recalling: "I'm sorry, OK, I . . . I . . . forgive me . . . all right . . . I'm going to . . . I kind of was back there" (Langer, p. 17).

A variety of stressful situations will produce intrusive images, as long as the episodes were infused with exceptionally strong negative emotions well above the range of normal human experience. Imagistic representations are by themselves intense enough to protrude from the ongoing stream of preconscious mentation, without purposeful retrieval efforts and even in the face of active avoidance or denial. The imagistic representational system temporarily supplants the narrative representational system as the dominant mode of thought. Unlike subtle disruptions that occur during normal cognition, such as transient shifts into the present verb tense, an abrupt and powerful loss of narrative control is psychologically damaging. Conversely, adding narrative description, interpretation, and authority to stark, unintegrated sensory images is a prominent component of psychotherapeutic treatment of trauma.

Integrating Image and Narrative

How can the agony caused by extreme trauma be alleviated? Many clinical researchers locate the disruptive power of trauma in concrete, specific, perceptual images that recur repeatedly and involuntarily (Herman, 1992; Harber and Pennebaker, 1992; Janoff-Bulman, 1992; Keane, Fairbank, Caddell, and Zimering, 1989; van der Kolk and Saporta, 1991). Accordingly, treatment usually focuses on re-experiencing and reinterpreting traumatic images within a supportive psychotherapeutic context.

Effective therapy requires that the victim of trauma consciously and deliberately construct narrative depictions of distinctive episodes. "Out of the fragmented components of frozen imagery and sensation, patient and therapist slowly reassemble an organized, detailed, verbal account, oriented in time and historical context" (Herman, 1992, p. 177). The description must focus on concrete perceptions and feelings: "A narrative that does not include traumatic imagery and bodily sensations is barren and incomplete. The ultimate goal, however, is to put the story, including its imagery, into words" (p. 177). Harber and Pennebaker (1992, p. 360) expressed a similar view: "victims must consciously confront the memories and emotions associated with their traumatic ordeals. This confrontation is best accomplished by translating the chaotic swirl of traumatic ideation and feelings into coherent language." Rozynko and Dondershine (1991, p. 159) also stressed the clinical importance of putting terrifying images into words: "Regardless of one's theoretical understanding with respect to trauma or its treatment, debriefing—the linguistic contextual analysis of the traumatic experience—is always central to therapy. The goal is to help the patient reconstruct his experience as completely and as accurately as possible. . . The goal is reached when the story is emotionally and cognitively complete and congruent."

The clinical emphasis on purposefully confronting specific perceptual and affective images is especially apparent in implosive (flooding) and eye movement desensitization and reprocessing (EMDR) therapies. With flooding, the therapist and patient prepare a script corresponding to each distinctive traumatic event. The patient then gives an oral description of each event and associated feelings, in the present tense, over a series of treatment sessions (Herman, 1992). Keane et al. (1989) used flooding to treat Vietnam veterans suffering from PTSD. Patients' trauma scripts were highly detailed: "Each traumatic scene involved the presentation of the entire context of the traumatic event, including the time period prior to the event, the traumatic event itself, and the immediate post-trauma environment. Central to the presentation would be details regarding the patients' behavioral, cognitive/subjective, and physiological response pattern during all three phases of the traumatic event" (p. 249).

EMDR, developed by Francine Shapiro, is a highly controversial new procedure for treating traumatic memories (Lipke and Botkin, 1992; Shapiro, 1989, 1991, 1993). Patients are instructed to "focus on the memory from which they wish relief and then to isolate a single picture representative of the entire memory (preferably the most traumatic point in the incident)" (Shapiro, 1989, p. 213). Unlike flooding procedures described by Keane et al. (1989), EMDR does not require that the patient construct an elaborate narrative script, but it does involve combining mental pictures with verbal labels and interpretations. Patients are asked for an associated belief statement: "What words about yourself or the incident best go with the picture?" (p. 213). Clients visualize the traumatic scene, rehearse the belief statement, concentrate on physical sensations accompanying the anxiety, and visually follow the therapist's finger as it moves rapidly side-to-side in front of the face. Patients are then asked about changes in their level of anxiety, thought content, and visual images: "Their answers are used as evidence of change, since they often reveal new insights, perceptions, or alterations in the picture. . . If the new cognition is a positive one, clients are directed to 'Think of that, along with the picture'" (p. 214). If new traumatic images arise during the course of therapy, they are treated individually with EMDR.

When treatment is successful, the patient experiences marked improvements in cognitive and affective functioning. The emotional power of the traumatic image diminishes, and patients report a sharp reduction in anxiety. Herman (1992, p. 183) described the impact of flooding as follows: "the 'action of telling a story' in the safety of a protected relationship can actually produce a change in the abnormal processing of the traumatic memory. With this transformation of memory comes relief of many of the major symptoms of post-traumatic stress disorder." Symptoms of involuntary re-experiencing are especially likely to be reduced by flooding techniques (Keane et al., 1989). Similarly, some patients who purposefully processed traumatic memories using EMDR reported "alteration or diminishing of the visual aspect of the memory," as well as reductions in distress (Lipke and Botkin, 1992, p. 593).

Although some reduction in anxiety may result from simple exposure to traumatic images in the absence of aversive consequences, psychological benefits also accrue from constructing an elaborate narrative and thereby gaining an enhanced sense of conscious control. Involuntary imagistic representations are supplemented with purposeful narrative representations: "Now words rather than images provide the mental medium for processing the powerful data" (Janoff-Bulman, 1992, p. 108). Verbal descriptions of trauma are less volatile than raw, perceptual images: "by putting their experiences into language, trauma victims can begin the reconstructive process of trauma assimilation. . . By evoking memories that carry emotional content, yet in a controlled and structured way, language gives victims stewardship over the course of traumatic assimilation" (Harber and Pennebaker, 1992, p. 383). Psychotherapy does not eliminate painful memories; rather, the memories become increasingly coherent, comprehensible, and controllable: "The goal of recounting the trauma story is integration, not exorcism" (Herman, p. 181). Narrative assimilation brings a reduction in symptoms: "Once the traumatic event is integrated into one's assumptive world, repetitive reexperiencing of the event essentially ceases . . . automatic, intrusive representations and an essentially forced need to talk about the event should not occur; rather, relatively nonthreatening recollections, images, and thoughts should occur naturally, in response to situations that are associated with the event" (Janoff-Bulman, 1992, p. 110).

Seventy years ago, Janet (1925) observed that intrusive memories lose much of their intensity when they come under conscious control. He presented a case study of a 30-year-old man who suffered from depression and mania. One troubling symptom involved memories which, according to Janet, were "too real": "He is continually tormented by an obsession [concerning an ended romantic relationship] which presents itself in the form of a visual image with an almost hallucinatory intensity" (pp. 143–144). According to Janet's patient, when the memories reappeared involuntarily, they were extraordinarily vivid and painful: "To be sure I almost always know that it is only a memory of the past, but it is a past which is so close to me . . . when the image appears, it seems to me that it was yesterday. . ." (p. 145). In contrast, when the patient purposefully recalled the same scenes, the memories "lost their peculiar character. They are reduced, faded, and the subject readily refers them to the past. . . The memories . . . only assume their abnormal strength . . . when they appear beyond the actual volition of the patient, that is to say, when they function in a dissociated manner" (pp. 147–148).

The psychological benefits of purposefully talking about traumatic memories are apparent in everyday as well as clinical contexts. When questioned about effective ways to cope with battlefield memories, World War II veterans frequently mentioned telling their story to others (Harvey et al., 1996). Victims of natural disasters also gain psychologically from talking about their experiences (Robb, 1989). Greenstein (1966) interviewed college students following the assassination of President Kennedy in 1963, and observed the positive effects of talking about the tragedy: "It was clear that the students *wanted* to talk. The interviews had a cathartic, confessional quality" (p. 194). Davis (1988) conducted a psychological experiment in which participants were required to recall highly emotional memories. One participant became very upset after she vividly imagined an intense anger experience. After one hour of talking with the researcher about a problem that she was having in an intimate relationship, she completed her participation in the research project. Following personal discussion and emotional outpouring, "both subjective and physiological measures revealed a substantial reduction in tension" (p. 19). Miller et al. (1993) observed that children "retell stories as a means of gaining relief from or resolution to some distressing past experience" (p. 90). For example, a 30-month-old child repeatedly recounted her experience of viewing a scary movie: "In the first [version] she fled from the scene, in the second she sought comfort from her parents, and in the third she was no longer scared" (p. 90).

In summary, memories of trauma are especially damaging when they intrude abruptly and automatically into consciousness and disrupt purposeful cognitive processing. When victims are encouraged to re-experience their most terrifying memories within a supportive clinical context, and to translate their perceptions and feelings into words, the balance shifts from image to narrative and from automaticity to conscious control. Once raw perceptual images are tied to narrative representations, feelings of dissociation diminish. The alien image becomes part of the self.

∗

Subversive Memory Images

Intrusive memories of trauma appear involuntarily, keep the perceptual characteristics of stressful events, and are experienced as disconnected from the self. But emotional memory manifests itself implicitly and indirectly as well as explicitly and intrusively. Specific memories can influence feelings and behaviors without invading consciousness. Because the underlying historical basis of present emotional reactivity is unrecognized, affective responses to nonconscious memories can be especially puzzling and maladaptive; the memories subvert rather than overwhelm purposeful cognitive processing.

One of the authors of *Emotion and Gender* (Crawford et al., 1992) provided a dramatic example of subversive memory. As a college student, she attended a statistics class which she enjoyed, taught by a professor she admired. One day the professor presented a statistics problem involving a laboratory experiment in which electrical stimulation was applied to muscles in rats' legs. During this particular lecture, the student became irritated and pointed out minor errors made by the instructor in an impatient and sarcastic manner. Later on, the student was puzzled by her intensely negative reaction to a favorite professor. On her way home, the student made a connection between the lecture and a dormant childhood experience: "She hadn't forgotten it in the sense that she would have remembered it clearly if anyone had reminded her of it. But she had pushed it away in her memory, and certainly had never spoken about it to anyone and had never even thought about it for eight or nine years" (p. 160).

The relevant childhood experiences involved treatment for polio. She was given electrical stimulation by an elderly masseur in a small, dingy room. She was naked with a cloth draped over her. The masseur rubbed the inside and outside of her leg with his hands, and he occasionally applied the stimulator to her genitals, commenting that "this is the most important part of the body. The energy comes from here" (p. 160). Although her mother remained in the room, the child felt embarrassed and repulsed by the intrusive and unorthodox medical procedures. This early humiliating experience apparently formed the basis for her unexplained anger years later, when a college professor described electrical stimulation applied to the legs of helpless animals.

A personal example also shows how emotions can be heightened by a nonconscious memory:

> When my wife proposed buying a tricycle for my 3-year-old daughter, my immediate reaction was concern. My thoughts and energies were focused on anxiety reduction: postponing the purchase, blocking off our driveway from the street, and so on. Sustained reflection produced a vivid memory image of my own early bike riding experience. I rode in the street without permission, and my father forcefully told me to stop. In my eagerness to comply, I fell off the bike. My childhood feelings of anxiety and embarrassment remain a prominent part of the memory. (Pillemer, 1992b, p. 258)

The uncomfortably and inexplicably high level of anxiety I felt when thinking about buying a tricycle for my daughter appeared to be attributable, at least in part, to the preconscious activation of this disturbing childhood memory.

Another personal example illustrates how inappropriately strong emotions are made understandable by conscious identification of preconscious memory images. On several occasions I have been intensely annoyed, even angered, when I have been lightly sprayed by water as cars unintentionally drove through puddles near where I was walking, and I am more keenly aware of this potential annoyance than other people with whom I walk. The operative underlying memory image refers to a childhood incident when I was intentionally soaked by teenagers who drove a car through a nearby puddle. I was embarrassed and had vivid fantasies of revenge, but my adversaries were older and I could not retaliate.

To account for occurences such as these, I proposed a speculative model in which specific preconscious memories incite emotional reactivity, (Pillemer, 1992b). The hypothesized causal sequence is as follows:

TRIGGERING SITUATION→PRECONSCIOUS MEMORY→
EMOTIONAL RESPONSE→ACTION

The term "preconscious" rather than "unconscious" is used because the memory is potentially accessible to focused attention and awareness.

This model differs from more common depictions of the relationship between mood and memory (Bower, 1981). The usual causal sequence portrays the effects of mood on memory in this manner:

TRIGGERING SITUATION→EMOTIONAL MOOD→
MOOD-CONSISTENT MEMORIES

In the model of preconscious memory images put forth here, the usual order of effects is reversed, with memories assuming an active rather than a passive role in emotional regulation. Memories are not simply activated when strong feelings are triggered by current circumstances; rather, present circumstances trigger related memory images and accompanying strong emotions. In the example provided by Crawford et al. (1992), the student's intensely negative feelings toward her instructor were not produced by the seemingly innocuous lecture content itself. Rather, the lecture triggered a preconscious memory of her unpleasant childhood encounter with electrical stimulation, which in turn triggered strong feelings of anger and irritation and the resulting inexplicably rude behavior.

The proposed model rests on the assumption that specific memories of emotionally salient events can exert their influence without reaching conscious awareness. As we saw in Chapter 4, memories of specific episodes can be activated implicitly rather than explicitly. Kihlstrom (1987) defined preconscious information as "percepts and memories" which, when activated by current perceptual inputs, are "able to influence ongoing experience, thought, and action," although "they do not cross the threshold required for representation in working memory, and thus for conscious awareness" (pp. 1450–51). Like the examples presented at the beginning of this section, some implicit memory images can be called up for conscious inspection. Brewin (1989) identified "preconscious stimuli" that are "accessible to consciousness if we are alerted to their presence. These stimuli have not been deliberately ignored, but are part of the enormous number of sensations, images, and so forth, which are automatically filtered out of the material potentially available to our limited consciousness" (p. 380). In an earlier work, Singer (1970) presented a similar model: "fleeting images and bits and pieces of uncoded material are held temporarily in iconic storage. . . Only if focal attention is brought to bear on the material . . . are we likely to get reportable content" (p. 143). These preconscious stimuli include "short-term memories, the elaborations upon events perceived and events drawn from long-term memory storage, and associations and combinations of old memories with recently perceived events or with images just aroused" (Singer, 1975, p. 77).

Both intrusive memories and subversive memories are activated involuntarily rather than deliberately. Whereas emotionally loaded memories of extreme trauma force their way into awareness, preconscious memories rest at the edge of consciousness; unless they are attended to intentionally, they may pass unnoticed. Berntsen (1996) conducted a diary study of involuntary memory, defined as "a memory of a personal life event that comes to consciousness without any preceding attempt at retrieving it" (p. 440). Participants reported being aware of having several involuntary memories per day, and they also acknowledged that "during a day, they might have had several involuntary memories that they did not really pay attention to" (p. 440). Spence (1988) made the similar clinical observation that memories often come to mind involuntarily or passively, and that passive memory "may speak in a whisper, and we may not notice its presence" (p. 314).

Negative emotional memories may fail to reach consciousness for reasons other than active avoidance or denial. The stream of internal stimuli, including memory images triggered by situational cues, often fails to reach the threshold of conscious awareness because it must compete for limited processing resources with attention-grabbing external inputs. When purposeful processing is directed to the current business at hand, automatically generated imagistic memory representations will remain outside of awareness: "most people simply do not recall a great deal of such [private mental] processing because they have moved on rapidly to new externally generated materials or to new thoughts" (Singer, 1978, p. 204). In the tricycle example I may not have focused initially on memory images because my cognitive processing was consumed by pressing external issues: deciding whether or not to buy the tricycle, and managing the anxiety caused by this decision. Because my related childhood experience was far removed from the adult decision I was facing, the memory may not have been identified initially as relevant to current concerns and may have been passed over even if it had received fleeting conscious attention.

Memory as a Cause of Emotional Upheaval

In most research studies of the relationship between emotion and memory, mood is manipulated experimentally and its effects on memory are observed. The direction of causality can also be reversed: perceptually vivid memories of specific episodes may produce changes in feelings (Pillemer, 1992b; Singer and Salovey, 1993). For example, hypnotized subjects put themselves into a good or bad mood by remembering a happy or sad occurrence (Bower, 1981). Koff, Borod, and White (1983) asked research participants to put on facial expressions corresponding to various feelings, such as sadness and happiness. When participants were asked how they went about adopting different expressions, most reported visualizing an emotionally appropriate scene. According to Singer (1970), "just as affects are evoked by the pattern of processing external stimuli, so too can they be evoked by the processing of material from long-term memory" (p. 140).

Although affectively salient memories may be retrieved purposefully in order to alter one's mood, feelings are also evoked without conscious recognition of internal cues. According to Brewin (1989, p. 382), "powerful emotional and behavioral effects can be observed without the necessity for representing relevant past experiences at a conscious level." This sort of involuntary episodic memory (discussed in earlier chapters) would have had important adaptive value in our early evolutionary history. In a world of limited environmental variation and clearly specified threats, automatic emotional and behavioral responsiveness to potentially dangerous situations would enhance the chances of survival.

In the complex and variable modern world, however, an involuntary preconscious memory system is a liability as well as an asset. Preconscious memories may be activated in structurally similar situations that are nevertheless quite remote from the original circumstances. Automatic remembering based on structural parallels rather than on surface similarities is elegant in its complexity, yet this is precisely where memory can go awry: the old emotions may not be valid in new and dramatically different life contexts. In Crawford et al.'s (1992) example presented earlier, the triggering situation—a college lecture on electrical stimulation of rats' muscles—was so far removed from the original experience of receiving inappropriate electrical stimulation for polio, that the evoked emotions—anger, annoyance—felt alien, and the resulting rude and hostile behavior towards the professor was inexplicable and maladaptive. Rather than providing an impetus to useful action, emotional memory actually subverted the student's valued classroom experiences.

In extreme instances, clinical intervention may be necessary to break the maladaptive link between preconscious memories and unexplained emotional distress. Some models of psychotherapeutic process link unwanted feelings and symptoms to powerful but unrecognized images of specific experiences. For example, Kantor (1980) described "critical identity images" that underlie negative behaviors and emotions. These images are "primarily visual and spatial," "their derivations are in past experience," and they "tend to have unusual vividness and intensity" (pp. 148–149). The images are cued by structural similarities between past and present circumstances: "Any new context similar in structure to the original identity image can invoke an emotional response and a behavioral response similar to what was experienced earlier" (p. 149). Although they "influence present and future events to a significant degree," the concrete images themselves "are beneath the surface of awareness, and usually remain there unless they spontaneously surface or are clinically elicited" (p. 150). The therapist helps the client to identify the underlying image and to pin down "enough of the concrete 'elements' to 'fix the picture' in awareness" (p. 157): "the therapist, while permitting and encouraging the expression of feelings, also explores and enlarges on other structural details—visual, behavioral, conceptual—how old are you in this scene? in what room of the house does the scene take place? who else is there? what is mother wearing? how do you feel about what your brother is doing?" (p. 158).

As in the treatment of intrusive memories of trauma, purposeful narrative processing of preconscious event memories helps to defuse their emotional power. Once inexplicable or troubling current feelings are attributed to an automatic reaction born out of past experience, the preconscious memory→emotion→action sequence can be consciously modified. The therapist attempts to specify "the exact content of the nonconscious memory in order to help the patient discriminate precisely which situational features elicit inappropriate fear, sadness, or other emotions" (Brewin, 1989, p. 387). Clients become increasingly skilled at identifying situations in which their emotional reactions are inappropriate, and at making connections between feelings and underlying images. In effect, they learn to treat preconscious mentation as a vital source of information about their emotions and actions. Disturbing emotional volatility is understandable and manageable when it is consciously linked to latent memory images.

To draw on analogies between past and present experience is useful, even essential, for successful adaptation and survival. Nevertheless, functional mismatches do occur. Preconscious memory can turn subversive when feelings and actions evoked by underlying memory images do not apply to present circumstances. Remembering based on analogy is central not only to understanding adaptive uses of memory, but also to explaining the role of memory in emotional dysfunction.

Chapter 6

*

Gender,
Culture, and
Personality

*N*ARRATIVE MEMORY—verbal depictions we use when thinking or talking about past events—does not evolve in the same way in all people. According to Bruner (1987, p. 16), "People anywhere can tell you some intelligible account of their lives. What varies is the cultural and linguistic perspective or narrative *form* in which it is formulated and expressed." The social and cultural context of early adult-child talk about the past clearly influences the form and content of children's narrative memories. Thus preschool children who actively engage in expansive memory talk will develop an elaborative personal memory style and a rich cache of personal event memories. Autobiographical memory *becomes* the activities or functions that are required of it, at least in part.

What sorts of social and cultural variations in life circumstances are likely to produce different demands on narrative memory? Boys and girls growing up in the United States are exposed to distinct but overlapping early environments; one distinction involves the frequency, extensiveness, and social meaning of talk about emotionally salient personal experiences. Similarly, memory sharing may be dramatically different in cultures that emphasize human individuality and uniqueness rather than collectivity and interpersonal enmeshment. In addition to between-group differences involving gender and culture, within-group differences in personal or cognitive styles may be associated with variations in predominant memory activities. These three potential sources of diversity in the organization and expression of personal event memories—gender, culture, and personality—will be considered in turn.

Although the idea of group differences in memory styles follows directly from the developmental model of autobiography presented in earlier chapters, a cautionary note is in order. Identifying gender or cultural differences in no way implies that *individuals* will conform to the group pattern. The magnitude of gender differences in memory is small, and the distributions for men and women overlap substantially. Gender correlates with variations in memory style, but it most assuredly is not the determining influence on individual memory styles. Similarly, culture is broadly associated with variations in autobiographical memory, but this does not mean that it is a strong predictor of individual memory styles. Overall patterns must be qualified further because most participants in research studies are middle class; gender and cultural differences may not hold up in more diverse samples. I will avoid repetitive use of cumbersome qualifiers ("some" men, "middle class" women), but the text should be read with these qualifiers in mind.

∗

Gender and Personal Event Memories

Researchers have only recently begun to explore gender differences in autobiographical memory (Loftus, Banaji, Schooler, and Foster, 1987). Gender influences may be most apparent when the analytic focus is on memory function. Girls and boys, and women and men, often use personal event memories for different purposes. These functional differences are apparent in adults' and children's memory talk, and in the use of personal journals or diaries. Men and women may adopt contrasting views about the importance of personal event memories and the value of autobiographical modes of expression.

The primary focus here is on potential gender differences in memory styles rather than content. Because men and women have distinctive life experiences, they may remember different things, or they may remember the same event differently. A more far-reaching and elusive issue involves possible gender differences in the functional organization of autobiographical memory. In her summary comments for a volume entitled *Women and Memory,* Catherine Stimpson juxtaposed the likelihood of gender differences in memory content with the intriguing possibility of differences in memory function: "The histories of men and women have not always mirrored each other. Because of that, the content of the public and private memories of men and women will not always be alike. . . However, what would it mean if we believed that the process of remembering itself was gender-marked? That the process was different for men and women because they were men and women? Is gender really to have that regulatory power?" (1987, p. 264). Recent case observations and systematic research point suggestively to gender differences in the ways that autobiographical memory is used.

Memory Style

Memory sharing serves several meta-communicative functions. The act of recounting detailed personal episodes signals emotionality, and it enhances the persuasiveness and believability of a communication. These interpersonal qualities of memory sharing appear to be more prominent in women's than in men's talk about the past. Women may be more likely than men to include personal memories in their conversations with others, to expect others to respond in kind, and to make attributions about the status of an interpersonal relationship on the basis of memory activities.

In her popular book, sociolinguist Deborah Tannen (1990) made the case for overarching gender differences in conversational styles. Tannen believes that memory talk, including small talk and gossip, is a critical aspect of social bonding for many women: "Telling what's happening in your life and the lives of those you talk to is a grown-up version of telling secrets, the essence of girls' and women's friendships" (p. 97). When a speaker freely recounts specific details of past events, the listener is "promoted" from acquaintance to friend. In contrast, men tend to disparage small talk, they are irritated by women's attention to personal details, and they respond to conversations about relationships by trying to solve the "problem." For many women, the act of talking about personal events is important in and of itself because it establishes intimacy and demonstrates caring: "Not only is providing solutions to minor problems beside the point, but it cuts short the conversation, which *is* the point" (p. 102).

Women quoted by Tannen were exasperated by men's reluctance to engage in detailed memory talk: "Men don't tell the whole story—who said what". . ."It's like pulling teeth to get him to tell me, 'What did she *say?* What did he *say?*'" (p. 116). If recounting the specifics of what was said is more strongly valued by girls and women, they may be more likely than men to attend to, rehearse, and remember such details. Loftus et al., (1987) asked people to predict who would be better, men or women, on a variety of memory tasks. In response to the item, "After having a conversation with a friend, subjects are asked to recall what they and the friend said," 58% of participants expected females to perform better than men, 36% expected the sexes to perform equally, and only 6% expected men to outperform women. Similarly, Crawford, Herrmann, Holdsworth, Randall, and Robbins (1989) found that women rated the accuracy of their memories for conversations more highly than men rated their own memories. Specific dialogue appears more prominently in girls' than in boys' memory narratives (Ely and McCabe, 1993). When describing past events, girls are more likely than boys to quote themselves, their mothers, and other children: "in a variety of ways, girls foreground conversational interchanges in depicting past events, a pattern that may reflect broader gender differences in the functions and goals of conversational narrative discourse" (Ely and McCabe, p. 688).

In contrast to women's revealing and detailed conversational style, Tannen describes men's memory sharing as guarded and general: men "tend to talk about political rather than personal relationships. . . If men do mention their wives and families, the mention is likely to be brief, not belabored and elaborated in depth or detail. If they make reference to a difficult personal situation, it will likely be minimal and vague" (1990, p. 101). Because women respond more favorably than men to self-disclosure, men's reticence may diminish when talking with women rather than with other men. When Lillian Rubin (1976) conducted her classic interview study of working-class families, she was surprised by men's willingness to open up to an unfamiliar woman. When asked, "Would it have been easier to talk about these personal issues with a man rather than a woman?" most men responded "No." One male participant offered this explanation: "Guys don't talk about things like that to each other. Me, I'm used to talking to women. I talked to my mother when I was a kid, not my father. When I got older, I talked to girls, not to guys. And now I have my wife to talk to." Rubin observed that "to the degree that the American culture approves male expression of closeness or intimacy, it is between a man and a woman, not between two men" (p. 21). Memory sharing may be strongly influenced by the gender composition of the dyad or group as well as by the gender of individual speakers.

Although men's conversations often focus on seemingly impersonal topics, such as work and sports, talk within these domains frequently includes stories about the past, including detailed references to specific episodes. Tannen (1990) described a dinner table conversation in which a father and sons recounted bicycle accidents or "wipe-outs." This memory talk indirectly communicated guidelines for how to behave: "Through attention to their stories, the boys are learning, and demonstrating for the youngest boy, that risking danger in riding a bike is good, getting hurt is unavoidable, sustaining injury bravely is commendable, technical knowledge and skill can be useful . . . and telling about risking danger, sustaining injury, and applying and displaying technical expertise is a good way to get attention and impress people" (p. 138).

It would be a mistake to assume that boys' and men's memory talk is devoid of emotional meaning because it often involves "impersonal" topics. For example, men frequently reminisce about sports, including both their own personal achievements and failures, and their firsthand experiences as witnesses to momentous public sporting events. Remembering these salient landmarks reactivates strong feelings not only about the events themselves, but also about emotional connections to peers and family members who shared in the experiences. In Tannen's bicycle example, the sons may continue to reminisce about their exploits as they grow older in part because the stories commanded their father's rapt attention and loving approval; although the specific memory content is not intimate, the associated feelings are.

The death of New York Yankee baseball great Mickey Mantle in 1995 triggered strong feelings and vivid memories among many fans who had grown up in the "Mantle era." In his eulogy at Mantle's funeral, sportscaster Bob Costas (1995) said that his phone's been ringing the past few weeks as Mickey fought for his life. I've heard from people I hadn't seen or talked to in years—guys I played stickball with. . . They're grown up now. They have their families. They're not even necessarily big baseball fans anymore. But they felt something hearing about Mickey, and they figured I did too." The strong feelings expressed by people who did not know Mantle personally emanated in part from remembered connections between Mantle's public accomplishments and fans' private lives: "There was The Mick's Triple Crown in '56 . . . the year a baby brother was born; The Mick's chase with Maris in '61 . . . when a sister graduated from high school; and the time Dick Radatz fanned The Mick with the bases loaded at Fenway in '62 . . . when a parent was recovering from a heart attack" (Shaughnessy, 1995, p. 42).

Professional football coach Bill Parcells also reminisced about Mantle's place in his early life: "I have been thinking about him. . . He provided me with a lot. . . I was in that place [Yankee Stadium] a lot." The Yankees served as a connection point between Parcells as a young boy and his hard-working father: father and son had a friendly rivalry, with Parcells rooting for the Boston Red Sox and his father for the Yankees. "They [the Yankees] were winning all the time. You start talking about 1950, they won all the time. My father would never be home from work until 6 p.m. because he was commuting from New York City. He would call me in the morning and ask me to handle the game for him to make sure the Yankees would win. I would be listening and want them to lose" (Blaudschun, 1995, p. 38).

Men's talk about sports or work provides only an indirect emotional linkage to other people. But the desire for interpersonal connection, so precious yet so elusive in some men's lives, may help to explain their passionate interest in sharing memories about topics that on the surface appear to be bereft of personal meaning.

Do stylistic variations in memory sharing reflect differences in the value assigned to memories of personal life events? Women may attend more closely to personal details associated with specific episodes, and they may come to view these details as crucial to understanding and as an important guide for future action. In describing her own classroom teaching style, Tannen (1991) stated that she frequently "offer(s) personal anecdotes illustrating the phenomena under discussion and praise(s) students' anecdotes as well as their critical acumen." Tannen informally observed that this teaching strategy is received quite differently by male and female students: "Male students are more likely to be comfortable attacking the readings and might find the inclusion of personal anecdotes irrelevant and 'soft' . . . it is women in my classes who are most likely to offer personal anecdotes" (p. B3).

Sehulster (1995) examined gender differences in memory styles more systematically. Memory profiles were constructed from college students' ratings of their own memory abilities and activities. Men and women differed on the autobiographical memory dimension, which included "memory for emotional experiences and personal past experiences" (Sehulster, 1981, p. 269): women's self-ratings were higher than men's. Sehulster speculated that "females more frequently access emotional material in conversation and therefore have it better rehearsed, organized, and accessible. . . We may find that the memory style of the individual develops through the exchange of the most 'valuable' or frequently needed information in that individual's social world" (p. 84).

Research also indicates that women tend to remember salient interactions with spouses more vividly than do their male partners, and that women assign greater personal importance to the episodes. Ross and Holmberg (1992) asked married couples to describe their first date together, a shared vacation, and a recent argument. Some couples recalled the events alone and other couples recalled the events together. Participants rated the clarity and vividness of the memory, the perceived importance of the event at the time of occurrence, and how often they had thought or talked about the event. Women's ratings of memory vividness were higher than men's ratings. Raters who were blind to the hypotheses of the study also scored women's memory transcripts as more vivid than men's. When couples recalled the events together, men reported more memory failures than did women. Wives assigned greater importance to the events than did their husbands, and wives reported reminiscing more frequently about them.

Ross and Holmberg (1992) speculated that women not only remember specific episodes in the relationship more clearly than do their spouses, but they also may be more strongly influenced by their recollections.

> If women's memories of past interactions in their marriage are often more vivid than men's, then spouses will sometimes misconstrue each other's responses to current events. In general, women may be more likely than their spouses to evaluate ongoing experiences in light of their vivid memories of past interactions. For example, a wife's extreme reaction to an oversight by her husband might appear inexplicable to her spouse. The wife may associate the current grievance with a vividly remembered sequence of irritations; in contrast, the husband may regard her annoyance as an unreasonable response to a single incident.   (p. 602)

Men's relative inattention to salient negative episodes could undermine the success of a marriage. Research on separation and divorce indicates that women are more likely to be the initiators (Pettit and Bloom, 1984), whereas men are frequently surprised by the sharply negative turn of events. According to clinical research psychologist Howard Markman, "Once the woman gives up, that's when she's likely to file for divorce or have an affair. . . And many men have no clue as to how bad things have got until they get the letter about divorce" (Bass,

1993, p. 23). Men's apparent obliviousness could be due in part to their failure to remember the trail of contributing episodes of marital discord, and to their failure to view particular episodes of discontent as compelling evidence that the marriage is faltering.

Taken together, research studies and anecdotal observations suggest that personal event memories are remembered more clearly and valued more strongly by women than by men. These findings are based largely on memories of personal relationships, an area in which girls and women invest a great deal of intellectual and emotional effort: "In this society, women are socialized to be the relationship 'experts,' more responsible, perhaps, for the outcomes of relationships. A logical consequence of this responsibility is thinking more frequently about relationships. Some of this thinking may take the form of reviewing past events, which may account for the finding that women have more vivid memories about relationship events than do their male partners" (Acitelli and Holmberg, 1993, p. 84). One might expect men's memories to be sharper in domains where they are similarly highly invested.

Do gender differences in personal memory extend beyond conversational styles and self-ratings? Gergen and Gergen (1993) observed that men's personal histories tend to be more purposeful and linear than women's accounts:

> Whereas men's stories concentrate on the pursuit of single goals, most often career oriented, women's are more complex. Women's stories usually weave together themes of achievement, along with themes of family obligations, personal development, love lives, children's welfare, and friendship. Whereas men's stories are rarely revealing about emotional experiences, traumas, self-depreciation, self-doubt, and self-destructiveness, women's stories express these aspects. Because of these multiple themes and self-expressions, the tone or movement of women's stories are never unidirectional, focused, or contained. (p. 196)

As part of a study of oral autobiographies, Bruner (1987) elicited short life histories from four family members. Two adult siblings, a brother and a sister, gave personal accounts that were consistent with Gergen and Gergen's gender differentiation. The woman's account contained "vivid analeptic flashbacks—as in an unbid memory of an injured chicken on the Long Island Expressway, the traffic too thick for rescue. Like so many of her images, this one was dense with plight and affect. It evoked her tenderness for helpless animals, she told us, then veering off to that topic. And so her order of telling is dominated not by real time sequences but by a going back and forth between what happens and what she feels and believes, and what she felt and believed" (pp. 30–31). In this, Bruner argued, the woman and her mother are both "locked in the same gender language" (p. 31). In contrast, her brother's account is "linear, from start to end . . . his narrative is progressive and sequential: the story tracks 'real time'" (p. 29).

Analyses of autobiography are consistent with gender differences in memory talk and vividness. For many men, general life themes, plans, and goals appear to predominate over seemingly inconsequential details accompanying concrete episodes. For many women, detailed personal memories reflect underlying values and beliefs and are indispensable to a narrative sense of self.

Although the data base supporting gender differences in personal memory is sparse, a recent large-scale research study also showed a female advantage in memory for specific information. Herlitz, Nilsson, and Bäckman (1997) examined memory abilities in a random sample of 530 women and 470 men living in Sweden. The tasks tapped episodic memory (memory for personally experienced unique information) as well as other types of memory (for example, general memory for facts). The episodic memory tasks included recall of particular words, statements, faces, and actions. At the end of the test session participants were asked to recall all the tasks they had performed, and the number of tasks remembered correctly served as an additional measure of episodic memory. Women consistently outperformed men on episodic tasks, although the magnitude of group differences was modest. In contrast, men and women performed similarly on all other types of memory tasks. The impersonal content of to-be-remembered material did not appear to favor women, yet a small but consistent female memory advantage was observed nevertheless.

Herlitz et al.'s findings indicate that women may indeed be slightly better than men at remembering specific information. The authors also pointed out that when gender differences have been found in other laboratory studies, women usually outperform men on episodic memory tasks. Women's advantage in the laboratory could be a result of more practice recounting details of past events. Alternatively, women could have an initial biological edge which is exploited further through extensive memory-related activities. In either case, women's vivid memories of detailed episodes, such as what was said in a recent conversation, may reflect more than their active engagement in personal topics. Women's memory styles may be more "episodic" than men's styles in part because they remember pinpointed events more clearly.

Childhood Origins

Researchers have identified an association between parents' and children's memory styles. Toddlers with parents who engage in elaborate memory talk frequently develop an elaborative autobiographical memory style themselves. Research also has documented notable variations in memory styles; some parent-child pairs adopt a highly elaborative style when discussing past events, whereas other pairs communicate in a more repetitive, factual, or instrumental style.

Is parent-child memory talk influenced by gender? Robyn Fivush and colleagues have conducted pioneering longitudinal research that points in this direction. Reese and Fivush (1993) asked mothers and fathers to discuss specific past events with their 40-month-old children. Parents who engaged in memory talk with daughters were more elaborative than were parents who reminisced with sons; and girls were correspondingly more active and elaborate rememberers than were boys. Early differences in memory style were not attributable to gender differences in basic linguistic abilities. In a longitudinal follow-up study when the children were 70 months old, girls provided more detailed memories than did boys in conversations with mothers, fathers, and an unfamiliar experimenter (Reese, Haden, & Fivush, 1996). These nascent gender differences may foreshadow variations in memory styles observed in adulthood: "Because parent-daughter dyads engage in lengthier and more detailed past event conversations, and because this style is associated with children's greater memory participation, daughters may very well grow up to value reminiscing more than sons and to produce more elaborate personal narratives" (Reese & Fivush, 1993, p. 605).

If young girls receive special encouragement to construct detailed and embellished accounts of personal episodes, then women's recall of early childhood events may be superior to men's recall. White and Pillemer (1979) reviewed older studies by Dudycha and Dudycha (1941), Waldfogel (1948), and Ruth Benedict (reported by Schachtel, 1947); in each instance women reported slightly earlier memories of childhood than did men.

Contemporary studies also support the idea that women have enhanced access to memories of early childhood. Mullen (1994) asked college students to give their age at the time of the earliest event they could remember, and girls were slightly younger than boys when the remembered events occurred. Cowan and Davidson (1984) had college students describe an early memory in which they "had a strong emotional reaction to another human being" (p. 102). Women's median age at the time of the remembered events (5.5 years) was 1 1/2 years earlier than men's median age (7 years). Friedman and Pines (1991) obtained the earliest gender-related memory from a sample of Israeli men and women. Each participant described his or her "earliest childhood memory that is related to the fact that you were a boy/girl or that people related to you as a boy/girl" (p. 27). Women's memories were of earlier events than were men's memories. Women's accounts also were longer and they contained more explicit expressions of emotion. Kuebli, Butler, and Fivush's (1995) analysis of parent-child memory conversations identified a parallel early gender difference in emotional expression: mothers talked more about emotions when discussing past events with daughters than with sons, and girls used more emotion terms and initiated more conversations about emotions than did boys. Crawford et al.'s (1989) survey of undergraduate students' beliefs about memory abilities was consistent with the slight female advantage found in studies of the age of early memories: participants expected women's memory for childhood events to be superior to men's memory for childhood.

Although gender differences in the age assigned to adults' early memories are not dramatic, when differences exist they consistently point to earlier memories for women than for men. In addition, women's memories for some childhood events appear to be more extensive and richer in affect. Research on parent-child memory talk provides one possible explanation: because parents more frequently engage girls than boys in elaborative memory conversations, women's early experiences are encoded in a detailed narrative form that enables their recall years later.

The connection between observed gender differences in the early socialization of memory and the form and content of adults' memories of childhood is indirect and tentative, but tantalizing nevertheless. Fivush and Reese (1992) reflected broadly on possible ties between parent-child memory talk and adult memory styles:

> the findings suggest that there may be individual differences in autobiographical memory, such that females, in contrast to males, have richer, more

embellished memories of past events and a life story that dates back further. Females may also be more interested in past events; they seem to reminisce more frequently, and to consider past events as more significant than do males. Most intriguing, these differences in the importance placed on auto-biographical memory may be related to early differences in parent-child conversations about the past. Because parents tend to be more elaborative with daughters than with sons, females may be learning more complex narrative forms for recounting and representing the past early in development, as well as learning that the past is valuable for understanding themselves and others. (p. 13)

Diaries

Gender differences are apparent in autobiographical writings as well as in spoken conversations about the past. Girls and women more frequently engage in and ascribe high social value to memory talk, and they also are far more likely than men to document their personal past in private diaries. Thompson (1982) surveyed college students about whether they kept a diary. Women were about four times as likely as men to keep a journal for personal reasons (33% of women versus 8% of men). Thompson and colleagues (Skowronski and Thompson, 1990; Thompson, Skowronski, Larsen, and Betz, 1996) also documented a female advantage with respect to the accuracy of dates assigned retrospectively to diary entries. Participating college students kept personal diaries as part of a research study and later dated the recorded events from memory; the results indicated that "females are more often exactly correct about the dates of autobiographical events than males" (Thompson et al., 1996, p. 160).

In 1993, Rebecca Morton and I gathered unpublished pilot data about gender differences in diary use among college students, most of whom were attending prestigious Eastern schools. In response to the question, "Do you presently keep a journal or diary?" 56% of women but only 12% of men answered affirmatively. In addition, most women (96%) but less than half of the men (44%) had kept a journal or diary at some point in the past.

Women's accounts of why they currently keep a diary, or why they have done so in the past, document the high premium placed on remembering personal episodes. Lifshin (1982) edited a collection of women's journals, and several of the contributors commented on the process of diary-keeping. Author Judith McDaniel portrayed her journal as an extension of autobiographical memory: "My journals are primarily for me. I use them to remember the hard things I need to remember in order to grow, to live a self-conscious life. . . I probably wouldn't need to keep [a journal] at all if I had total recall of those most difficult learning moments, but since I find them hard to remember, I expect I'll be keeping a journal for a long time" (p. 168). Writer Rachel De Vries "began with a desire to remember, and that continues to be her main purpose in journal writing" (p. 37). An entry in Sylvia Plath's diary revealed her purpose in writing about herself: "As of today I have decided to keep a diary again—just a place where I can write my thoughts and opinions when I have a moment. Somehow I have to keep and hold the rapture of being seventeen. Every day is so precious and I feel infinitely sad at the thought of all of this melting farther and farther away from me as I grow older" (p. 89).

The view expressed by these female authors and diarists—that it is essential to keep in touch with the personal past—also is apparent in the comments of some college women who participated in our Wellesley pilot study. One student wrote that she kept a diary "to record my thoughts and feelings and events that have happened to me. I want to be able to look back 20 years from now and see how I got to where I will be." Another student stated that she writes in her journal "as a way of recording important moments in my life that I can look back on and remember exactly how I felt at that moment." A third student kept a diary "to have a way to ensure that I will always be able to remember important parts of my life."

Other reasons that women gave for keeping diaries illustrate some of the same functions that Tannen and others have attributed to women's memory conversations: enhancing intimacy, analyzing people and situations, and expressing emotions. In the case of diaries, the intended audience is the self rather than others. Kay Morgan explicitly mentioned the conversational quality of diary-writing: "I use my diaries to talk to myself" (Lifshin, p. 8). Writer Gail Godwin used her journal for "confiding secrets, for working out answers to events or people who puzzle me, for wailing and bitching (naturally) . . . for recording interesting conversation and details I know I would forget later" (Lifshin, p. 9). For some women diarists, writing is an invaluable source of emotional release. Dancer Darlene Myers wrote in her journal to effect her own "personal catharsis" (Lifshin, p. 220), and several college students in our pilot study also listed emotional expression as a vital function of keeping a diary.

Although studies of diary keeping are not definitive, they fit well with analyses of gender differences in memory talk. Women tend to place a higher value than men on remembering salient personal episodes, on talking about them with others, and on recording them so that they can be revisited at a later time. Anecdotal evidence suggests that when men keep written records of their life experiences, the narratives—like spoken exchanges between males—are comparatively bereft of intimate details and explicit emotions. For example, Schaefer (1993) analyzed a diary written by Denton Geyer, which recorded Geyer's travels through Europe in 1928–29. Geyer's diary was notable for the striking absence of personal details and emotional expression: "There is nothing much personal in the diary. He met just about everybody who was anybody in education from Adler in Vienna to Claparede in Paris, but he does not mention even once that he misses his wife and newborn child. The only way we know they exist is that he writes in the very last paragraph that they await him at the railroad station" (Schaefer, 1993, p. 7).

Men's relative lack of interest in diary-keeping mirrors their reticence in personal conversations about the past. Although rigid gender roles appear to have loosened in the last 30 years, many boys still grow up in social milieus that fail to encourage—or actively discourage—intimate and emotional talk about the personal past. In contrast, many girls grow up in milieus that encourage memory talk, and as women they come to value and cherish the opportunity to express their memories of emotion-laden personal experiences—both verbally and in writing.

Narrative Approaches to Scholarship

As girls begin to converse actively about the personal past, first with parents and later with peers, they may extract several overarching beliefs from these exchanges. First, learning from past events is an interactive, shared enterprise. Second, telling stories constructed from personal experience enhances interpersonal connection and strengthens the force of argument and persuasion. Third, attention to contextual details and unique aspects of events is essential for effective self expression, informed action, and deep understanding.

These values are embedded in descriptions of women's "ways of knowing" (Belenky, Clinchy, Goldberger, and Tarule, 1986). Clinchy (1995) identified women's intellectual styles that are "personal rather than detached, subjective rather than objective, concrete rather than abstract, and intimate rather than distant" (p. 259). This type of knowing "relies on narrative, rather than argument, as a mode of discourse, but narrative is used as a collaborative way of thinking—thinking with, rather than against, the position one is examining, and using story-telling as a way not just of illuminating but of developing concepts" (p. 260).

Values embodied in girls' and women's memory activities also are echoed in more general feminist approaches to scholarship (Conway, 1992; Crawford et al., 1992; Personal Narratives Group, 1989; Stivers, 1993; West, 1992). Some feminists have embraced narrative forms of autobiographical expression as core components of empirical social science as well as the humanities. "Since feminist theory is grounded in women's lives . . . women's personal narratives are essential primary documents for feminist research. These narratives present and interpret women's life experiences. They can take many forms, including biography, autobiography, life history—a life story told to a second person who records it—diaries, journals, and letters" (Personal Narratives Group, 1989, p. 4).

Stivers (1993) observed that from a postmodern perspective, all knowledge is interpretative to some extent. That being the case, "feminists can say coherently that individual, contextual accounts such as are found in personal narratives are 'real knowledge' in as weighty a sense as the knowledge claims of positivism though the blend of subjectivity and objectivity is different for each" (p. 410). "The feminist interest in personal narrative is grounded in the claim that the subject's understanding of her life is inherently valid" (p. 420). Although memories are reconstructions rather than exact replications of experience, they have meaning and truth value nevertheless: "When talking about their lives, people lie sometimes, forget a lot, exaggerate, become confused, and get things wrong. Yet they *are* revealing truths. These truths don't reveal the past 'as it actually was,' aspiring to a standard of objectivity. They give us instead the truths of our experiences" (Personal Narratives Group, 1989, p. 261).

Some feminists argue that an exclusive focus on objectivity at the expense of personal experience actually undermines discovery of underlying truths, because detailed recollections sharpen interpretation and unearth subtle meanings. "Detail is important because in detail we recognize constraints placed on our understandings by the notion of 'relevance'; the so-called 'irrelevant' aspects of episodes or events point to the hidden moral or normative aspects of our actions" (Crawford et al., 1992, p. 46). Similarly, autobiography is central to a valid understanding of self: because "the sense of self is an essentially narrative phenomenon," in which "people conceive of themselves in terms of stories about their actions in the world," then "a narrative approach to self-understanding is not a distortion of reality but a confirmation of it" (Stivers, p. 412). Analyzing personal stories not only deepens self-understanding; autobiographical episodes also convey lessons that are generalizable to the lives of others. Reading other people's autobiographies "will make us both more reflective and more decisive about working on the inner script with which we construct the meaning of our own lives. . . It is valuable to examine our own inner texts with these powerful models in mind, for they can both instruct and call forth a more confident inner voice of our own" (Conway, 1992, pp. xii–xiii).

Although women's informal memory styles are compatible with certain feminist approaches to scholarship, a causal connection between memory activities and scholarly attitudes is uncertain. Embracing narrative as a formal analytic tool could be a natural outgrowth of a distinctive, gender-linked elaborative memory style fostered first by parents encouraging young girls to express and share personal memories, and sustained by women engaging actively in memory talk and writing. From this perspective, women are the "personal interviewers of everyday life" (Jourard, 1979, p. 33), and as such they may be drawn to narrative and autobiography as scientific methodologies.

Another view holds that some feminists have adopted narrative modes of scholarship in opposition to logical positivism, with its emphasis on discovering general, testable principles and its "disdain for the particular, the contigent, the nongeneralizable" (Stivers, 1993, p. 417). Feminist scholarship can be interpreted as a confrontational or even subversive response to male control over science: "feminism demands that those who have been objectified now be able to define themselves, to tell their own stories. This is essentially a claim that each human being occupies a legitimate position from which to experience, interpret, and constitute the world" (Stivers, p. 411). Autobiographical narrative provides, in this view, an alternative mode of scholarly inquiry.

These two perspectives are not mutually exclusive. In the historical context of modern Western science, women have been marginalized as scholars, and women's lives have too infrequently been the focus of scientific work. Nevertheless, some women may gravitate towards narrative modes of expression not because they represent an alternative to a male-dominated scientific monolith, but because they are compatible with life-long memory activities and corresponding world views. Speaking about women's conceptions of morality and epistemology, Clinchy (1995) made the case that women's intellectual perspectives need not be born out of oppression: "Some argue that these are intrinsically powerless modes that women, as victims of oppression, are forced to adopt, but it is equally possible that these modes are seen as powerless simply because women use them" (p. 261). What many scholars seek is not an exclusive, alternative, female vision and methodology, but rather an openness to multiple visions and methodologies (Stivers, 1993, p. 421). In a world in which multiple perspectives on scientific truth are tolerated or even encouraged, some women may be especially receptive to narrative approaches because they complement a positive view of personal memory as an essential component of effective communication, problem-solving, and understanding.

*

Culture and Personal Event Memories

In Western cultures, talk about the past often promotes an increasingly independent or autonomous sense of self. For example, Nelson (1989b) and colleagues conducted an extraordinarily detailed analysis of individual memory performance. They examined the pre-sleep crib talk of Emily, the precocious daughter of university professors (white, middle class, living in the United States). Emily's bedtime dialogues with her parents, as well as her spontaneous utterances when left alone, were collected for fifteen months, spanning Emily's third year of life. Her narrative constructions were surprisingly well formed and elaborate even at this very young age.

One prominent theme in the bedtime narratives is "what happened" (Nelson, 1989a, p. 28), including descriptions of specific episodes as well as everyday routines. Parents occasionally modeled autobiographical construction. For a period of two months, "her father recounted the day's events to her as a pre-bed routine, and Emily contributed to these recounts" (Nelson, p. 32). In Emily's own monologues, however, talk with parents was rarely repeated; she focused on other topics. Nelson speculated that "when her parents discussed with her an event that she had experienced, that experience received sufficient attention that she did not then need to recapitulate it in her own talk" (p. 32). Feldman's

(1989) analysis of Emily's monologues revealed a problem-solving function: "Often, she arrives at her time alone in bed with an unsolved puzzle in hand and goes to work on it in monologue" (p. 98). Bruner and Lucariello (1989) focused on Emily's increasingly successful attempts to impose meaning on her daily activities: "Emily learns how to tell about these events in her soliloquies in a way that captures their sequencing and gives a sense of how usual or unusual they are, what stance she takes towards them, what her intentions were at the time, and how she reflects upon them" (p. 96).

The authors took special note of the significance of Emily's working independently, through spoken narratives, to make sense of her world: "She manages not only to convert her world into manageable narrative but also to do so on her own terms—alone, in her crib, and without intervention by adults or anybody else. She has begun not only to master her developmental talk but to master it *on her own*" (Bruner and Lucariello, pp. 96–97). Similarly, Feldman observed that Emily's self-narratives serve a special, individuating function: "It is *her* world that constitutes the domain of monologue, her *father's* that provides the basis for dialogic discourse. It may be in this respect that monologic speech is a necessary step toward Emily's construction of her own working representation of the world" (p. 119).

Emily's memory talk appears to promote the development of an individual identity and autonomous self-concept. But what about the development of toddlers who grow up in cultures in which few opportunities exist for pre-sleep memory talk, in part because nighttime separations are believed to be harmful to the child and divisive for the family? What happens when the primary goals of socialization within a given culture favor strengthening familial interdependence and group cohesion, rather than developing autonomy and individuality?

Morelli, Rogoff, Oppenheim, and Goldsmith (1992) contrasted the sleeping arrangements of children growing up in the United States with those of Mayan children in Guatemala. Like Emily, children in most middle-class Caucasian families living in the United States sleep apart from their parents, usually beginning in the first year of life. In Morelli et al.'s sample, 80% of U.S. babies slept in a room separate from their parents by 6 months of age. In sharp contrast, 100% of Mayan infants slept with their mother into the second year. The practice of children sharing a bed with parents for the first few years of life is common in Japan, India, Korea, Italy, and many if not most other countries of the world (Morelli et al., 1992; Roland, 1991). Not surprisingly, middle-class Caucasian U.S. parents and infants develop elaborate bedtime routines in response to the stress of separation, whereas families living in co-sleeping cultures have a smoother nighttime transition.

Although co-sleeping may be merely a practical response to cramped living quarters, it may also reflect a positive cultural value placed on interdependence. Whereas U.S. parents view separate sleeping arrangements as an important form of independence training, and move the infant from the parents' bedroom on the basis of perceived developmental readiness, Mayan parents regard early separations as "tantamount to child neglect"; when told about U.S. infants sleeping apart from their parents, one Mayan mother could not believe it. "But there's someone else in there with them, isn't there?" (Morelli et al., p. 608). Similarly, many Japanese families believe that children are born separate and must be socialized into interdependence, and that co-sleeping contributes to this process (Morelli et al., p. 611). In middle-class U.S. families, most parents apparently believe that children are born dependent and that autonomy must be encouraged beginning at an early age, even if the process of individuation is a stressful one. According to one U.S. mother, "It was time to give him his own room . . . his own territory. That's the American way" (Morelli et al., p. 604).

What is the function of bedtime dialogues and monologues from the child's and parents' perspectives? Nelson, Bruner, Lucariello, and Feldman admired Emily's evolving narrative sense of self and individuality, but the transition to separate sleeping arrangements also takes an emotional toll: "During the second year of life, sleeping disturbances are far and away the most common reason for psychological consultation among the 'psychofunctional' problems of childhood. And the majority of these include a going-to-sleep problem as well as repeated awakenings, nightmares, and so on. . . The going-to-sleep ritual is very widely used to help the child make the transition to sleep—or to simply being alone" (Stern, 1989, p. 312). Emily's pre-sleep talk with her parents "includes the deploying of various strategies to get her parents to remain in the room . . . the fact that the dialogue is leading up to separation is almost never out of Emily's or her parents' minds" (p. 312).

One way to cope with separation is to activate memories of loved ones in their absence, and this may be part of the motivation for Emily's nightly memory work: "one can construe both Emily's future talk and her past talk as types of activation of internalized others to help her self-regulate under anxiety of separation. This kind of self-regulation need not be very specific . . . a nonspecific mental peopling of her world will do" (Stern, p. 314). At least some of Emily's narrative constructions "may be designed to 'hold onto' the parents, via their words, phrases, topics, or 'voices' . . . whatever the other purposes of monologue, if it recreates the 'presence' of others by activating internal representation of self-with-others, it will have served the self-regulating function of mitigating separation anxiety to some extent" (pp. 314–315). It seems likely that part of her parents' motivation for participating in extended bedtime dialogues is to provide Emily with mental images that will soothe and sustain her in their absence.

Emily's nightly rituals contrast sharply with the ease with which Mayan children pass from wakefulness to sleep: "There was not a separate routine to coax the baby to sleep. Most of the babies simply fell asleep when sleepy, along with the rest of the family or before if they got tired" (Morelli et al., p. 607). In many non-Western cultures, separation of very young children from parents is a relatively infrequent occurrence (Roland, 1991). In cultures where parents do not feel a sense of urgency about promoting their children's autonomy, a strong impetus for the construction of elaborate individualized self-narratives beginning in infancy and toddlerhood may not exist.

Independence versus Interdependence

How might differing cultural values foster the development of distinctive memory styles? Some researchers have identified two overarching cultural approaches to socialization: individualism and collectivism. Countries identified as strongly individualistic include the United States, Canada, Australia, and Western European nations; countries identified as strongly collectivistic include many Asian, African, Latin American, and some Southern European nations (Dion and Dion, 1993; Markus and Kitayama, 1991; Triandis, 1989) Nevertheless, considerable variation exists among people within countries: "on average, relatively more individuals in Western cultures will hold this [individualistic] view than will individuals in non-Western cultures," but "within a given culture . . . individuals will vary in the extent to which they are good cultural representatives and construe the self in the mandated way" (Markus and Kitayama, 1991, p. 226). People who adopt an individualistic perspective are labeled independent (Markus and Kitayama,

1991), idiocentric (Triandis, 1989), or individualized (Roland, 1991). People who adopt a collectivistic perspective are labeled interdependent (Markus and Kitayama, 1991), allocentric (Triandis, 1989), or familial (Roland, 1991).

Individualistic cultures value and promote self-actualization, individuation, and autonomy. They stress "attending to the self, the appreciation of one's difference from others, and the importance of asserting the self" (Markus and Kitayama, p. 224). Individualists "give priority to personal goals over the goals of collectives" (Triandis, p. 509). Collectivistic cultures value the pursuit of common goals, group harmony, and shared identities. They favor an approach that involves "attending to and fitting in with others and the importance of harmonious interdependence with them" (Markus and Kitayama, p. 224). Collectivists "either make no distinctions between personal and collective goals, or if they do make such distinctions, they subordinate their personal goals to the collective goals" (Triandis, p. 509). In some Asian cultures, "self-experience is that of a we-self in contrast to the highly individualistic I-self of Westerners that forms a dualistic relationship between 'I' and 'you' (Roland, p. 165). These contrasting cultural perspectives are reflected in conceptions of social achievement: "the Japanese nightmare is exclusion, meaning that one is failing the normative goal of connecting to others. This is in sharp contrast to the American nightmare which is to fail at separating from others, as can occur when one is unduly influenced by others, or does not stand up for what one believes, or when one goes unnoticed or undistinguished" (Markus and Kitayama, 1991, p. 228).

Cultural perspectives on collectivism and individualism ought to be apparent not only in overt behaviors and activities, but also in the organization of thought, including memory: "A second consequence of having an interdependent self as opposed to an independent self concerns the ways in which knowledge about self and other is processed, organized, and retrieved from memory" (Markus and Kitayama, 1991, p. 232). Because individualistic cultures stress "elements of identity that reflect possessions—what do I own, what experiences have I had, what are my accomplishments" (Triandis, 1989, p. 515), self-referenced memories may be prominently represented in conversations and in life histories. Because collectivistic cultures emphasize interpersonal connection rather than individuation, personal episodes may be less prominent in memory talk and autobiography.

Although individualism and collectivism have been interpreted as components of a single bipolar construct, recent analyses suggest that they may represent two separate dimensions. Some cultural groups are on average more collectivistic and less individualistic than other groups, but many groups will exhibit both qualities. Similarly, individuals within cultures are not uniformly high on one dimension and low on the other. Wink (1997) gave tests of individualism and collectivism to students attending college in the United States who were of Chinese, Korean, or European descent. Asian-Americans scored higher on collectivism than did Euro-Americans. Group differences in individualism were smaller and less consistent, but Chinese- and Korean-American students were "somewhat less likely than Euro-Americans to report engagement in public displays of individuality through self-assertiveness or overt expression of one's uniqueness." Although collectivism and, to a lesser extent, individualism varied predictably across cultural groups, measures of collectivism and individualism were not correlated at the individual level of analysis. Accordingly, the terms "individualist" and "collectivist" are used in this chapter to indicate general tendencies of cultures and individuals rather than absolute, dichotomous categories.

Autobiographical Expression

Individualistic and collectivistic cultures offer different perspectives on autobiography. Individualists may be more willing or even eager to tell about their own experiences and feelings, and they are intrigued by others' intimate life stories: "autobiography is closely linked in Western culture with the emerging value of the unique and independent individual" (Gergen and Gergen, 1993, p. 195). The fascination with individual lives in the United States is confirmed by the *New York Times Book Review*'s list of bestsellers; one or more self-revealing autobiographies are invariably present on the list. A number one bestseller in 1996 was basketball star Dennis Rodman's autobiography, *Bad As I Wanna Be*. Rodman's exaggerated individuality—brightly dyed hair, extravagant tattoos, outlandish behavior on the basketball court, outspokenness—is a primary source of the public's interest in his personal life.

Whereas individualists place a premium on uniqueness, collectivists respond to "the press not to stand out and to fit in" (Markus and Kitayama, 1991, p. 244). Accordingly, collectivists may not share individualists' enthusiasm for highly personalized life stories. Autobiography is rare in traditional Asian cultures: "Autobiography as such was unknown, since for a scholar to write a book about himself would have been deemed egotistical in the extreme" (Kim, 1990, p. 153). In Jade Snow Wong's autobiography, *Fifth Chinese Daughter*, the author uses the third person to refer to herself throughout the book. Although the book was published in the United States, Wong explains that "this story is written in the third person from Chinese habit. The submergence of the individual is literally practiced. In written Chinese, prose or poetry, the word 'I' almost never appears. . . Even written in English, an 'I' book by a Chinese would seem outrageously immodest to anyone raised in the spirit of Chinese propriety" (1945, p. vii). Chinese language also communicates a tacit disdain for individualistic propensities: "the Chinese term for *individualism (geren juyi)* is understood to mean something closer to *selfishness*" (Pomerantz, 1991, p. 8).

Cultures differ with respect to the form and extensiveness of memory talk. It is not uncommon for people from individualistic cultures to freely recount personal anecdotes and even intimate details of their private lives; they appear to have the "need to express [their] own thoughts, feelings, and actions to others" (Markus and Kitayama, 1991, p. 246). In contrast, free-flowing conversations about the personal past may occur less frequently in collectivistic cultures. Collectivists often communicate indirectly or nonverbally, under the implicit assumption that other people will know or can infer their intentions (Roland, 1991; Triandis, 1994). Even in psychotherapy sessions, Japanese patients expect the therapist to understand their private selves without probing: "For the therapist to ask questions of the patient is considered to be intrusive at best and insulting at worst" (Roland, p. 168). Individualists pursue intimacy by exchanging detailed personal information; collectivists achieve intimacy through implicit, empathic understanding.

In the United States, parents and children frequently co-construct embellished narrative accounts of daily experiences. Children growing up in collectivistic societies may have fewer opportunities for memory sharing and autobiographical co-construction. Minami and McCabe (1991) observed that "Japanese children are not usually encouraged to narrate details of experiences that adults can and are expected to infer empathically" (p. 577). Rogoff and Mistry (1990) attributed Mayan children's halting story recall to the fact that "it was an unfamiliar and stressful situation for Mayan children to attempt to narrate a story to an adult" (p. 213).

Mullen and Yi (1995) conducted the most detailed and systematic cross-cultural comparison of parent-child memory talk to date. Conversations between mothers and their 3-year-old children were recorded during normal activities for one day. Both mother and child wore a vest containing a small tape recorder. One-half of the mother-child pairs were Asians living in Seoul, Korea, and one-half were Caucasians living near Boston, Massachusetts; all were from middle-class backgrounds, and all mothers were college graduates. Transcripts were coded for episodes of past event talk, defined as "an instance of the mother and child talking about a specific past event which the child had experienced or witnessed" (p. 411). The frequency of past event talk differed markedly, with Caucasian pairs engaging in such talk almost three times as often as Korean pairs. Additional analyses confirmed that episodes discussed by Caucasian dyads more often featured the child as a primary actor, described thoughts or feelings, and referred to the child's attributes. Events discussed by Korean dyads more often mentioned behavioral expectations or social norms.

Having one's everyday conversations tape-recorded is an unusual occurrence, and Mullen and Yi's results need to be replicated using other test procedures. Nevertheless, Caucasian mothers and preschoolers appear to talk more about personal events from the child's past than do Korean mother-child pairs. The authors concluded that U.S. children "are being taught that each person has a collection of individual attributes that makes them unique, and that it is important to discover and give expression to this individuality. The construction of accounts of one's experiences is an important avenue towards achieving this goal" (p. 417). In contrast, Korean children "are learning that each person has a collection of roles within the social network, and that there are behavioral expectations associated with these roles. The sense of self comes from one's success at performing these roles. There may be less need to differentiate oneself in terms of personal attributes, and thus less need for an elaborated autobiographical narrative" (p. 417).

Echoes of culture are apparent not only in patterns of memory talk but also in children's own memory productions. Minami and McCabe (1991) identified uniformities in Japanese children's personal event narratives. Children between the ages of 5 and 9 years who had lived in the United States for less than two years were interviewed in their native tongue. The topic was personal injuries, and children were asked questions such as, "Have you ever gotten hurt?" or "Did you ever get stung by a bee?" Children were encouraged to elaborate on one specific experience. In contrast to the lengthy stories typically produced by U.S. children, event narratives recounted by Japanese children were short, and they closely followed a conventional mode of presentation, apparently influenced by haiku and related forms of discourse. The researchers concluded that Japanese children's event descriptions reflected cultural expectations for narrative expression marked by brevity and regularity rather than by individuality. "A prerequisite of *haiku* is to abbreviate the essentials. . . The same characteristic was observed in Japanese children's narratives, in which they tended to succinctly talk about several isolated, similar events . . . most Japanese children made their stories straight to the point and very comprehensible" (p. 595).

Han, Leichtman, and Wang (in press) examined autobiographical memory and story recall of 4- and 6-year old children living in China, Korea, and the United States; all U.S. children were white, and most parents of children from all three countries had a college degree. On the first day of testing, children were interviewed in their native language about several personally experienced events (for example, "How did you spend your last birthday?"; "Now, I'd like you to tell me just one thing you did recently that was really special and fun"). Then they saw a narrated slide show of a children's story. The next day, children were questioned about the children's story. Although the three groups of children performed similarly on the objective test of story recall, their personal event memories differed systematically by country of origin. U.S. children's memories were more detailed, and they were more likely to describe distinctive events as opposed to general occurrences. They more often mentioned personal preferences, voiced their opinions about remembered events, and described internal cognitive and emotional processes. When a ratio of self-mentions to other-mentions was computed, American children referred to themselves most frequently in their memory narratives.

Cultural differences in children's predominant memory activities could influence the extensiveness of childhood amnesia. Adults' memories of early childhood would thus be more detailed and readily accessible in cultures where parent-child memory talk is frequent and elaborate, where parent and child eagerly co-construct the child's developing narrative sense of self, and where memories of distinctive childhood events are repeatedly revisited in conversation. Mullen (1994) tested this hypothesis by comparing the earliest memories of Asian and Caucasian college students studying in the United States. In three separate studies, the average age of the earliest memory for Caucasian students was between 5 and 9 months younger than for Asian students. Because the Asian samples in these studies combined foreign Asians and Asian-Americans, a fourth study included only Korean students studying in the U.S. but who grew up in Korea; these students responded in Korean. The mean age of the earliest memory for Korean students was 55.5 months compared to an average of 38.8 months for Caucasian students. Mullen linked cultural differences in adults' memories of childhood to stylistic differences in early parent-child memory talk: "socialization goals may influence the ways in which adults structure conversations with children about their experiences and these styles of talk in turn shape the development of autobiographical memory" (p. 77).

Although the link between cultural imperatives and memory styles is indirect, research is consistent with the idea that preferred forms of autobiographical expression reflect values embedded in the surrounding society. To achieve the goal of autonomy, individualistic families may enthusiastically engage young children in elaborative memory talk and help them construct distinctive life stories, including self-referenced episodes which contribute to a sense of independence and uniqueness. To achieve the goal of interdependence, collectivistic families may emphasize social norms and foster empathic understanding, and they may downplay uses of memory that promote a separate, and potentially divisive, view of the self.

∗

Personality and Personal Event Memories

Although gender and cultural group differences in memory are apparent, other sorts of variations cut across these broad groups. Here I focus on two aspects of memory style: the tendency to recount general rather than specific qualities of past events, and to report early childhood events in a disjointed rather than a coherent manner. I also outline possible connections between these stylistic qualities and dimensions of personality.

When a situation requires that a person supply personal information from autobiographical memory, he or she often has considerable leeway with respect to the form of the response. For example, if asked to describe what happened during the college years, a former student could focus on general experiences—classes were difficult, lifelong friendships were formed, things improved greatly after a tumultuous first year—or she could recount pinpointed events such as saying good-bye to parents on the first day, the agony of failing an important exam, or the chance meeting of her future spouse. When my colleagues and I asked current students and alumnae to write out their salient memories of Wellesley College, we obtained some narratives that were specific, others that were general, and still others that featured both specific and general information (Pillemer et al., 1986; Pillemer et al., 1988; Pillemer et al., 1996; these studies are described in Chapter 4). Our instructions to participants appeared on the surface to encourage reporting of specific episodes: we asked for separate written descriptions of individual memories and requested that writers make their accounts as detailed as possible. Although specific memories were frequently given both by current students and by alumnae who had graduated as long as 22 years earlier, a substantial proportion of memories (between 26% and 58% in different samples) were primarily general or contained a mixture of general and specific components.

Other researchers have obtained memories using test procedures that pull even more strongly and explicitly for specific episodes. McCabe et al. (1991) asked young adults to recount three early childhood memories and three adolescent memories; the instructions stated that each memory "must be of a *specific* experience that you can *clearly visualize* even today." Even after extensive prompting, some participants persisted in giving general or scripted memories. For example, one person described her memory of "when I started high school." After she gave an extended general account, the interviewer asked, "Can you narrow it down to a more particular incident of one thing that happened concerning the beginning of high school?" The response remained general: "I remember how crowded things were, you know, people going through the halls. You had to push your way through and you had five minutes to get from one end to the other, and there was just like clutters of people everywhere. That's one of the main things that I remember about when I first started school. It seemed like so much chaos and turmoil." The interviewer probed further: "You have the general idea, but I have the impression that what you just gave is an overall description of that whole time period. I would like it if you could narrow it to one particular incident that happened concerning this time period." Nevertheless, the person was unable to fulfill this request: "Um, I don't,

I don't really know how to narrow it down to one particular incident, but the main, the thing that most sticks with me is, you know, like the first week where just the crowding, the crowding, the chaos. . . I was comfortable with my teachers and my surroundings in the classrooms, but it was just in the hallways between classes, having to try and find your way and get there on time and things like that. . ." (pp. 148–149). Despite repeated probes for specific memories, almost 20% of all memories obtained by McCabe et al. were general.

Thorne and Klohnen (1993) also observed marked individual differences in the ease with which young adults in a memory study recalled specific episodes. Participants were asked to provide 10 specific memories of "personally important or problematic encounters" with another person. Despite a clear request for "memories of specific encounters rather than memories of events that happened frequently," some respondents found the task to be confusing and difficult: "some subjects seemed to feel at home, whereas others seemed nearly baffled at first and wanted to know exactly what kinds of memories to recount. Once they got started, some subjects were able to remember many events; others seemed to struggle" (p. 235).

Singer and Salovey (1993) identified two broad categories of written and spoken autobiographical memories that correspond closely to the specific-general distinction: the "single-event memory narrative" and the "summary memory narrative." For example, a participant in a memory study produced the following single event narrative: "I was having a swimming lesson, and the instructor knew that I had a fear of going under deep water. She tried to solve this by sitting on the side of the pool and having me hold onto her legs and pushing me in and out of the water—so long that my head went under. I wanted to stop after a couple of minutes (I was out of breath), but she wouldn't let me—she kept pushing my head under. I panicked and tried to get out, then failing to do so, tried to pull her in. I made so much noise that eventually she let me go, and I ran outside where my mother was waiting. I remember thinking that I was going to drown" (p. 85). Singer and Salovey noted that the narrator "has chosen to tell us about a particular swimming lesson, but this certainly was not her only one. . . One could imagine the participant telling a summarized memory about her 'Dreaded swimming lessons'" (p. 85). This preferred mode of responding, the authors argued, may reflect a deeper underlying memory style: "Her choice to speak of a singular event may be due to the unique terror of the incident, but it may also be due to her style as a person. Is it possible that some people move from general memories to specific ones more easily than other people? Some individuals may be more comfortable with the powerful emotions that can be evoked by recalling the imagery and sensory details of a particular past experience" (p. 85).

Williams (1996; Williams and Broadbent, 1986; Williams and Dritschel, 1988) discovered what he termed "overgeneral" recall, in which people chronically produce general memories even when instructed to recount specific episodes. Williams and colleagues presented people with cue words and asked them to recall an associated specific event, "something that happened at a particular place and time and took no longer than a day" (1996, p. 246). An example of a specific response to the cue word "happy" is "The day we left to go on holiday," whereas an example of a general response is "When I'm playing squash" (p. 247). Pronounced individual differences on this memory task were apparent: some people readily reported specific memories, whereas others frequently gave general memories despite strong encouragement to search for particular instances.

Williams (1996) attributed overgeneral memory in part to "a more long-term cognitive style . . . some individuals may learn to use overgeneral encoding and retrieval styles as a means to control affect, and more specifically to minimize negative affect" (p. 255). Accordingly, overgeneral memory is more prevalent among individuals with certain types of emotional disturbance. Williams and colleagues showed that depressed and suicidal people are especially likely to produce general memories in response to a request for specific memories. McNally and colleagues (McNally, Litz, Prassas, Shin, and Weathers, 1994; McNally, Lasko, Macklin, and Pittman, 1995) used a similar word-cued memory task and identified overgeneral memory in Vietnam war veterans with a clinical diagnosis of Post-traumatic stress disorder (PTSD).

Difficulties in moving from generalities to specifics may impair interpersonal problem-solving, because finding effective solutions frequently requires access to episodic memories. For example, a college student who is faced with the dilemma of loneliness may fail to identify successful strategies for meeting people if she can muster only general event descriptions, such as "I am happy when I'm with my boyfriend." Memories of specific instances in which she was happy contain more detailed and prescriptive information about particular activities that may bring her into contact with other people and elevate her mood (Williams, 1996, p. 252).

Although possible explanations for the overgenerality effect among clinical patients remain speculative at this time, Williams (1996) offered a tentative developmental account for severe depression. Williams posited that an early history of extremely negative life events could have lasting effects on narrative memory styles: "the person growing up in such an environment may learn that specific episodic information is too negative, so the person passively avoids this punishing consequence of recollection. . . Whenever a mnemonic cue activates categoric intermediate descriptions that begin to retrieve fragments of a negative specific episode, the search is aborted" (p. 260). The individual's encoding and retrieval processes become habitually "locked" at a generic level of event representation, and this overgeneral memory style even spills over to experiences unrelated to trauma. In fact, if severely depressed adults have a paucity of positive mnemonic cues in their current environment, then memories of specific positive events may be even harder to access than negative episodes (Williams, 1996, p. 262). Because emotional disturbance severely taps attentional resources, purposeful efforts to move beyond the generic level of retrieval are further impeded.

According to Williams's developmental explanation, early trauma can foster a life-long predisposition toward thematic rather than episodic remembering. Depressed people have on average experienced many more negative life events than have nondepressed people (Williams, 1996). Kuyken and Brewin (1995) found that depressed individuals who have a reported history of childhood sexual abuse are especially likely to exhibit overgeneral memory. Adult combat veterans who experienced significant childhood trauma are at greatest risk for PTSD, and PTSD sufferers also demonstrate overgeneral retrieval on autobiographical memory tasks (McNally et al., 1994). Of course, an explanation based partly on traumatic early experiences does not deny the potential importance of genetic predispositions toward emotional disturbance or, for that matter, overgeneral memory.

Singer and Salovey (1993) also argued that the habitual activation of general rather than specific memories may dampen negative affect associated with painful past events. "We propose that some people may use highly abstract and summarized memories as a means to ward off unwanted images and emotional reactions from their past . . . the organization of memory narratives, representing one aspect of a cognitive style, may be employed for defensive purposes" (p. 105). In support of the idea that avoiding specific memories serves a defensive function, people who are classified as having a repressive personality style are especially likely to produce general rather than specific memories and to have limited access to emotional or early childhood memories (Davis, 1987; Kihlstrom and Harackiewicz, 1982; Singer and Salovey, 1993). From this perspective, "repression" may be construed as failure to move from a general to a specific level of memory processing.

Overly general memory is apparent not only on autobiographical memory tests, but also in the course of psychotherapy. Consider the following exchange between a patient and a therapist (Williams, 1996, pp. 245–246):

Therapist: When you were young, what sorts of things made you happy?
Patient: Well, things used to be alright then; I mean, better than they are now, I think. When my dad was there, he used to take me for walks on the Common sometimes after lunch on a Sunday.
Therapist: Can you tell me about one such a walk?
Patient: Well, we used to go out after lunch, sometimes we would take a ball and play around. Afterwards, we might go and see my granny who lived on the other side of the Common.
Therapist: When you think back, now, can you remember any particular time? I want you to try and recall any one of these times. Any time will do, it doesn't have to be particularly important or special.
Patient: I remember there used to be other children on the Common sometimes. Sometimes they would be friends of mine and I would stop and chat to them for a while.
Therapist: Can you remember any particular time when you met any of your friends?
Patient: If it was winter, there weren't usually many people about.

Because many types of clinical treatment involve recall of specific events, people with a chronically general memory style pose a special psychotherapeutic challenge, one that may inspire new memory-based interventions (Williams, 1996).

Specificity-generality is not the only dimension of memory style associated with variations in personality. Research on emotional attachment has focused on memory coherence rather than specificity per se. Main, Kaplan, and Cassidy (1985) constructed the Adult Attachment Interview (AAI), in which people describe memories of their early attachment relationships with parents. Pronounced individual differences on this measure are apparent: some narrative accounts are coherent and consistent, whereas other accounts are disjointed, rambling, or sparse.

Main et al. identified a strong relationship between U.S. mothers' memory styles on the AAI and the quality of their children's emotional attachment status. Attachment had been assessed at 1 year of age using the well-known Ainsworth Strange Situation procedure (Ainsworth, Blehar, Waters, and Wall, 1978), in which mothers and infants undergo brief separations and reunions. Following separations, securely attached infants actively seek proximity to and comfort from the parent, after which they return to productive play. Insecurely attached infants avoid or ignore the parent, show ambivalent behavior, or appear disorganized or disoriented.

Parents completed the AAI when their children were 6 years old. When parents of securely attached children were asked about their own early attachment histories, their stories had several characteristics in common. They valued attachment relationships, they had ready access to attachment-related early memories, and their interview narratives were coherent and realistic. In contrast, parents of children who had been classified as insecure were "relatively incoherent in their interview transcripts, exhibiting logical and factual contradictions; inability to stay with the interview topic; contradictions between the general descriptions of their relationships with their parents and actual autobiographical episodes offered; apparent inability to access early memories," and so forth (Main, 1991, p. 143). In support of Main et al.'s original study, a recent analysis combining the results of 18 separate samples demonstrated a strong overall relationship between adults' narrative memories of attachment-related experiences and the quality of their infants' attachment (van IJzendoorn, 1995a).

Researchers working with the AAI stress that it is the coherence and organization of adults' attachment narratives, rather than the positive or negative valence of the specific events described, that is predictive of infants' attachment status (Bakermans-Kranenburg and van IJzendoorn, 1993; van IJzendoorn, 1995a, 1995b; Main, 1991; Main et al., 1985; Steele, Steele, and Fonagy, 1996). According to van IJzendoorn, "In the AAI coding system, the content of adults' autobiographical story is irrelevant; the classification of the transcribed interviews depends on the form in which the story has been told, particularly the degree of coherence in a linguistic sense" (1995b, p. 411). Parents with a secure adult attachment style can and do report negative and even traumatic early life experiences, but they do so in a way that illustrates that negative events have been understood and thoughtfully incorporated into the life narrative: "In the parents of secure babies, unfavorable attachment experiences seemed to have been considered and integrated into mental process long before the interview took place" (Main et al., 1985, p. 96).

What accounts for the strong correspondence between the quality of parents' own attachment narratives and their children's attachment behaviors? Parents who have a coherent and confident sense of their own attachment history may interact with their infants in a way that encourages secure bonding. "Parents' mental representations of their childhood experiences with attachment relationships are thought to determine the degree to which information concerning their infants' attachment needs can be processed freely and without distortion. . . Secure parents are believed to have worked through their past negative attachment experiences or to have had secure experiences and, therefore, to be able to focus undivided attention on their infants' attachment signals" (Bakermans-Kranenburg and van IJzendoorn, 1993, p. 870). Research has supported the expected connection between parents' performance on the AAI and their reponsiveness to children's attachment-seeking behaviors (van IJzendoorn, 1995a).

One parental strategy for providing children with emotional security involves talking about present and past events (Bretherton, 1993, 1995). As we have seen, parent-child memory talk contributes to the child's evolving autobiographical sense of self. Open parent-child conversations may be most important when the child has experienced events that are unexpected, emotionally painful and difficult to comprehend. Children and adults who demonstrate secure attachment profiles are not untouched by troubling early episodes, but these negative events are mentally situated within a broader and more reflective life perspective. Oppenheim and Waters posited that parents of insecure children may "fail to provide them with the appropriate emotional support or scaffolding that is needed to process or integrate a complex, negative situation" (1995, p. 206). Siegel offered a similar view from a clinical perspective: "Early remembering is enhanced by parent-child interactions that involve shared construction of stories about remembered events. Inhibition of this memory talk may be part of memory disturbances in childhood trauma" (1996, p. 46).

Why are some parents able to describe their early attachment-related experiences fluidly and coherently, while others give accounts that are disjointed or rambling, with apparent omissions or distortions? Although conclusive data are still lacking, one possibility is that, secure adults engaged in supportive memory talk with their own parents, and that these verbal activities are reflected in their internal working models of attachment. A second possibility is that they had the opportunity to reconstruct their autobiographies successfully later in life. Adult attachment styles reflect not only early interactions with parents, but also later efforts to understand and reinterpret the past. In adulthood, "a trusted friend, spouse, or therapist can provide a 'secure base' for exploring and working through adverse childhood experiences and can enable the adult to 'earn' a coherent and autonomous attachment representation" (van IJzendoorn, 1995a, p. 399). Oppenheim and Waters (1995) made a similar observation: "supportive relationships later in life can help provide a benign perspective on early insecure attachments and dampen some of their negative effects. One aspect of such supportive relationships may be that they provide a co-construction context in which new ways to view the past are explored and articulated" (p. 213).

Elaborate parent-child memory talk is not the only way to promote emotional security. Although all cultural groups value infant-parent attachment and expect children to use mothers as a secure emotional base, differences in specific attachment-related behaviors are apparent (Miyake et al., 1985; Posada et al., 1995). Cultures also may diverge in the realm of attachment-related communication. Families within cultures that promote connection and enmeshment rather than separation and autonomy may rely heavily on nonverbal modes of emotional support. If family members were to discuss personal episodes vigorously, and to reconstrue past experiences in ways that promote individuation, this could be considered symptomatic of a flawed rather than a healthy underlying attachment system. Internal working models of healthy attachment in collectivistic cultures may emphasize implicit interpersonal connections and mutuality. Open and frequent communication about the personal past may be an indicator of secure attachment primarily in individualistic cultures, where memory serves to bridge parent-child separations and where achieving a clearly articulated autonomous sense of self is a marker of successful development.

Even within Western cultures, it would be a mistake to conclude that free and open verbal communication and active memory sharing are essential components of emotional security in all families. For example, Constantine and Israel (1985), following Kantor and Lehr (1975), observed that successfully functioning families may adopt very different interactive styles. One such style, termed *synchronous,* resembles the communicative style of families in collectivistic cultures in some respects. A synchronous family "would rely less on communication, which would be minimal, than on implicit understanding and shared points of view" (p. 528). Whereas an open family "wants things clearly and explicitly stated, the synchronous one prefers things to be left implicit and 'just understood'" (pp. 529–530). A highly functioning synchronous family "works with quiet efficiency" (p. 531). In contrast to children growing up in families where free-flowing conversations are the rule, children in synchronous families "must develop high interpersonal sensitivity, exceptional ability to decipher nonverbal communication, and a knack for discerning unstated expectations or implicit demands" (pp. 535–536). An emphasis on elaborate personal memory talk will surely be missing from synchronous families' models of successful emotional relationships.

Variations in attachment styles and in family systems highlight the adaptive flexibility of the narrative memory system. Narrative memory does not emerge in identical fashion in all cultures, or in men and women, or even in different families within cultures. Rather, memory is used in the service of broad cultural values and within-family proclivities. Definitions of positive change in narrative memory are meaningful only within the perspective of a particular cultural and familial framework.

*

Autobiographical Intelligence

When I began work on this book it did not occur to me to describe autobiographical memory as a form of intelligence. Traditionally, psychologists have portrayed intelligence as a general capacity that can be measured by verbal or mathematical tests. These tests tap memory for abstract knowledge rather than specific episodes. Recently, disenchantment with standard conceptions of IQ has led to alternative models of social, practical, personal, or emotional intelligence. For example, Gardner's multi-faceted conception of intelligence includes self-understanding: "an emerging sense of self proves to be a key element in the realm of the personal intelligences" (1993, p. 242). Although social and personal intelligence would seem to draw on autobiographical experiences, memory for personal events is not yet a formal part of the IQ equation.

Nevertheless, as the book progressed and especially as I completed this chapter, I became more and more convinced that personal event memory is an essential component of practical intelligence. Using the memory of a momentous success or failure as positive motivation, or to avoid disaster, is intelligent behavior. Skillfully recounting a specific memory at just the right time in order to enhance the persuasive weight of an argument is intelligent behavior. Revisiting and reconstruing traumatic past episodes so as to diminish their negative emotional toll is intelligent behavior. And acknowledging that other people may have different memory styles and tailoring interpersonal interactions accordingly is intelligent behavior.

It is tempting to identify particular memory styles as more desirable, or intelligent, than other styles. Comparisons involving gender, culture, and personality indicate that adaptive value does not lie in any one style, but rather in the match between memory activities and external demands imposed by particular life situations. Narrative memory does not evolve in isolation, according to an internally driven formula; it is created in part by the social conditions that surround it.

References

A very brief history of time. (1993, August). *University of Chicago Magazine*, p. 36.

Abelson, R. P. (1981). Psychological status of the script concept. *American Psychologist, 36*, 715–729.

Abrams, M. H. (1988). *A glossary of literary terms* (5th ed.). Fort Worth: Holt, Rinehart and Winston.

Acitelli, L. K., and Holmberg, D. (1993). Reflecting on relationships: The role of thoughts and memories. *Advances in Personal Relationships, 4*, 71–100.

Adams, J. M. (1992, February 17). Captive memories. *The Boston Globe*, pp. 1, 4.

Addams, J. (1992). Twenty years at Hull-House. In J. K. Conway (Ed.) (1992, pp. 506–525).

Ainsworth, M. D. S., Blehar, M. C., Waters, E., and Wall, S. (1978). *Patterns of attachment: A psychological study of the strange situation*. Hillsdale, N.J.: Erlbaum.

Archer, R. L. (1980). Self-disclosure. In D. M. Wegner and R. R. Vallacher (Eds.), *The self in social psychology* (pp. 183–205). New York: Oxford University Press.

Arnold, M. B. (1969). Human emotion and action. In T. Mischel (Ed.), *Human action: Conceptual and empirical issues* (pp. 167–197). New York: Academic Press.

Atlas, J. (1991, June 23). Stranger than fiction. *The New York Times Magazine*, pp. 22, 41, 43.

Bakermans-Kranenburg, M. J., and van IJzendoorn, M. H. (1993). A psychometric study of the adult attachment interview: Reliability and discriminant validity. *Developmental Psychology, 29*, 870–879.

Banaji, M. R., and Crowder, R. G. (1989). The bankrupcy of everyday memory. *American Psychologist, 44*, 1185–1193.

Bandura, A. (1982). The psychology of chance encounters and life paths. *American Psychologist, 37*, 747–755.

Barsalou, L. W. (1988). The content and organization of autobiographical memories. In U. Neisser and E. Winograd (Eds.), *Remembering reconsidered: Ecological and traditional approaches to the study of memory* (pp. 193–243). New York: Cambridge University Press.

Bass, A. (1991, September 30). 'Date rape' victims bear scars longer, study finds. *The Boston Globe*, pp. 1, 6.

Bass, A. (1993, November 22). Resisting the forces that pull couples apart. *The Boston Globe*, pp. 21, 23.

Bass, A. (1995, June 3). Measuring TV news' toll on children. *The Boston Globe*, pp. 1, 9.

Bauer, P. J., and Wewerka, S. S. (1997). Saying is revealing: Verbal expression of event memory in the transition from infancy to early childhood. In P. W. van den Broek, P. J. Bauer, and T. Bourg (Eds.), *Developmental spans in event comprehension and representation: Bridging fictional and actual events* (pp. 139–168). Mahwah, N.J.: Erlbaum.

Beals, D. E. (1991). Stories from the classroom: Rate of response to personal event narratives told by beginning teachers. *The Quarterly Newsletter of the Laboratory of Comparative Human Cognition, 13,* 31–38.

Belenky, M. F., Clinchy, B. M., Goldberger, N. R., and Tarule, J. M. (1986). *Women's ways of knowing: The development of self, voice, and mind.* New York: Basic Books.

Bell, B. E., Loftus, E. F. (1989). Trivial persuasion in the courtroom: The power of (a few) minor details. *Journal of Personality and Social Psychology, 56,* 669–679.

Belove, L. (1980). First encounters of the close kind (FECK): The use of the story of the first interaction as an early recollection of a marriage. *Journal of Individual Psychology, 36,* 191–208.

Bennett, P. (1991, November 9). Magic opens a window on AIDS. *The Boston Globe,* pp. 1, 8.

Bernstein, J. (1983). A child's garden of science. *The American Scholar, 52,* 295–298.

Berntsen, D. (1996). Involuntary autobiographical memories. *Applied Cognitive Psychology, 10,* 435–454.

Blaudschun, M. (1995, August 16). Parcells gives hero farewell. *The Boston Globe,* p. 38.

Bohannon, J. N., III. (1988). Flashbulb memories for the Space Shuttle disaster: A tale of two theories. *Cognition, 29,* 179–196.

Bohannon, J. N., III, and Symons, V. L. (1992). Flashbulb memories: Confidence, consistency, and quantity. In E. Winograd and U. Neisser (Eds.) (1992, pp. 65–91).

Bourke-White, M. (1992). Portrait of myself. In J. K. Conway (Ed.) (1992, pp. 425–453).

Bower, G. H. (1981). Mood and memory. *American Psychologist, 36,* 129–148.

Boyd, C. (1993, May 31). The children have not forgotten. *The Boston Globe,* pp. 25, 27

Bretherton, I. (1993). From dialogue to internal working models: The co-construction of self in relationships. In C. A. Nelson (Ed.), *Memory and affect in development: The Minnesota Symposia on Child Psychology,* Vol. 26 (pp. 237–263). Hillsdale, N.J. : Erlbaum.

Bretherton, I. (1995). A communication perspective on attachment relationships and internal working models. *Monographs of the Society for Research in Child Development, 60,* 310–329.

Brewer, W. F. (1986). What is autobiographical memory? In D. C. Rubin (Ed.), *Autobiographical memory* (pp. 25–49). New York: Cambridge University Press.

Brewer, W. F. (1988). Memory for randomly sampled autobiographical events. In U.

Neisser and E. Winograd (Eds.), *Remembering reconsidered: Ecological and traditional approaches to the study of memory* (pp. 21–90). New York: Cambridge University Press.

Brewer, W. F. (1992). The theoretical and empirical status of the flashbulb memory hypothesis. In E. Winograd and U. Neisser (Eds.) (1992, pp. 274–305).

Brewer, W. F. (1996). What is recollective memory? In D. C. Rubin (Ed.), *Remembering our past: Studies in autobiographical memory.* (pp. 19–66). New York: Cambridge University Press.

Brewin, C. R. (1989). Cognitive change processes in psychotherapy. *Psychological Review, 96,* 379–394.

Brewin, C. R., Andrews, B., and Gotlib, I. H. (1993). Psychopathology and early experience: A reappraisal of retrospective reports. *Psychological Bulletin, 113,* 82–98.

Britton, B. K., and Pellegrini, A. D. (Eds.). (1990). *Narrative thought and narrative language.* Hillsdale, N.J.: Erlbaum.

Brokaw, T. (1991, June 16). Of fathers and children and sports. *The New York Times,* p. S 9.

Bronner, E. (1994, January 11). "More to life than money." *The Boston Globe,* pp. 25, 28.

Brooks, L. R., Norman, G. R., and Allen, S. W. (1991). Role of specific similarity in a medical diagnostic task. *Journal of Experimental Psychology: General, 120,* 278–287.

Brown, R. (1990). Politeness theory: Exemplar and exemplary. In I. Rock (Ed.), *The legacy of Solomon Asch: Essays in cognition and social psychology* (pp. 23–38). Hillsdale, N.J.: Erlbaum.

Brown, R., and Kulik, J. (1977). Flashbulb memories. *Cognition, 5,* 73–99.

Bruce, D. (1989). Functional explanations of memory. In L. W. Poon, D. C. Rubin, and B. A. Wilson (Eds.), *Everyday cognition in adulthood and late life* (pp. 44–58). New York: Cambridge University Press.

Bruner, J. S. (1986). *Actual minds, possible worlds.* Cambridge, MA: Harvard University Press.

Bruner, J. S. (1987). Life as narrative. *Social Research, 54,* 11–32.

Bruner, J. S. (1990). *Acts of meaning.* Cambridge, MA: Harvard University Press.

Bruner, J. S., and Lucariello, J. (1989). Monologue as narrative recreation of the world. In K. Nelson (Ed.) (1989b, pp. 73–97).

Buckner, N., and Whittlesey, R. (Co-Producers and Directors). (1994). *Apollo 13: To the edge and back* [film].

Buehlman, K. T., Gottman, J. M., and Katz, L. F. (1992). How a couple views their past predicts their future: Predicting divorce from an oral history interview. *Journal of Family Psychology, 5,* 295–318.

Campbell, B. A., and Spear, N. E. (1972). Ontogeny of memory. *Psychological Review, 79,* 215–236.

Campion, N. R. (1994). From the White House—Reflections on Wellesley: Hillary Rodham Clinton '69 remembers. *Wellesley, 78,* 8–11.

Capps, L., and Ochs, E. (1995). Out of place: Narrative insights into agoraphobia. *Discourse Processes, 19,* 407–439.

Carter, K. (1993). The place of story in the study of teaching and teacher education. *Educational Researcher, 22,* 5–12.

Ceci, S. J., and Bruck, M. (1993). Suggestibility of the child witness: A historical review and synthesis. *Psychological Bulletin, 113,* 403–439.

Chandler, D. L. (1993, October 14). Pair's binary pulsar discovery in UMass research earns Nobel. *The Boston Globe,* pp. 1, 8.

Christianson, S-Å. (1989). Flashbulb memories: Special, but not so special. *Memory & Cognition, 17,* 435–443.

Claffey, C. E. (1989, December 19). Robert Coles. *The Boston Globe,* pp. 69, 72–73.

Clinchy, B. M. (1995). Commentary. *Human Development, 38,* 258–264.

Colegrove, F. W. (1899). Individual memories. *American Journal of Psychology, 10,* 228–255.

Connelly, F. M., and Clandinin, D. J. (1990). Stories of experience and narrative inquiry. *Educational Researcher, 19,* 2–14.

Constantine, L. L., and Israel, J. T. (1985). The family void: Treatment and theoretical aspects of the synchronous family paradigm. *Family Process, 24,* 525–547.

Conway, J. K. (Ed.). (1992). *Written by herself.* New York: Vintage.

Conway, M. A. (1995). *Flashbulb memories.* Hillsdale, N.J.: Lawrence Erlbaum.

Conway, M. A., Anderson, S. J., Larsen, S. F., Donnelly, C. M., McDaniel, M. A., McClelland, A. G. R., Rawles, R. E., and Logie, R. H. (1994). The formation of flashbulb memories. *Memory & Cognition, 22,* 326–343.

Conway, M. A., Gardiner, J. M., Perfect, T. J., Anderson, S. J., and Cohen, G. M. (1997). *Changes in memory awareness during learning: The acquisition of knowledge by psychology undergraduates. Journal of Experimental Psychology: General, 126,* 393–413.

Costas, B. (1995). Text of Bob Costas' eulogy at the funeral. ESPNET SportsZone/Major League Baseball/Memories of the Mick. *espnet.sportszone@starwave.com.*

Cowan, N., and Davidson, G. (1984). Salient childhood memories. *The Journal of Genetic Psychology, 145,* 101–107.

Crawford, J., Kippax, S., Onyx, J., Gault, U., and Benton, P. (1992). *Emotion and gender: Constructing meaning from memory.* Newbury Park, CA: Sage.

Crawford, M., Herrmann, D. J., Holdsworth, M. J., Randall, E. P., and Robbins, D. (1989). Gender and beliefs about memory. *British Journal of Psychology, 80,* 391–401.

David, A. S., and Howard, R. (1994). An experimental phenomenological approach to delusional memory in schizophrenia and late paraphrenia. *Psychological Medicine, 24,* 515–524.

Davis, P. J. (1987). Repression and the inaccessibility of affective memories. *Journal of Personality and Social Psychology, 53,* 585–593.

Davis, P. J. (1988). Physiological and subjective effects of catharsis: A case report. *Cognition and Emotion, 2,* 19–28.

Davis, W. A. (1992, October 14). Predicting divorce. *The Boston Globe,* pp. 75, 81.

De Negri, G. G. (Producer), Taviani, P., and Taviani, V. (Directors). (1982). *The night of the shooting stars* [film].

Dickens, C. (1956). *Great Expectations.* New York: Pocket Books.

Dion, K. K., and Dion, K. L. (1993). Individualistic and collectivistic perspectives on gender and the cultural context of love and intimacy. *Journal of Social Issues, 49,* 53–69.

Donald, M. *Origins of the modern mind.* (1991). Cambridge, MA: Harvard University Press.

Dudycha, G. J., and Dudycha, M. M. (1933a). Adolescents' memories of preschool experiences. *Journal of Genetic Psychology, 42,* 468–480.

Dudycha, G. J., and Dudycha, M. M. (1933b), Some factors and characteristics of childhood memories. *Child Development, 4,* 265–278.

Dudycha, G. J., and Dudycha, M. M. (1941). Childhood memories: A review of the literature. *Psychological Bulletin, 36,* 34–50.

Edwards, D., and Middleton, D. (1986). Joint remembering: Constructing an account of shared experience through conversational discourse. *Discourse Processes, 9,* 423–459.

Edwards, D., and Middleton, D. (1988). Conversational remembering and family relationships: How children learn to remember. *Journal of Social and Personal Relationships, 5,* 3–25.

Eisenberg, A. R. (1985). Learning to describe past experiences in conversation. *Discourse Processes, 8,* 177–204.

Ellement, J., and Coakley, T. (1993, September 18). "A memory we live with forever." *The Boston Globe,* pp. 1, 6.

Ely, R., and McCabe, A. (1993). Remembered voices. *Journal of Child Language, 20,* 671–696.

Epstein, S. (1994). Integration of the cognitive and the psychodynamic unconscious. *American Psychologist, 49,* 709–724.

Erikson, E. H. (1969). *Ghandi's truth.* New York: Norton.

Erikson, E. H. (1975). *Life history and the historical moment.* New York: Norton.

Fearn, A. W. (1992). My days of strength: An American woman doctor's forty years in China. In J. K. Conway (Ed.), (1992, pp. 527–547).

Feldman, C. F. (1989). Monologue as problem-solving narrative. In K. Nelson (Ed.), (1989b, pp. 98–119).

Fivush, R. (1988). The functions of event memory: Some comments on Nelson and Barsalou. In U. Neisser and E. Winograd (Eds.), *Remembering reconsidered: Ecological and traditional approaches to the study of memory* (pp. 277–282). New York: Cambridge University Press.

Fivush, R. (1991). The social construction of personal narratives. *Merrill-Palmer Quarterly, 37,* 59–81.

Fivush, R., and Fromhoff, F. A. (1988). Style and structure in mother-child conversations about the past. *Discourse Processes, 11,* 337–355.

Fivush, R, Haden, C., and Adam, S. (1995). Structure and coherence of preschoolers' personal narratives over time: Implications for childhood amnesia. *Journal of Experimental Child Psychology, 60,* 32–56.

Fivush, R., and Hamond, N. R. (1990). Autobiographical memory across the pre-school years: Toward reconceptualizing childhood amnesia. In R. Fivush and J. A. Hudson (Eds.), *Knowing and remembering in young children* (pp. 223–248). New York: Cambridge University Press.

Fivush, R., and Reese, E. (1992). The social construction of autobiographical memory. In M. A. Conway, D. C. Rubin, and W. Wagenaar, (Eds.), *Theoretical perspectives on autobiographical memory* (pp. 1–28). Dordrecht, Netherlands: Kluwer Academic Publishers.

Franklin, J. L., and Matchan, L. (1993, December 7). Porter gets 18–20 years. *The Boston Globe,* pp. 1, 29.

French Jews' kin retrace rail journey to Auschwitz. (1992, April 7). *The Boston Globe,* p. 12.

Freud, S. (1953). Three essays on the theory of sexuality. In J. Strachey (Ed.), *The standard edition of the complete psychological works of Sigmund Freud.* Vol. 7 (pp. 135–243). London: Hogarth Press. (Original work published 1905)

Freud, S. (1963). Introductory lectures on psycho-analysis. In J. Strachey (Ed.), *The standard edition of the complete psychological works of Sigmund Freud.* Vols. 15–16. London: Hogarth Press. (Original work published 1916–1917)

Friedman, A., and Pines, A. (1991). Sex differences in gender-related memories. *Sex Roles, 25,* 25–32.

Galbraith, J. K. (1990). *A short history of financial euphoria.* New York: Viking.

Gaposchkin, C. P. (1992). An autobiography and other recollections. In J. K. Conway (Ed.) (1992, pp. 248–282).

Gardner, H. (1993). *Frames of mind: The theory of multiple intelligences (tenth-anniversary edition).* New York: Basic Books.

Garner, R., Gillingham, M. G., and White, C. S. (1989). Effects of "seductive details" on macroprocessing and microprocessing in adults and children. *Cognition and Instruction, 6,* 41–57.

Gee, J. P. (1991). A linguistic approach to narrative. *Journal of Narrative and Life History, 1,* 15–39.

Gergen, M. M., and Gergen, K. J. (1993). Narratives of the gendered body in popular autobiography. In R. Josselson and A. Lieblich (Eds.), (1993, pp. 191–218).

Glasgow, E. A. G. (1992). The woman within. In J. K. Conway (Ed.), (1992, pp. 372–400).

Gold-Steinberg, S. (1994). Personal choices in political climates: Coping with legal and illegal abortion. In C. E. Franz and A. J. Stewart (Eds.), *Women creating lives: Identities, resilience, and resistance* (pp. 263–272). Boulder, CO: Westview Press.

Goldsmith, L. R., and Pillemer, D. B. (1988). Memories of statements spoken in every-day contexts. *Applied Cognitive Psychology, 2,* 273–286.

Goleman, D. (1987, October 20). Leading psychologist expands the boundaries. *The New York Times,* pp. C1, C13.

Goleman, D. (1992, Jan/Feb). Wounds that never heal: How trauma changes your brain. *Psychology Today, 88,* pp. 62–66.

Goodman, G. S., Quas, J. A., Batterman-Faunce, J. M., Riddlesberger, M. M., and Kuhn, J. (1994). Predictors of accurate and inaccurate memories of traumatic events experienced in childhood. *Consciousness and Cognition, 3,* 269–294.

Goodwin, P. (1991, November 13). Olympic dream remains in Magic's mind. *The Boston Globe,* p. 41.

Greenstein, F. I. (1966). Young men and the death of a young president. In M. Wolfenstein and G. Kliman (Eds.), *Children and the death of a president* (pp. 193–216). Garden City, N. Y.: Anchor Books.

Grice, H. P. (1975). Logic and conversation. In P. Cole and J. L. Morgan (Eds.), *Syntax and semantics.* Vol. 3. *Speech acts* (pp. 41–58). New York: Academic Press.

Han, J. J., Leichtman, M.D., and Wang, Q. (in press). Autobiographical memory in Korean, Chinese, and American children. *Developmental Psychology.*

Harber, K. D., and Pennebaker, J. W. (1992). Overcoming traumatic memories. In S A. Christianson (Ed.), *The handbook of emotion and memory: Research and theory* (pp. 359–387). Hillsdale, N.J.: Erlbaum.

Harvey, A. D. (1986). Evidence of a tense shift in personal experience narratives. *Empirical Studies of the Arts, 4,* 151–162.

Harvey, J. H., Stein, S. K., and Scott, P. K. (1996). Fifty years of grief: Accounts and reported psychological reactions of Normandy invasion veterans. *Journal of Narrative and Life History, 5,* 315–332.

Hatcher, S. L. (1994). Personal rites of passage. In A. Lieblich and R. Josselson (Eds.), *Exploring identity and gender: The narrative study of lives.* Vol. 2 (pp. 169–194). Thousand Oaks, CA: Sage.

Hauser, T. (1992). *Muhammad Ali memories.* New York: Rizzoli.

Hayne, H., and Rovee-Collier, C. (1995). The organization of reactivated memory in infancy. *Child Development, 66,* 893–906.

Heider, F. (1989). Fritz Heider. In G. Lindzey (Ed.), *A history of psychology in autobiography.* Vol. 8 (pp. 127–155). Stanford: Stanford University Press.

Herlitz, A., Nilsson, L.-G., and Backman, L. (1997). Gender differences in episodic memory. *Memory & Cognition, 25,* 801–811.

Herman, J. L. (1992). *Trauma and recovery.* New York: Basic Books.

Hermans, H. J. M., Kempen, H. J. G., and van Loon, R. J. P. (1992). The dialogical self: Beyond individualism and rationalism. *American Psychologist, 47,* 23–33.

Heuer, F., and Reisberg, D. (1992). Emotion, arousal, and memory for detail. In S. Christianson (Ed.), *The handbook of emotion and memory: Research and theory* (pp. 151–180). Hillsdale, N.J.: Erlbaum.

Hoffman, A. M., and Hoffman, H. S. (1990). *Archives of memory: A soldier recalls World War II.* Lexington, KY: The University Press of Kentucky.

Howard, G. S. (1991). Culture tales: A narrative approach to thinking, cross-cultural psychology, and psychotherapy. *American Psychologist, 46,* 187–197.

Howe, M. L., and Courage, M. L. (1993). On resolving the enigma of infantile amnesia. *Psychological Bulletin, 113,* 305–326.

Howe, M. L., Courage, M. L., and Peterson, C. (1994). How can I remember when "I" wasn't there: Long-term retention of traumatic experiences and emergence of the cognitive self. *Consciousness and Cognition, 3,* 327–355.

Howes, M., Siegel, M., and Brown, F. (1993). Early childhood memories: Accuracy and affect. *Cognition, 47,* 95–119.

Hudson, J. A. (1990). The emergence of autobiographical memory in mother-child conversation. In R. Fivush and J. A. Hudson (Eds.), *Knowing and remembering in young children* (pp. 166–196). New York: Cambridge University Press.

Hudson, J. A. (1993). Reminiscing with mothers and others: Autobiographical memory in young two-year-olds. *Journal of Narrative and Life History, 3,* 1–32.

Inhelder, B. (1989). Barbel Inhelder. In G. Lindzey (Ed.), *A history of psychology in autobiography.* Vol. 8 (pp. 208–243). Stanford: Stanford University Press.

Jacoby, L. L. (1988). Memory observed and memory unobserved. In U. Neisser and E. Winograd (Eds.), *Remembering reconsidered: Ecological and traditional approaches to the study of memory* (pp.145–177). New York: Cambridge University Press.

Jacoby, L. L., Marriott, M. J., and Collins, J. G. (1990). The specifics of memory and cognition. In T. K. Srull and R. S. Wyer (Eds.), *Advances in social cognition.* Vol. 3. *Content and process specificity in the effects of prior experiences* (pp. 111–121). Hillsdale, N.J.: Erlbaum.

Jacoby, O. (Producer and Director). (1986). *Benny Goodman: Adventures in the kingdom of swing* [film].

Janet, P. (1925). Memories which are too real. In Campblee, C. M., Langfeld, H. S., McDougall, W., Roback, A. A., and Taylor, E. W. (Eds.), *Problems of personality.* New York: Harcourt, Brace.

Janet, P. (1928). *L'evolution de la memoire et de la notion du temps.* Vol. 1. Paris: Chahine.

Janoff-Bulman, R. (1992). *Shattered assumptions: Towards a new psychology of trauma.* New York: Free Press.

Johnson, F. (1991, June 23). The limitless heart. *The New York Times Magazine,* pp. 10, 12.

Johnson, G. (1991). *In the palaces of memory.* New York: Alfred A. Knopf.

Johnson, M. K. (1988). Reality monitoring: An experimental phenomenological approach. *Journal of Experimental Psychology: General, 117,* 390–394.

Johnson, M. K., and Multhaup, K. S. (1992). Emotion and MEM. In S-A Christianson (Ed.), *The handbook of emotion and memory: Research and theory* (pp. 33–66). Hillsdale, N.J.: Erlbaum.

Josselson, R., and Lieblich, A. (Eds.). (1993). *The narrative study of lives.* Vol. 1. Newbury Park, CA: Sage.

Jourard, S. M. (1979). *Self-disclosure: An experimental analysis of the transparent self.* Huntington, N.Y.: Robert E. Krieger.

Kahn, J. P. (1991, November 8). A lesson about vulnerability hits Americans hard. *The Boston Globe,* pp. 1, 54.

Kagan, J. (1972). A psychologist's account at mid-career. In T. S. Krawiec (Ed.), *The psychologists.* Vol. 1 (pp. 137–165). New York: Oxford University Press.

Kahneman, D., Fredrickson, B. L., Schreiber, C. A., and Redelmeier, D. A. (1993). When more pain is preferred to less: Adding a better end. *Psychological Science, 4,* 401–405.

Kantor, D. (1980). Critical identity image: A concept linking individual, couple, and family development. In J. K. Pearce and L. J. Friedman (Eds.), *Family therapy: Combining psychodynamic and family systems approaches* (pp. 137–167). New York: Grune and Stratton.

Kantor, D., and Lehr, W. (1975). *Inside the family: Toward a theory of family process.* San Francisco: Jossey-Bass.

Kaye, G. (1991). A certain Simon Schama. *Harvard Magazine, 94,* 46–53.

Keane, T. M., Fairbank, J. A., Caddell, J. M., and Zimering, R. T. (1989). Implosive (flooding) therapy reduces symptoms of PTSD in Vietnam combat veterans. *Behavior Therapy, 20,* 245–260.

Kihlstrom, J. F. (1987). The cognitive unconscious. *Science, 237,* 1445–1452.

Kihlstrom, J. F., and Harackiewicz, J. M. (1982). The earliest recollection: A new survey. *Journal of Personality, 50,* 134–148.

Kilmann, R. H. (1985). Corporate culture. *Psychology Today, 19,* 62–68.

Kim, E. H. (1990). Defining Asian American realities through literature. In A. R. Jan-Mohamed and D. Lloyd (Eds.), *The nature and context of minority discourse* (pp. 146–170). New York: Oxford University Press.

Kinzie, J. D., Fredrickson, R. H., R. Ben, J. Fleck, and W. Karls. (1984). Posttraumatic stress disorder among survivors of Cambodian concentration camps. *The American Journal of Psychiatry, 141,* 645–650.

Kiser, L. J., Ackerman, B. J., Brown, E., Edwards, N. B., McColgan, E., Pugh, R., and Pruitt, D. B. (1988). Post-traumatic stress disorder in young children: A reaction to purported sexual abuse. *Journal of the American Academy of Child and Adolescent Psychiatry, 27,* 645–649.

Knapp, M. L., Stohl, C., and Reardon, K. K. (1981, Autumn). "Memorable" messages. *Journal of Communication,* 27–41.

Knowles, M. S. (1989). *The making of an adult educator.* San Francisco: Jossey-Bass.

Kott, E., Borod, J. C., and White, B. (1983). A left hemisphere bias for visualizing emotional situations. *Neuropsychologia, 21,* 273–275.

Koppel, T. (Host). (1996, April 25). Mr. Ambassador [television interview of Robert Krueger on ABC News Nightline]

Kosslyn, S. M. (1994). *Image and brain: The resolution of the Imagery debate.* Cambridge, MA: MIT Press.

Kuebli, J., Butler, S., and Fivush, R. (1995). Mother-child talk about past emotions: Relations of maternal language and child gender over time. *Cognition and Emotion, 9,* 265–283.

Kurbat, M. A., Shevell, S. K., and Rips, L. J. (in press). A year's memories: The calendar effect in autobiographical recall. *Memory & Cognition.*

Kuyken, W., and Brewin, C. R. (1995). Autobiographical memory functioning in depression and reports of early abuse. *Journal of Abnormal Psychology, 104,* 585–591.

Labov, W. (1982). Speech actions and reactions in personal narrative. In D. Tannen (Ed.), *Analyzing discourse: Text and talk* (pp. 219–247). Washington, D.C.: Georgetown University Press.

Labov, W., and Waletzky, J. (1967). Narrative analysis: Oral versions of personal experience. In J. Helm (Ed.), *Essays on the verbal and visual arts* (pp. 12–44). Seattle: University of Washington Press.

Langer, L. L. (1991). *Holocaust testimonies: The ruins of memory.* New Haven: Yale University Press.

Larsen, S. F. (1988). Remembering without experiencing: Memory for reported events. In U. Neisser and E. Winograd (Eds.), *Remembering reconsidered* (pp. 326–355). New York: Cambridge University Press.

Larsen, S. F., and Plunkett, K. (1987). Remembering experienced and reported events. *Applied Cognitive Psychology, 1,* 15–26.

Lazarus, B. (1990, Summer). Bruno Bettelheim and the uses of freedom. *University of Chicago Magazine,* pp. 31–32.

LeDoux, J. E. (1992). Emotion as memory: Anatomical systems underlying indelible neural traces. In S-A. Christianson (Ed.), *The handbook of emotion and memory: Research and theory (pp. 269–288).* Hillsdale, N.J.: Erlbaum.

LeDoux, J. E. (1996). *The emotional brain.* New York: Simon & Schuster.

Lewicki, P. (1985). Nonconscious biasing effects of single instances on subsequent judgments. *Journal of Personality and Social Psychology, 48,* 563–574.

Lie, E., and Newcombe, N. (1995, November). *Childhood amnesia: Memory for faces of preschool classmates.* Presented at the annual meeting of the Psychonomic Society, Los Angeles, CA.

Lifshin, L. (Ed.). (1982). *Ariadne's thread.* New York: Harper and Row.

Lipke, H. J., and Botkin, A. L. (1992). Case studies of eye movement desensitization and reprocessing (EMDR) with chronic post-traumatic stress disorder. *Psychotherapy, 29,* 591–595.

Loftus, E. F. (1993). The reality of repressed memories. *American Psychologist, 48,* 518–537.

Loftus, E. F., Banaji, M. R., Schooler, J. W., and Foster, R. A. (1987). Who remembers what? Gender differences in memory. *Michigan Quarterly Review, 26,* 64–85.

Loftus, E. F., and Kaufman, L. (1992). Why do traumatic experiences sometimes produce good memory (flashbulbs) and sometimes no memory (repression)? In E. Winograd and U. Neisser (Eds.) (1992, pp. 212–223).

Loftus, E. F., and Ketcham, K. (1991). *Witness for the defense.* New York: St. Martin's Press.

Logan, G. D. (1990). Social cognition gets specific. In T. K. Srull and R. S. Wyer (Eds.), *Advances in social cognition.* Vol. 3. *Content and process specificity in the effects of prior experiences* (pp. 141–151). Hillsdale, N.J.: Erlbaum.

Mack, J. E. (1971). Psychoanalysis and historical biography. *Journal of the American Psychoanalytic Association, 19,* 143–179.

Mackavey, W. R., Malley, J. E., and Stewart, A. J. (1991). Remembering autobiographically consequential experiences: Content analysis of psychologists' accounts of their lives. *Psychology and Aging, 6,* 50–59.

Madden, M. (1991, November 8). Grieving is unbelievable. *The Boston Globe,* pp. 51, 55.

Madden, M. (1993, July 30). The pall will linger for as long as the questions remain. *The Boston Globe,* pp. 41, 51.

Main, M. (1991). Metacognitive knowledge, metacognitive monitoring, and singular (coherent) vs. multiple (incoherent) model of attachment. In C. M. Parkes, J. Stevenson-Hinde, and P. Marris (Eds.), *Attachment across the life cycle* (pp. 127–159). New York: Tavistock/Routledge.

Main, M., Kaplan, N., and Cassidy, J. (1985). Security in infancy, childhood, and adulthood: A move to the level of representation. *Monographs of the Society for Research in Child Development, 50,* 66–104.

Malcolm X. (1965). *The autobiography of Malcolm X.* New York: Grove Press.

Mandler, J. M. (1990). Recall and its verbal expression. In R. Fivush and J. A. Hudson (Eds.), *Knowing and remembering in young children* (pp. 317–330). New York: Cambridge University Press.

Marks, D. F. (1983). Mental imagery and consciousness: A theoretical review. In A. A. Sheikh (Ed.), *Imagery: Current theory, research, and application* (pp. 96–130). New York: Wiley.

Markus, H. R., and Kitayama, S. (1991). Culture and the self: Implications for cognition, emotion, and motivation. *Psychological Review, 98,* 224–253.

May, P. (1991, June 11). The man who beat out Jordan. *The Boston Globe,* pp. 105, 110.

McAdams, D. P. (1988). *Power, intimacy, and the life story.* New York: Guilford.

McAdams, D. P. (1993). *The stories we live by: Personal myths and the making of the self.* New York: Morrow.

McCabe, A., Capron, E., and Peterson, C. (1991). The voice of experience: The recall of early childhood and adolescent memories by young adults. In A. McCabe and C. Peterson (Eds.), *Developing narrative structure* (pp. 137–173). Hillsdale, N.J.: Erlbaum.

McCabe, A., and Peterson, C. (1991). Getting the story: A longitudinal study of parental styles in eliciting narratives and developing narrative skill. In A. McCabe and C. Peterson (Eds.), *Developing narrative structure* (pp. 217–253). Hillsdale, N.J.: Erlbaum.

McCann, I. L., and Pearlman, L. A. (1990). Vicarious traumatization: A framework for understanding the psychological effects of working with victims. *Journal of Traumatic Stress, 3,* 131–149.

McCloskey, M., Wible, C. G., and Cohen, N. J. (1988). Is there a special flashbulb-memory mechanism? *Journal of Experimental Psychology: General, 117,* 171–181.

McDonough, W. (1993, July 30). Exact cause may prove elusive. *The Boston Globe,* p. 49.

McKee, R. D., and Squire, L. D. (1993). On the development of declarative memory. *Journal of Experimental Psychology: Learning, Memory, and Cognition, 19,* 397–404.

McNally, R. J. (1992). Psychopathology of post-traumatic stress disorder (PTSD): Boundaries of the syndrome. In M. Basoglu (Ed.), *Torture and its consequences: Current treatment approaches* (pp. 229–252). Cambridge: Cambridge University Press.

McNally, R. J., Lasko, N. B., Macklin, M. L., and Pittman, R. K. (1995). Autobiographical memory disturbance in combat-related posttraumatic stress disorder. *Behavior Research and Therapy, 33,* 619–630.

McNally, R. J., Litz, B. T., Prassas, A., Shin, L. M., and Weathers, F. W. (1994). Emotional priming of autobiographical memory in post-traumatic stress disorder. *Cognition and Emotion, 8,* 351–367.

Mead, M. (1974). Margaret Mead. In G. Lindzey (Ed.), *A history of psychology in autobiography,* Vol. 6 (pp. 293–326). Englewood Cliffs, N.J.: Prentice-Hall.

Mead, M. (1992). Blackberry winter: My earlier years. In J. K. Conway (Ed.), (1992, pp. 285–308).

Meier, D. (1986). Learning in small moments. *Harvard Educational Review, 56,* 298–300.

Meltzoff, A. N. (1995). What infant memory tells us about infantile amnesia: Long-term recall and deferred imitation. *Journal of Experimental Child Psychology, 59,* 497–515.

Mendenhall, D. R. (1992). Unpublished memoir. In J. K. Conway (Ed.) (1992, pp. 172–199).

Middleton, D., and Buchanan, K. (1994, August). *Collective remembering: Some cultural issues in reminiscence.* Paper presented at the 3rd International Conference on Practical Aspects of Memory, University of Maryland, College Park, MD.

Miller, G. A. (1989). George A. Miller. In G. Lindzey (Ed.), *A history of psychology in autobiography.* Vol. 8 (pp. 390–418). Stanford: Stanford University Press.

Miller, P. J., Hoogstra, L., Mintz, J., Fung, H., and Williams, K. (1993). Troubles in the garden and how they get resolved: A young child's transformation of his favorite story. In C. A. Nelson (Ed.), *Memory and affect in development: The Minnesota Symposia on Child Psychology,* Vol. 26 (pp. 87–114). Hillsdale, N.J.: Erlbaum.

Miller, P. J., Mintz, J., Hoogstra, L., Fung, H., and Potts, R. (1992). The narrated self: Young children's construction of self in relation to others in conversational stories of personal experience. *Merrill-Palmer Quarterly, 38,* 45–67.

Miller, P. J., Potts, R., Fung, H., Hoogstra, L., and Mintz, J. (1990). Narrative practices and the social construction of self in childhood. *American Ethnologist, 17,* 292–311.

Minami, M., and McCabe, A. (1991). *Haiku* as a discourse regulation device: A stanza analysis of Japanese children's personal narratives. *Language in Society, 20,* 577–599.

Miyake, K., Chen, S., and Campos, J. J. (1985). Infant temperament, mother's mode of interaction, and attachment in Japan: An interim report. *Monographs of the Society for Research in Child Development, 50,* 276–297.

Montgomery, M. R. (1992, May 25). Recalling Cocoanut Grove. *The Boston Globe,* pp. 30, 34

Morelli, G. A., Rogoff, B., Oppenheim, D., and Goldsmith, D. (1992). Cultural variation in infants' sleeping arrangements: Questions of independence. *Developmental Psychology, 28,* 604–613.

Mullen, M. K. (1994). Earliest recollections of childhood: A demographic analysis. *Cognition, 52,* 55–79.

Mullen, M. K., and Yi, S. (1995). The cultural context of talk about the past: Implications for the development of autobiographical memory. *Cognitive Development, 10,* 407–419.

Murphy, K. R., and Balzer, W. K. (1986). Systematic distortions in memory-based behavior ratings and performance evaluations: Consequences for rating accuracy. *Journal of Applied Psychology, 71,* 39–44.

Myers, N. A., Clifton, R. K., and Clarkson, M. G. (1987). When they were very young: Almost-threes remember two years ago. *Infant Behavior and Development, 10,* 123–132.

Myllyniemi, R. (1986). Conversation as a system of social interaction. *Language and Communication, 6,* 147–169.

Neisser, U. (1962). Cultural and cognitive discontinuity. In T. E. Gladwin and W. Sturtevant (Eds.), *Anthropology and human behavior* (pp. 54–71). Washington, D.C.: Anthropological Society of Washington.

Neisser, U. (1967). *Cognitive psychology.* Englewood Cliffs, N.J.: Prentice-Hall.

Neisser, U. (1981). John Dean's memory: A case study. *Cognition, 9,* 1–22.

Neisser, U. (1982a). *Memory observed: Remembering in natural contexts.* San Francisco: Freeman.

Neisser, U. (1982b). Memory: What are the important questions? In U. Neisser (Ed.) (1982a, pp. 3–19).

Neisser, U. (1985). The role of theory in the ecological study of memory: Comment on Bruce. *Journal of Experimental Psychology: General, 114,* 272–276.

Neisser, U., and Harsch, N. (1992). Phantom flashbulbs: False recollections of hearing the news about *Challenger.* In E. Winograd and U. Neisser (Eds.), (1992, pp. 9–31).

Neisser, U., Winograd, E., Bergman, E. T., Schreiber, C. A., Palmer, S. E., and Weldon, M. S. (1996). Remembering the earthquake: Direct experience vs. hearing the news. *Memory, 4,* 337–357.

Nelson, K. (1988). The ontogeny of memory for real events. In U. Neisser and E. Winograd (Eds.), *Remembering reconsidered: Ecological and traditional approaches to the study of memory* (pp. 244–276). New York: Cambridge University Press.

Nelson, K. (1989a). Monologue as representation of real-life experience. In K. Nelson (Ed.), (1989b, pp. 27–72).

Nelson, K. (Ed.). (1989b). *Narratives from the crib*. Cambridge, MA: Harvard University Press.

Nelson, K. (1993). The psychological and social origins of autobiographical memory. *Psychological Science, 4,* 7–14.

Newcomb, T. M. (1974). Theodore M. Newcomb. In G. Lindzey (Ed.), *A history of psychology in autobiography.* Vol. 6 (pp. 367–391). Englewood Cliffs, N.J.: Prentice-Hall.

Newmeyer, F. J. (1986). *Linguistic theory in America* (2nd ed.). Orlando, FL: Academic Press.

Nuthall, G., and Alton-Lee, A. (1995). Assessing classroom learning: How students use their knowledge and experience to answer classroom achievement test questions in science and social studies. *American Educational Research Journal, 32,* 185–223.

Oppenheim, D., and Waters, H. S. (1995). Narrative processes and attachment representations: Issues of development and assessment. *Monographs of the Society for Research in Child Development, 60,* 197–215.

Oshinsky, D. (1991, October 20). What became of the Democrats? [Review of *Chain reaction,* T. B. Edsall with M. D. Edsall]. *The New York Times Book Review,* pp. 1, 24, 26–27.

Perner, J., and Ruffman, T. (1995). Episodic memory and autonoetic consciousness: Developmental evidence and a theory of childhood amnesia. *Journal of Experimental Child Psychology, 59,* 516–548.

Perris, E. E., Myers, N. A., and Clifton, R. K. (1990). Long-term memory for a single infancy experience. *Child Development, 61,* 1796–1807.

Personal Narratives Group (Eds.). (1989). *Interpreting women's lives: Feminist theory and personal narratives.* Bloomington, IN: Indiana University Press.

Peterson, C., and Rideout, R. (1997, April). Do 2- and 3-year-olds recall pre-language stressful experiences? In P. Bauer and M.-E. Pipe (Chairs), *Telling it like it was: Relations between language and memory in early childhood.* Symposium conducted at the biennial meetings of the Society for Research in Child Development, Washington, D.C.

Pettit, E. J., and Bloom, B. L. (1984). Whose decision was it? The effects of initiator status on adjustment to marital disruption. *Journal of Marriage and the Family, 46,* 587–595.

Peyer, T., and Seely, H. (1993, November). The day the stars cried. *The New Yorker, 69,* p. 128.

Pillemer, D. B. (1984). Flashbulb memories of the assassination attempt on President Reagan. *Cognition, 16,* 63–80.

Pillemer, D. B. (1990). Clarifying the flashbulb memory concept: Comment on McCloskey, Wible, and Cohen (1988). *Journal of Experimental Psychology: General, 119,* 92–96.

Pillemer, D. B. (1992a). Preschool children's memories of personal circumstances: The fire alarm study. In E. Winograd and U. Neisser (Eds.) (1992, pp. 121–137).

Pillemer, D. B. (1992b). Remembering personal circumstances: A functional analysis. In E. Winograd and U. Neisser (Eds.) (1992, pp. 236–264).

Pillemer, D. B., Desrochers, A. B., and Ebanks, C. M. (1998). Remembering the past in the present: Verb tense shifts in autobiographical memory narratives. In C. P. Thompson, D. J. Herrmann, D. Bruce, J. D. Read, D. G. Payne, and M. P. Toglia (Eds.), *Autobiographical memory: Theoretical and applied perspectives.* Mahwah, N.J.: Erlbaum.

Pillemer, D. B., Goldsmith, L. R., Panter, A. T., and White, S. H. (1988). Very long-term memories of the first year in college. *Journal of Experimental Psychology: Learning, Memory, and Cognition, 14,* 709–715.

Pillemer, D. B., Koff, E., Rhinehart, E. D., and Rierdan, J. (1987). Flashbulb memories of menarche and adult menstrual distress. *Journal of Adolescence, 10,* 187–199.

Pillemer, D. B., Krensky, L., Kleinman, S. N., Goldsmith, L. R., and White, S. H. (1991). Chapters in narratives: Evidence from oral histories of the first year in college. *Journal of Narrative and Life History, 1,* 3–14.

Pillemer, D. B., Picariello, M. L., Law, A. B., and Reichman, J. S. (1996). Memories of college: The importance of specific educational episodes. In D. C. Rubin (Ed.), *Remembering our past: Studies in autobiographical memory* (pp. 318–337). New York: Cambridge University Press.

Pillemer, D. B., Picariello, M. L., and Pruett, J. C. (1994). Very long-term memories of a salient preschool event. *Applied Cognitive Psychology, 8,* 95–106.

Pillemer, D. B., Rhinehart, E. D., and White, S. H. (1986). Memories of life transitions: The first year in college. *Human Learning, 5,* 109–123.

Pillemer, D. B., and White, S. H. (1989). Childhood events recalled by children and adults. In H. W. Reese (Ed.), *Advances in child development and behavior.* Vol. 21 (pp. 297–340). Orlando, FL: Academic Press.

Platt, W., and Baker, R. A. (1931). The relation of the scientific "hunch" to research. *Journal of Chemical Education, 8,* 1969–2002.

Pomerantz, M. (1991, September-October). Chinese (non-) individualism. *Harvard Magazine,* p. 8.

Posada, G., Gao, Y., Wu, F., Posada, R., Tascon, M., Schoelmerich, A., Sagi, A., Kondo-Ikemura, K., Haaland, W., and Synnevaag, B. (1995). The secure-base phenomenon across cultures: Children's behavior, mothers' preferences, and experts' concepts. *Monographs of the Society for Research in Child Development, 60,* 27–48.

Price, S. L. (1995, July 17). The return. *Sports Illustrated, 83,* 22–26.

Raskin, D. C., and Esplin, P. W. (1991). Statement validity assessment: Interview procedures and content analysis of children's statements of sexual abuse. *Behavioral Assessment, 13,* 265–291.

Rasley, J. S. (1993, August). Barbaric derivations. *University of Chicago Magazine,* p. 6.

Reese, E., and Fivush, R. (1993). Parental styles of talking about the past. *Developmental Psychology, 29,* 596–606.

Reese, E, Haden, C. A., and Fivush, R. (1993). Mother-child conversations about the past: Relationships of style and memory over time. *Cognitive Development, 8,* 403–430.

Reese, E., Haden, C. A., and Fivush, R. (1996). Mothers, fathers, daughters, sons: Gender differences in autobiographical reminiscing. *Research on Language and Social Interaction, 29,* 27–56.

Reidy, C. (1990, November 13). Why we love Natalie. *The Boston Globe,* pp. 55, 59.

Reisberg, D., Heuer, F., McLean, J., and O'Shaughnessy, M. (1988). The quantity, not the quality, of affect predicts memory vividness. *Bulletin of the Psychonomic Society, 26,* 100–103.

Ribadeneira, D. (1991, November 8). Young hoop players voice sorrow, disbelief. *The Boston Globe,* pp. 1, 53.

Richmond, T. (1995). *Konin: A quest.* New York: Pantheon.

Rierdan, J., Losardo, M., Pillemer, D. B, and Penk, W. E. (1995). *Stability in three measures of PTSD symptomatology: A longitudinal study of civilian crime victims.* Unpublished manuscript.

Robb, C. (1989, October 19). For survivors of earthquakes, the shocks linger on. *The Boston Globe,* pp. 93, 98.

Robinson, J. A. (1986). Temporal reference systems and autobiographical memory. In D. C. Rubin (Ed.), *Autobiographical memory* (pp. 159–188). New York: Cambridge University Press.

Robinson, W., Jr. (1993). Interview for United Airlines in-flight entertainment network.

Rodman, D. (1996). *Bad as I wanna be.* New York: Delacorte.

Roediger, H. L. (1990). Implicit memory: Retention without remembering. *American Psychologist, 45,* 1043–1056.

Roediger, H. L. (1991). They read an article? A commentary on the everyday memory controversy. *American Psychologist, 46,* 37–40.

Rogoff, B., and Mistry, J. (1990). The social and functional context of children's remembering. In R. Fivush and J. A. Hudson (Eds.), *Knowing and remembering in young children* (pp. 197–222). New York: Cambridge University Press.

Roland, A. (1991). The self in cross-civilizational perspective: An Indian-Japanese-American comparison. In R. C. Curtis (Ed.), *The relational self* (pp. 160–180). New York: Guilford.

Romano, R. (1991, November 9). Friends, fans express support. *The Boston Globe,* p. 30.

Rose, C. (Producer and Host). (1994, July 19). Comet Shoemaker-Levy 9 [television interview by Charlie Rose]

Ross, B. H. (1984). Remindings and their effect in learning a cognitive skill. *Cognitive Psychology, 16,* 371–416.

Ross, B. M. (1991). *Remembering the personal past: Descriptions of autobiographical memory.* New York: Oxford.

Ross, M., and Holmberg, D. (1992). Are wives' memories for events in relationships more vivid than their husbands' memories? *Journal of Social and Personal Relationships, 9,* 585–604.

Rozynko, V., and Dondershine, H. E. (1991). Trauma focus group therapy for Vietnam veterans with PTSD. *Psychotherapy, 28,* 157–161.

Rubin, D. C. (1982). On the retention function for autobiographical memory. *Journal of Verbal Learning and Verbal Behavior, 21,* 21–38.

Rubin, D. C. (1995a). *Memory in oral traditions.* New York: Oxford University Press.

Rubin, D. C. (1995b). Stories about stories. In R. S. Wyer, Jr. (Ed.), *Advances in social cognition.* Vol. 8. *Knowledge and memory: The real story* (pp. 153–164). Hillsdale, N.J.: Erlbaum.

Rubin. D. C., and Kozin, M. (1984). Vivid memories. *Cognition, 16,* 81–95.

Rubin, D. C., and Schulkind, M. D. (1997). Distribution of important and word-cued autobiographical memories in 20-, 35-, and 70-year-old adults. *Psychology and Aging, 12,* 524–535.

Rubin, L. B. (1976). *Worlds of pain: Life in the working-class family.* New York: Basic Books.

Runyan, W. M. (1982). *Life histories and psychobiography.* New York: Oxford University Press.

Ryan, B. (1990, June 8). Detroit's character was built in Boston. *The Boston Globe,* pp. 81, 88.

Ryan, B. (1994, March 11). Kruk's misfortune is a large dose of real life. *The Boston Globe,* pp. 41–42.

Sarason, S. B. (1993). *The case for change.* San Francisco: Jossey-Bass.

Schachtel, E. (1947). On memory and childhood amnesia. *Psychiatry, 10,* 1–26.

Schacter, D. L. (1987). Implicit memory: History and current status. *Journal of Experimental Psychology: Learning, Memory, and Cognition, 13,* 501–518.

Schacter, D. L. (1994). Priming and multiple memory systems: Perceptual mechanisms of implicit memory. In D. L. Schacter and E. Tulving (Eds.), *Memory systems 1994.* Cambridge, MA: MIT Press.

Schacter, D. L. (1996). *Searching for memory: The brain, the mind, and the past.* New York: Basic Books

Schaefer, H. (1993, February). A scholar's diary. *University of Chicago Magazine,* p. 7.

Schank R. C. (1980). Failure-driven memory. *Cognition and Brain Theory, 4,* 41–60.

Schank, R. C. (1990). *Tell me a story: A new look at real and artificial memory.* New York: Scribners.

Schank, R. C., and Abelson, R. P. (1995). Knowledge and memory: The real story. In R. S. Wyer, Jr. (Ed.), *Advances in Social Cognition.* Vol. 8 (pp. 1–85). Hillsdale, N.J.: Erlbaum.

Schooler, J. W., Gerhard, D., and Loftus, E. F. (1986). Qualities of the unreal. *Journal of Experimental Psychology: Learning, Memory and Cognition, 12,* 171–181.

Schwarz, R., and Gilligan, S. (1995). The devil is in the details. *The Family Therapy Networker, 19,* 21–23.

Scudder, J. (1992). Modeling my life. In J. K. Conway (Ed.) (1992, pp. 349–371).

Sehulster, J. R. (1981). Structure and pragmatics of a self-theory of memory. *Memory & Cognition, 9,* 263–276.

Sehulster, J. R. (1995). Memory styles and related abilities in presentation of self. *American Journal of Psychology, 108,* 67–88.

Select Committees on the Iran-Contra Investigation. (1988a). *Testimony of John M. Poindexter.* Washington, D.C.: U.S. Government Printing Office.

Select Committees on the Iran-Contra Investigation. (1988b). *Testimony of George P. Shultz and Edwin Meese, III.* Washington, D.C.: U.S. Government Printing Office.

Shapiro, F. (1989). Eye movement desensitization: A new treatment for post-traumatic stress disorder. *Journal of Behavior Therapy and Experimental Psychiatry, 20,* 211–217.

Shapiro, F. (1991). Eye movement desensitization and reprocessing procedure: From EMD to EMD/R—A new treatment model for anxiety and related traumata. *The Behavior Therapist, 14,* 133–135, 128.

Shapiro, F. (1993). Eye movement desensitization and reprocessing (EMDR) in 1992. *Journal of Traumatic Stress, 6,* 417–421.

Shaughnessy, D. (1989, July 20). Donnie Moore's tragedy. *The Boston Globe,* pp. 33, 37.

Shaughnessy, D. (1993, July 14). The error of our ways: Buckner forced to move. *The Boston Globe,* pp. 53, 56.

Shaughnessy, D. (1995, August 14). Mickey Mantle dead of cancer. *The Boston Globe,* pp. 1, 42.

Shaw, A. H. (1992). The story of a pioneer. In J. K. Conway (Ed.) (1992, pp. 475–503).

Sheingold, K, and Tenney, Y. J. (1982). Memory for a salient childhood event. In U. Neisser (Ed.) (1982a, pp. 201–212).

Sherry, D. F., and Schacter, D. L. (1987). The evolution of multiple memory systems. *Psychological Review, 94,* 439–454.

Siegel, D.J. (1996). Dissociation, psychotherapy, and the cognitive sciences. In J. L. Spira and I. D. Yalom (Eds.), *Treating dissociative identity disorder* (pp. 39–79). San Francisco: Jossey-Bass.

Silberner, J. (1981). Psychological A-bomb wounds. *Science News, 120,* 296–298.

Simon, J. (1993, September 26). The Fuhrer's movie maker. *The New York Times Book Review,* pp. 1, 26–29.

Simonton, D. K. (1988). *Scientific genius: A psychology of science.* New York: Cambridge University Press.

Singer, J. A., and Salovey, P. (1993). *The remembered self: Emotion and memory in personality.* New York: The Free Press.

Singer, J. L. (1970). Drives, affects, and daydreams: The adaptive role of spontaneous imagery or stimulus-independent mentation. In J. S. Antrobus (Ed.), *Cognition and affect* (pp. 131–158). Boston: Little, Brown.

Singer, J. L. (1975). *The inner world of daydreaming.* New York: Harper and Row.

Singer, J. L. (1978). Experimental studies of daydreaming and the stream of thought.

In K. S. Pope and J. L. Singer (Eds.), *The stream of consciousness* (pp. 187–223). New York: Plenum.

Skowronski, J. J., and Thompson, C. P. (1990). Reconstructing the dates of personal events: Gender differences in accuracy. *Applied Cognitive Psychology, 4,* 371–381.

Smith, E. R. (1990). Content and process specificity in the effects of prior experiences. In T. K. Srull and R. S. Wyer (Eds.), *Advances in social cognition.* Vol. 3. *Content and process specificity in the effects of prior experiences* (pp. 1–59). Hillsdale, N.J.: Erlbaum.

Spence, D. P. (1982). *Narrative truth and historical truth.* New York: Norton.

Spence, D. P. (1988). Passive remembering. In U. Neisser and E. Winograd (Eds.), *Remembering reconsidered: Ecological and traditional approaches to the study of memory* (pp. 311–325). New York: Cambridge University Press.

Srull, T. K., and Wyer, R. S. (1990). Content and process specificity: Where do we go from here? In T. K. Srull and R. S. Wyer (Eds.), *Advances in social cognition.* Vol. 3. *Content and process specificity in the effects of prior experiences* (pp. 165–180). Hillsdale, N.J.: Erlbaum.

Steele, H., Steele, M., and Fonagy, P. (1996). Associations among attachment classifications of mothers, fathers, and their infants. *Child Development, 67,* 541–555.

Steinem, G. (1992). Outrageous acts and everyday rebellions: Ruth's song (because she could not sing it). In J. K. Conway (Ed.) (1992, pp. 658–672).

Stern, D. N. (1989). Crib monologues from a psychoanalytic perspective. In K. Nelson (Ed.) (1989b, pp. 309–319).

Stewart, A. J., Sokol, M., Healy, Jr., J. M., Chester, N. L., and Weinstock-Savoy, D. (1982). Adaptation to life changes in children and adults: Cross-sectional studies. *Journal of Personality and Social Psychology, 43,* 1270–1281.

Stimpson, C. R. (1987, Winter). The future of memory: A summary. *Michigan Quarterly Review, 26,* 259–265.

Stivers, C. (1993). Reflections on the role of personal narrative in social science. *Signs: Journal of Women in Culture and Society, 18,* 408–425.

Strong, A. L. (1992). I change worlds: The remaking of an American. In J. K. Conway (Ed.) (1992, pp. 612–637).

Tannen. D. (1990). *You just don't understand: Women and men in conversation.* New York: Ballantine.

Tannen, D. (1991, June 19). Teachers' classroom strategies should recognize that men and women use language differently. *The Chronicle of Higher Education, 37,* pp. B1, B3.

Tenney, Y. J. (1989). Predicting conversational reports of a personal event. *Cognitive Science, 13,* 213–233.

Terr, L. (1988). What happens to early memories of trauma? A study of twenty children under age five at the time of documented traumatic events. *Journal of the American Academy of Child and Adolescent Psychiatry, 27,* 96–104.

Terr, L. (1990). *Too scared to cry*. New York: Basic Books.

Tessler, M., and Nelson, K. (1994). Making memories: The influence of joint encoding on later recall by young children. *Consciousness and Cognition, 3,* 307–326.

Thompson, C. P. (1982). Diary-keeping as a sex-role behavior. *Bulletin of the Psychonomic Society, 20,* 11–13.

Thompson, C. P., Skowronski, J. J., Larsen, S. F., and Betz, A. L. (1996). *Autobiographical memory: Remembering what and remembering when*. Mahwah, N.J.: Erlbaum.

Thorne, A., and Klohnen, E. (1993). Interpersonal memories as maps for personality consistency. In D. C. Funder, R. D. Parke, C. Tomlinson-Keasey and K. Widaman (Eds.), *Studying lives through time* (pp. 223–253). Washington, D.C.: American Psychological Association.

Thurlow, S. (1982). Nuclear war in human perspective: A survivor's report. *American Journal of Orthopsychiatry, 52,* 638–645.

Tlumacki, J. (1993, November 21). Where we were. *The Boston Globe,* pp. 76–77.

Tobias, B. A., Kihlstrom, J. F., and Schacter, D. L. (1992). Emotion and implicit memory. In S-A. Christianson (Ed.), *The handbook of emotion and memory: Research and theory*. Hillsdale, N.J.: Erlbaum.

Toombs, M. (1995, May 25). Vandross orchestrates starry nights. *Night and Day* (The weekly guide), *The San Diego Union-Tribune,* p. 13.

Triandis, H. C. (1989). The self and social behavior in differing cultural contexts. *Psychological Review, 96,* 506–520.

Triandis, H. C. (1994). Major cultural syndromes and emotion. In S. Kitayama and H. R. Markus (Eds.), *Emotion and culture* (pp. 285–306). Washington, D.C.: American Psychological Association.

Tulving, E. (1983). *Elements of episodic memory*. New York: Clarendon Press.

Tulving, E. (1993). What is episodic memory? *Current Directions in Psychological Science, 2,* 67–70.

Tulving, E, and Schacter, D. L. (1990). Priming and human memory systems. *Science, 247,* 301–306.

Updike, J. (1990, August 5). Why Rabbit had to go. *The New York Times Book Review,* pp. 1, 24–25.

Usher, J. A., and Neisser, U. (1993). Childhood amnesia and the beginnings of memory for four early life events. *Journal of Experimental Psychology: General, 122,* 155–165.

van IJzendoorn, M. H. (1995a). Adult attachment representations, parental responsiveness, and infant attachment: A meta-analysis on the predictive validity of the adult attachment interview. *Psychological Bulletin, 117,* 387–403.

van IJzendoorn, M. H. (1995b). Of the way we were: On temperament, attachment, and the transmission gap: A rejoinder to Fox (1995). *Psychological Bulletin, 117,* 411–415.

Van Der Kolk, B. A., and Saporta, J. (1991). The biological response to psychic trauma: Mechanisms and treatment of intrusion and numbing. *Anxiety Research, 4,* 199–212.

Vecchione, J. (Producer and Director). (1986). *Eyes on the prize: America's civil rights years,* Episode 1: *Awakenings (1954–56)* [film].

Vitz, P. C. (1990). The use of stories on moral development: New psychological reasons for an old educational method. *American Psychologist, 45,* 709–720.

Waldfogel, S. (1948). The frequency and affective character of childhood memories. *Psychological Monographs, 62,* Whole No. 291.

Wallerstein, J. S. (1980). *Surviving the breakup.* New York: Basic Books.

Wapner, S. (1981). Transactions of persons-in-environments: Some critical transitions. *Journal of Environmental Psychology, 1,* 223–239.

Wapner, S., Ciottone, R. A., Hornstein, G. A., McNeil, O. V., and Pacheco, A. M. (1983). An examination of studies of critical transitions through the life cycle. In S. Wapner and B. Kaplan (Eds.), *Toward a holistic developmental psychology* (pp. 111–132). Hillsdale, N.J.: Erlbaum.

Warren, A. R., and Swartwood, J. N. (1992). Developmental issues in flashbulb memory research: Children recall the *Challenger* event. In E. Winograd and U. Neisser (Eds.) (1992, pp. 95–120).

Washburn, M. F. (1992). A history of psychology in autobiography. In J. K. Conway (Ed.), (1992, pp. 130–142).

Weaver, C. A. (1993). Do you need a "flash" to form a flashbulb memory? *Journal of Experimental Psychology: General, 122,* 39–46.

Weaver, R. L., II, and Cotrell, H. W. (1987). Lecturing: Essential communication strategies. In M. G. Weimer (Ed.), *Teaching large classes well: New directions for teaching and learning,* No. 32. (pp. 57–69). San Francisco: Jossey-Bass.

West, B. A. (1992). Women's diaries as ethnographic resources. *Journal of Narrative and Life History, 2,* 333–354.

Wetzler, S. E., and Sweeney, J. A. (1986). Childhood amnesia: An empirical demonstration. In D. C. Rubin (Ed.), *Autobiographical memory* (pp. 191–221). New York: Cambridge University Press.

White, M., and Epston, D. (1990). *Narrative means to therapeutic ends.* New York: Norton.

White, S. H., and Pillemer, D. B. (1979). Childhood amnesia and the development of a socially accessible memory system. In J. F. Kihlstrom and F. J. Evans (Eds.), *Functional disorders of memory* (pp. 29–73). Hillsdale, N.J.: Erlbaum.

Whittlesea, B. W. A., and Dorken, M. D. (1993a). Incidentally, things in general are particularly determined: An episodic-processing account of implicit learning. *Journal of Experimental Psychology: General, 122,* 227–248.

Whittlesea, B. W. A., and Dorken, M. D. (1993b). Potential power of coding particular experiences: Reply to Mathews and Roussel (1993). *Journal of Experimental Psychology: General, 122,* 401–404.

Wiener, J. (1991, May 26). The last game. *The New York Times Magazine,* pp. 10, 30.

Wilkie, C. (1990, July 19). Storm swirls around Silber remarks on health-care rationing. *The Boston Globe,* pp. 1, 22.

Williams, J. (1987). *Eyes on the prize: America's civil rights years, 1954-1965.* New York: Viking.

Williams, J. M. G. (1996). Depression and the specificity of autobiographical memory. In D. C. Rubin (Ed.), *Remembering our past: Studies in autobiographical memory* (pp. 244–267). New York: Cambridge University Press.

Williams, J. M. G., and Broadbent, K. (1986). Autobiographical memory in suicide attempters. *Journal of Abnormal Psychology, 95,* 144–149.

Williams, J. M. G., and Dritschel, B. H. (1988). Emotional disturbance and the specificity of autobiographical memory. *Cognition and Emotion, 2,* 221–234.

Wink, P. (1997). Beyond ethnic differences: Contextualizing the influence of ethnicity on individualism and collectivism. *Journal of Social Issues, 53,* 329–350.

Winograd, E., and Killinger, W. A., Jr. (1983). Relating age at encoding in early childhood to adult recall: Development of flashbulb memories. *Journal of Experimental Psychology: General, 112,* 413–422.

Winograd, E., and Neisser, U. (Eds.) (1992). *Affect and accuracy in recall: Studies of "flashbulb" memories.* New York: Cambridge University Press.

Wolfe, J. A. (1991). Palaeobotanical evidence for a June "impact winter" at the Cretaceous/Tertiary boundary. *Nature, 352,* pp. 420–423.

Wolfenstein, M., and Kliman, G. (Eds.). (1966). *Children and the death of a president.* Garden City, N.Y.: Anchor Books.

Wong, J. S. (1945). *Fifth Chinese daughter.* New York: Harper and Row.

Wong, P. T. P., and Weiner, B. (1981). When people ask "why" questions, and the heuristics of attributional search. *Journal of Personality and Social Psychology, 40,* 650–663.

Wright, D. B. (1993). Recall of the Hillsborough disaster over time: Systematic biases of "flashbulb" memories. *Applied Cognitive Psychology, 7,* 129–138.

Yuille, J. C., and Cutshall, J. L. (1986). A case study of eyewitness memory of a crime. *Journal of Applied Psychology, 71,* 291–301.

Index

Abelson, R. P., 5, 15–16, 63, 126–127, 139, 143
Abrams, M. H., 44
Abstractions, 5–6, 12, 63, 96
Accuracy, 8, 10–11, 17, 55–59
Achievement tests, 14–15
Acitelli, L. K., 184
Acquaintance rape, 31
Adam, S., 117
Adams, J. M., 33
Adaptive significance, 17
Addams, Jane, 2, 75–76
Adult Attachment Interview, 205–209
Adult-child memory talk. *See* Memory talk
Affective memories, 104
African Americans, 36, 98
AIDS, 38, 79
Ainsworth, M. D. S., 208
Ainsworth Strange Situation procedure, 208
Ali, Muhammad, 144–145
Allen, S. W., 14
Alton-Lee, A., 14–15
Amnesia, childhood, 20, 100, 108–115, 133–135, 201
Analogous events, 79–83
Anchoring events, 73–76
Anderson, S. J., 15
Andrews, B., 56–57
Archer, R. L., 139
Arnold, Magna, 104
Atlas, J., 148
Attachment, 208–211
Attention, 140–142
Atwater, Lee, 149
Auschwitz concentration camp, 2, 32–33, 101, 165
Authority, 141–142
Autobiographical intelligence, 211–212

Autobiographically consequential experiences, 83
Autobiographical memories, 19, 21–22, 49–51, 56–60, 63, 96, 100, 116–119, 125, 127, 129, 155, 160, 177–178, 201–202, 206–207, 211
Autobiographies, 9, 11, 83, 86, 96–97, 127, 129, 138, 177, 185, 192, 197–202, 204

Baker, R. A., 47
Bakermans-Kranenburg, M. J., 208–209
Balzer, W. K., 60
Banaji, M. R., 9, 178
Bandura, A., 43, 87
Barsalou, L. W., 130
Bass, A., 31, 37, 183–184
Batterman-Faunce, J. M., 126
Bauer, P. J., 114
Beals, D. E., 152–153
Belenky, M. F., 190
Beliefs, 10–11, 18–19, 52, 74
Believability, 144–145
Bell, B. E., 146
Belove, L., 2
Benchoan, Henri, 2
Benedict, Ruth, 186
Bennett, P., 79
Bernstein, J., 71
Berntsen, D., 173
Bettelheim, Bruno, 142
Betz, A. L., 188
Big Bang theory, 28
Bird, Larry, 38, 78
Blaudschun, M., 182
Blehar, M. C., 208
Bloom, B. L., 183
Bohannon, J. N., 35, 57
Borod, J. C., 174
Botkin, A. L., 167–168
Bourke-White, Margaret, 3, 77–78

Bower, G. H., 174
Boyd, C., 32
Bretherton, I., 209
Brewer, W. F., 49–50, 53–54, 57–58
Brewin, C. R., 56–57, 164, 172, 174–175, 206
Britton, B. K., 9
Broadbent, K., 52, 205
Brokaw, Tom, 41
Bronner, E., 40–41
Brooks, L. R., 14
Brown, F., 56
Brown, Roger, 7–9, 34–36, 61–62, 100–101, 139
Brown v. Board of Education, 98
Bruce, D., 16–17, 143, 147
Bruner, Jerome, 9, 11, 21, 71, 86, 119, 124, 139, 148, 155, 177, 184–185, 194–195
Buchanan, K., 141
Buckner, Bill, 39–40
Buckner, N., 158
Buehlman, K. T., 151
Bush, George, 149

Caddell, J. M., 166
California, earthquake in, 35–36
Cambodia, holocaust in, 31, 165
Campbell, B. A., 109
Campion, N. R., 81
Capps, L., 157
Carter, K., 11, 94
Cassidy, J., 207
Causality, retrospective, 83–87
Central themes, 59–62
Challenger, explosion of, 35–36, 57–58
Chance, 87
Chandler, D. L., 46
Chester, N. L., 88
Childhood amnesia. See Amnesia, childhood
Chile, earthquake in, 27
Chinese children, 199, 201
Chomsky, Noam, 46–47
Chowchilla bus kidnapping, 84
Christianson, S-Å., 35
Ciottone, R. A., 88
Civil rights movement, 97–98
Claffey, C. E., 65
Clandinin, D. J., 9, 84

Clarkson, M. G., 114
Clifton, R. K., 13, 23, 114
Clinchy, B. M., 190, 193
Clinical psychology, 100–101
Clinton, Hillary Rodham, 81
Coakley, T., 36
Cocoanut Grove nightclub fire, 37
Cognition, 8
Cognitive constraints on narrative memory, 129–133
Cognitive processing, 12–16
Cognitive psychology, 4–7, 12, 14–15, 63, 95, 100, 102, 104–105
Cohen, G. M., 15
Cohen, N. J., 35
Colegrove, F. W., 34–35
Coles, Robert, 65
Collective memories, 82–83
Collectivism, 196–198, 210
Collins, J. G., 5, 14
Communicative frame, 139
Communicative functions, 19
Connelly, F. M., 9, 84
Constantine, L. L., 210
Conversational styles, 179–181
Conway, M. A., 15, 35, 57–58, 191–192
Cosell, Howard, 144
Costas, Bob, 181
Cotrell, H. W., 141
Courage, M. L., 20, 113
Cowan, N., 187
Crawford, J.: Emotion and Gender, 84, 170, 172, 174, 191
Crawford, M., 134–135, 180, 187
Critical identity images, 175
Critical incidents, 40–44
Critical junctures, 87–95
Critical period fallacy, 83
Crowder, R. G., 9
Culture, 21–22, 177–178, 193–202
Cutshall, J. L., 57

Darwin, Charles, 27, 46
David, A. S., 55
Davidson, G., 187
Davis, P. J., 169, 207
Davis, W. A., 151
Dean, John, 147
Delbo, Charlotte, 101
Demjanjuk, John, 67

De Negri, G. G., 59
Depression, 206
Desrochers, A. B., 19, 155, 157
Details, peripheral, 59–62
Development, memory, 19–21
Developmental psychology, 100
De Vries, Rachel, 189
Diaries, 188–190
Dickens, Charles: *Great Expectations,* 83
Dinosaurs, extinction of, 29
Dion, K. K., 196
Dion, K. L., 196
Directive functions, 18, 42, 63–64, 66, 68, 70, 87–88
Divorce, 84
Donald, Merlin, 106–108
Dondershine, H. E., 166
Dorken, M. D., 14
Dritschel, B. H., 205
Dualistic memory representations, 100–104
Dudycha, G. J., 110, 186
Dudycha, M. M., 110, 186
Dukakis, Michael, 149

Earliest memories, 110–111, 208
Ebanks, C. M., 19, 155, 157
Educational episodes, 6
Edwards, D., 119–121, 139
Einstein, Albert, 71
Eisenberg, A. R., 117–118
Ellement, J., 36
Ely, R., 66, 180
Emerson, Ralph Waldo, 67
Emotion, 55–56, 149–155, 170–176
Emotional functions, 18
Empathy, 151–153
Environmental cues, 88
Epiphanies, 44
Episodes: life, 3–16; educational, 6; specific, 24, 86, 88, 138–145; nuclear, 40, 71; of continuity, 71; interconnected, 97–98. *See also* Events
Episodic culture, 106–107
Episodic memories, 4–16, 49, 63, 67–68, 70
Epstein, S., 102
Epston, D., 10
Erikson, E. H., 80, 83
Esplin, P. W., 147

Eventism, 83–84
Events: originating, 3, 70–73; life, 4–16; momentous, 26–49, 94; traumatic, 30–33; newsworthy, 33–40; transitional, 43–44, 88, 93–95; anchoring, 73–76; turning points, 76–79; analogous, 79–83. *See also* Episodes
Evolutionary analyses, 104–108
Experimental control, 4–5
Experimental psychology, 12–16
Explicit memories, 102–104
Eye movement desensitization and reprocessing, 167–168

Fairbank, J. A., 166
Fearn, Anne Walter, 72, 96–97
Feldman, C. F., 193–195
Fivush, Robin, 20–21, 113, 116–117, 119, 121, 124–125, 186–188
Flashbulb memories, 7–9, 34–36, 38, 50, 53–54, 57–58, 100
Flooding, 167–168
Fonagy, P., 208
Ford, Gerald, 8
Foster, R. A., 178
Franklin, J. L., 31
Fredrickson, B. L., 95
Freud, Sigmund, 10, 20, 104, 108–110
Friedman, A., 187
Frisch, Dean, 81
Fromhoff, F. A., 121
Fung, H., 116

Galbraith, John Kenneth, 82, 85
Gaposchkin, Cecilia Payne, 47–48, 65–66, 86
Gardiner, J. M., 15
Gardner, H., 211
Garner, R., 60–61
Gee, J. P., 158
Gender, 21–22, 177–193
Gergen, K. J., 184–185, 198
Gergen, M. M., 184–185, 198
Gerhard, D., 146
Geyer, Denton, 190
Gilligan, S., 55
Gillingham, M. G., 60–61
Glasgow, Ellen, 45
Godwin, Gail, 189
Goldberger, N. R., 190

Goldsmith, D., 194
Goldsmith, L. R., 43, 54, 66, 88, 90
Gold-Steinberg, S., 53
Goleman, D., 30, 71
Goodman, Benny, 3
Goodman, G. S., 126
Goodwin, P., 38
Gotlib, I. H., 56–57
Gottman, John, 151
Greenstein, F. I., 169
Grice, H. P., 139
Group differences, 21–22

Haden, C., 117, 121, 186
Haldeman, H. R., 147
Hall, Arsenio, 38
Hamond, N. R., 20, 117
Han, J. J., 201
Harackiewicz, J. M., 20, 110, 207
Harber, K. D., 164, 166, 168
Harsch, N., 35, 54, 57–58
Harvard Center for Cognitive Studies, 11
Harvey, A. D., 156–157
Harvey, J. H., 164–165, 169
Hatcher, S. L., 88
Hayne, H., 113, 116
Healy, J. M., 88
Hearing news, 33–40
Heider, Fritz, 45–46
Henderson, Dave, 39
Herlitz, A., 185
Herman, Judith, 18, 30, 32, 101, 164,
    166–168
Hermans, H. J. M., 66
Herrmann, D. J., 180
Heuer, F., 55–56, 149
Hillsborough football disaster, 35
Hiroshima, atomic bombing of, 25–29,
    31, 59, 87, 99
Historical truth, 10–11, 86
Hitler, Adolf, 44
Hoffman, Alice: *Archives of Memory*, 2,
    156, 159–161
Hoffman, Howard: *Archives of Memory*,
    1–2, 156, 158–161
Holdsworth, M. J., 180
Holmberg, D., 183–184
Holmes, Larry, 144–145
Hoogstra, L., 116
Hornstein, G. A., 88

Horton, Willie, 149
Howard, G. S., 9–10
Howard, R., 55
Howe, M. L., 20, 113
Howes, M., 56, 110
Hudson, J. A., 21, 116–117, 121, 125
Hulse, Russell, 46
Hurricane Andrew, 32

Identity images, 175
Idiosyncratic responsiveness, 87
Illumination, moments of, 44–49
Images: memory, 52–55, 104–105, 108,
    138; versus narratives, 100–102; inte-
    grated with narratives, 166–170
Implicit memories, 102–104
Implosive therapy, 167–168
Independence/interdependence, 196–
    198
Individual differences, 21–22
Individualism, 196–198, 210
Information-processing approach, 6
Inhelder, Barbel, 47
Insights, 40, 44–49
Intelligence, autobiographical, 211–212
Intimacy, 149–151, 153, 155
Intrusive memories, 162–170, 173
IQ, 211
Iran-Contra affair, 145–146
Iraq, bombing of, 35
Israel, J. T., 210

Jacobson, Natalie, 44
Jacoby, L. L., 5, 14, 103, 105
Jacoby, O., 3
Janet, P., 168–169
Janoff-Bulman, R., 27, 53, 164, 166, 168
Japanese-Americans, internment of,
    33
Japanese children, 199–201
Johnson, Earvin "Magic," 38, 79
Johnson, Fenton, 150
Johnson, G., 46
Johnson, M. K., 54, 102, 105–106, 144,
    147
Jordan, Michael, 38, 41–42
Josselson, R., 9
Jourard, S. M., 139, 192
Journals, 188–190
Junctures, critical, 87–95

Kagan, Jerome, 76–77
Kahn, J. P., 79
Kahneman, D., 95
Kantor, D., 175, 210–211
Kaplan, N., 207
Katz, L. F., 151
Kaufman, L., 62
Kaye, G., 65
Keane, T. M., 166–168
Kempen, H. J. G., 66
Kennedy, John, 2, 7–8, 20, 34, 36–37, 110, 133, 169
Ketcham, K., 67
Kidnapping, 84
Kihlstrom, J. F., 20, 103–104, 110, 172, 207
Killinger, W. A., Jr., 20, 110–111
Kilmann, R. H., 82
King, Coretta Scott, 98
King, Martin Luther, Jr., 98
Kinzie, J. D., 31, 165
Kiser, L. J., 32
Kitayama, S., 196–199
Klaas, Polly, 37
Kleinman, S. N., 88
Kliman, G., 37
Klohnen, E., 204
Knapp, M. L., 66, 88
Knowles, Malcolm, 96
Koff, E., 2, 174
Koppel, Ted, 158
Korean children, 200–202
Kosslyn, S. M., 161
Kozin, M., 53
Krensky, L., 88
Krueger, Robert, 157–158
Kruk, John, 36–37
Kuhn, J., 126
Kulik, James, 7–9, 34–36, 61–62, 100–101
Kurbat, M. A., 91
Kuyken, W., 206

Labov, W., 11, 139, 148, 156–157
Landmarks, memory, 95–98
Langer, L. L., 32–33, 101, 165
Language development, 115–116
Larsen, S. F., 35, 144, 188
Larson, Gary: *The Far Side,* 38–39
Lasko, N. B., 205

Law, A. B., 2
Lazarus, B., 142
LeDoux, J. E., 104, 113
Lehr, W., 210–211
Leichtman, M. D., 201
Levy, David, 159
Lewicki, P., 12–13
Lewis, Reggie, 85
Lie, E., 115
Lieblich, A., 9
Life episodes, 4–16
Life histories. *See* Autobiographies
Lifshin, L., 188–189
Lincoln, Abraham, 2, 34–35
Lipke, H. J., 167–168
Litz, B. T., 205
Loftus, Elizabeth, 56, 62, 67, 135, 146, 178–179
Logan, G. D., 12
Long-term memories, 173
Losardo, M., 38
Lovell, James, 158
Lucariello, J., 194–195
Lund, Charles, 37
Lynch, Gary, 46

Mack, J. E., 83
Mackavey, W. R., 83, 95
Macklin, M. L., 205
Madden, Michael, 38, 85
Main, M., 207–209
Malcolm X, 36, 75–76
Malley, J. E., 83
Mandler, J. M., 133
Mantle, Mickey, 181–182
March on Washington, 98
Markman, Howard, 183–184
Marks, D. F., 161
Markus, H. R., 196–199
Marriott, M. J., 5, 14
Matchan, L., 31
Mayan children, 194–196, 199
McAdams, D. P., 9, 40–41, 71, 76
McCabe, A., 66, 116, 124–125, 180, 199–200, 203–204
McCann, I. L., 38
McCloskey, M., 35, 57
McDaniel, Judith, 188–189
McDonough, Will, 85
McKee, R. D., 105, 113

McLean, J., 149
McNally, R. J., 164, 205–206
McNeil, O. V., 88
Mead, Margaret, 72, 77
Media sensationalism, 39–40
Meier, D., 94
Meltzoff, A. N., 114
Memorability, 142–143
Memorable messages, 65–68
Memories: personal event, 1–24, 50–52, 65–83, 86, 96, 119, 140, 143, 162, 178, 193, 202; self-defining, 3; episodic, 4–16, 49, 63, 67–68, 70; flashbulb, 7–9, 34–36, 38, 50, 53–54, 57–58, 100; autobiographical, 19, 21–22, 49–51, 56–57, 59–60, 63, 96, 100, 116–119, 125, 127, 129, 155, 160, 177–178, 201–202, 206–207; personal, 49–50; recollective, 50; vivid, 52–55, 95; semantic, 63; collective, 82–83; implicit/explicit, 102–104; affective, 104; earliest, 110–111, 208; intrusive, 162–170, 173; subversive, 170–176; preconscious, 171–173; short-term/long-term, 173; overgeneral, 205–207
Memory accuracy, 8, 10–11, 17, 55–59
Memory development, 19–21
Memory directives, 18, 63–98
Memory function, 16–19
Memory images, 52–55, 100–102, 104–105, 108, 138, 166–170
Memory landmarks, 95–98
Memory narratives, 52–55, 100–102, 104–105, 108, 129–133, 138, 166–170
Memory in natural contexts, 7–9
Memory questions, 117–129
Memory representations, 49–62
Memory research, 7–16
Memory sharing, 117–118, 138–140, 149, 151, 155, 179–186, 210–211
Memory structure/content, 116–118
Memory talk, 20–21, 115–135, 153, 186–188, 209–210
Mendenhall, Dorothy Reed, 72
Merrill, Robert, 8
Messages: memorable, 65–68; symbolic, 68–70
Middleton, D., 119–121, 139, 141
Miller, George, 11, 43, 80

Miller, P. J., 116, 118–119, 127–128, 142, 169
Mimetic culture, 106–107
Minami, M., 199–200
Mintz, J., 116
Mistry, J., 199
Miyake, K., 210
Mnemonic cues, 206
Momentous events, 26–49, 94
Moments of illumination, 44–49
Montgomery, M. R., 37
Montgomery bus boycott, 98
Moore, Donnie, 39–40
Moore, Marylyn, 8
Morelli, G. A., 194–196
Morgan, Kay, 189
Morris, Edmund, 148
Morton, Rebecca, 188
Mosko, Sarah, 46
Moskowitz, Benjamin, 77–78
Mullen, M. K., 20, 110, 186–187, 200–201
Multhaup, K. S., 102, 105–106
Multiple-Entry Modular memory system, 102
Multiple levels of representation, 22–23
Multiple memory systems, 104–108
Murphy, K. R., 60
Myers, Darlene, 189
Myers, N. A., 13, 23, 114
Myllyniemi, R., 139
Mythic culture, 106–107

Nagasaki, atomic bombing of, 27
Narrative memory style, 124, 126
Narratives: life, 9–11, 96–97; memory, 52–55, 104–105, 108, 129–133, 138; versus images, 100–102; integrated with images, 166–170
Narrative studies, 9–11
Narrative truth, 10–11, 86
Natural contexts, memory in, 7–9
Nazis, 2, 32–33, 136–139, 142–143, 161
Neiderbach, Shelley, 30
Neisser, Ulric, 5, 11, 20, 34–36, 54, 56–59, 95, 113, 147; *Cognitive Psychology*, 9; *Memory Observed*, 7–9
Nelson, K., 6, 20–21, 49–51, 63, 113, 116–119, 124–127, 130, 193
Newcomb, Theodore, 77

Newcombe, N., 115
Newmeyer, F. J., 47
Newsworthy events, 33–40
Night of the Shooting Stars, 59–60
Nixon, Richard, 147
Norman, G. R., 14
Nuclear scenes/episodes, 40, 71
Nuthall, G., 14–15

Ochs, E., 157
Oppenheim, D., 194, 210
Oral traditions, 96, 184
Originating events, 3, 70–73
Originological fallacy, 83, 85–86
O'Shaughnessy, M., 149
Oshinsky, D., 149
Overgeneral memories, 205–207

Pacheco, A. M., 88
Palme, Olaf, 35
Panter, A. T., 43, 90
Paradigmatic memory style, 124, 126
Parcells, Bill, 181–182
Parche, Gunther, 163
Parent-child memory talk. *See* Memory talk
Parks, Rosa, 98
Pearlman, L. A., 38
Pellegrini, A. D., 9
Penk, W. E., 38
Pennebaker, J. W., 164, 166, 168
Perceptual memory system, 102
Perceptual representation system, 103
Perfect, T. J., 15
Peripheral details, 59–62
Perner, J., 113, 116, 130
Perris, E. E., 13, 23, 114
Personal event memories, 1–24, 50–52, 65–83, 86, 96, 119, 140, 143, 162, 178, 193, 202
Personality, 21–22, 177, 202–211
Personal memories, 49–50
Personal narratives, 9–11
Persuasion, 143–149
Peterson, C., 115–116, 124–125, 130
Pettit, E. J., 183
Peyer, T., 8
Piaget, Jean, 47
Picariello, M. L., 2
Pillemer, D. B., 2–3, 6, 11, 18–20, 34–35,
38, 41, 43, 45, 50, 52–54, 57, 62, 64, 66, 68, 73–74, 78, 80, 82, 86–92, 94, 100–101, 109–110, 113, 116–117, 127, 130, 132, 134, 139–140, 143, 149–150, 155–158, 160, 170–171, 173–174, 186, 203
Pines, A., 187
Pittman, R. K., 205
Plath, Sylvia, 189
Platoon, 87
Platt, W., 47
Plunkett, K., 144
Poindexter, John, 146
Polk, Margaret, 97
Pomerantz, M., 199
Porter, James R., 31
Posada, G., 210
Post-traumatic stress disorder, 32, 164, 167, 205 206
Potts, R., 116
Power, Katherine Ann, 36
Prassas, A., 205
Preconscious memories, 171–173
Predictive functions, 63–64, 66–68, 70, 88
Present tense descriptions, 155–162
Price, S. L., 163
Pruett, J. C., 110
Psychic trauma, 30, 53
Psychotherapeutic functions, 18
Psychotherapy, 10, 18, 66, 168, 207

Quas, J. A., 126
Questions, memory, 117–129

Radatz, Dick, 181
Randall, E. P., 180
Rape, 31
Raskin, D. C., 147
Rasley, J. S., 93
Reagan, Ronald, 34, 53, 145–146, 148
Real-world usefulness, 17
Reardon, K. K., 66
Recollective memories, 50
Redelmeier, D. A., 95
Reese, E., 116–117, 121, 123–125, 186–188
Reflective memory system, 102
Reichman, J. S., 2
Reidy, C., 44

Reisberg, D., 55–56, 149
Religious beliefs, 19
Representation: multiple levels of, 22–23; dualistic memory, 100–104
Repression, 133–135
Retrospective causality, 83–87
Rhinehart, E. D., 2, 43, 89
Ribadeneira, D., 79
Richmond, T., 162
Riddlesberger, M. M., 126
Rideout, R., 115, 130
Riefenstahl, Leni, 44
Rierdan, J., 2, 38
Riley, Chris, 157–158
Riley, Pat, 38
Rips, L. J., 91
Robb, C., 165, 169
Robbins, D., 180
Robinson, J. A., 91
Robinson, William "Smokey," 48
Rodman, Dennis: *Bad As I Wanna Be,* 198
Roediger, H. L., 5, 103, 105, 115
Rogoff, B., 194, 199
Roland, A., 195–197, 199
Romano, R., 38
Roosevelt, Theodore, 148
Rose, Charlie, 159
Ross, B. H., 80
Ross, B. M., 60, 119
Ross, M., 183
Rovee-Collier, C., 113, 116
Rozynko, V., 166
Rubin, D. C., 53–54, 96, 108, 111–112
Rubin, Lillian, 180
Rudman, Warren, 145–146
Ruffman, T., 113, 116, 130
Runyan, W. M., 86
Ryan, B., 78–79
Ryan, Ken, 36–37

Salovey, P., 3, 9–10, 174, 204, 206–207
Saporta, J., 166
Sarason, S. B., 11
Schachtel, E., 20, 113, 186
Schacter, D. L., 23, 59, 103–106, 108
Schaefer, H., 190
Schama, Simon, 65
Schank, R. C., 9, 15–16, 63, 80–81, 88, 126–127, 139, 141–144, 176

Schemas, 5–6, 63
Schooler, J. W., 146, 178
Schreiber, C. A., 95
Schroeder, Walter, 36
Schulkind, M. D., 111–112
Schwarz, R., 55
Scott, P. K., 164–165
Scripts, 5–6, 24, 63–64, 88
Scudder, Janet, 71
Seely, H., 8
Sehulster, J. R., 182–183
Seles, Monica, 163–164
Self, sense of, 117, 119
Self-defining memories, 3
Self-reflection, 45–46
Semantic memories, 63
Sexual assault/abuse, 31–32, 134–135, 206
Shakespeare, William, 65, 68
Shapiro, Francine, 167
Shaughnessy, D., 39–40, 181
Shaw, Anna Howard, 70
Sheingold, K., 20, 56, 110
Sherry, D. F., 23, 106, 108
Shevell, S. K., 91
Shilts, Randy, 79
Shin, L. M., 205
Short-term memories, 173
Shultz, George, 145–146
Siegel, M., 56
Silber, John, 44, 148
Silberner, J., 28
Simon, J., 44
Simonton, D. K., 46–47
Singer, J. A., 3, 9–10, 174, 204, 206–207
Singer, J. L., 172–174
Situational cues, 43
Skinner, B. F., 43
Skowronski, J. J., 188
Smith, E. R., 6, 12
Smith, Leroy, 41
Smith, Morris, 40–43
Social behavior, 12–16
Social interaction model, 116, 127, 138
Social psychology, 12, 15
Sokol, M., 88
Spear, N. E., 109
Specific episodes, 24, 86, 88, 138–155
Spence, Donald: *Narrative Truth and Historical Truth,* 10–11, 22, 102, 134, 173

Squire, L. D., 105, 113
Srull, T. K., 5, 81
Steele, H., 208
Steele, M., 208
Stein, S. K., 164–165
Stein, Sara, 37
Steinem, Gloria, 70
Stern, D. N., 195–196
Stewart, A. J., 83, 88
Stimpson, Catherine: *Women and Memory*, 178–179
Stivers, C., 191–193
Stohl, C., 66
Storytelling, 127, 155–157, 179–180
Stress, 164–165
Strong, Anna Louise, 69
Subversive memories, 170–176
Sugano, Toyoko, 28
Swartwood, J. N., 35
Sweeney, J. A., 111
Symbolic messages, 68–70
Symons, V. L., 57
Synchronous families, 210–211

Tannen, Deborah, 62, 150–151, 155, 179–182
Tarule, J. M., 190
Tenney, Y. J., 20, 56, 110, 140
Terr, Lenore, 20, 22–23, 101, 110, 113–115; *Too Scared to Cry*, 25–26, 28–29, 31, 37–38, 53, 59, 84–85, 87, 99
Tessler, M., 117, 119, 124–126
Thatcher, Margaret, 35, 58
Themes, central, 59–62
Theoretic culture, 107
Thomas, Isaiah, 38
Thompson, C. P., 188
Thorne, A., 204
Thurlow, S., 31
Till, Emmett, 98
Titchener, E. B., 60
Tlumacki, J., 8
Tobias, B. A., 103–104
Tokyo, fire bombing of, 28
Toombs, M., 72
Torture, 32
Transitional events, 43–44, 88, 93–95
Trauma, 18, 20, 22–23, 25–26, 28–33, 37–38, 42, 53, 58–59, 84, 101, 104, 134–135, 163–170, 173, 206

Traumatic events, 30–33
Triandis, H. C., 196–197, 199
Truth, narrative/historical, 10–11, 86
Tulving, Endel, 4–6, 28, 49, 64, 67–68, 86, 103, 105
Turner, Michael, 28
Turning points, 76–79

Unconscious memories, 172
Unexpected illumination, 46–47
Updike, John, 157
Usher, J. A., 20, 56, 111

Van der Kolk, B. A., 166
Vandross, Luther, 72
Van IJzendoorn, M. H., 2–8–210
Van Loon, R. J. P., 66
Vecchione, J., 98
Verb tense, 155–162
Vietnam war, 87, 205
Vitz, P. C., 9
Vivid memories, 52–55, 95

Waldfogel, S., 110–112, 186
Waletzky, J., 11, 148, 156–157
Wall, S., 208
Wallau, Alex, 144–145
Wallerstein, J. S., 84
Wang, Q., 201
Wapner, S., 88
Ward, Helen, 3
Warren, A. R., 35
Warwick, Dionne, 72
Washburn, Margaret, 46
Watergate scandal, 147
Waters, E., 208
Waters, H. S., 210
Watts riots, 98
Weathers, F. W., 205
Weaver, C. A., 35
Weaver, R. L., 141
Webster, Noah, 27
Weiner, B., 84
Weinstock-Savoy, D., 88
Weld, William, 44
West, B. A., 191
Wetzler, S. E., 111
Wewerka, S. S., 114
White, B., 174
White, C. S., 60–61

White, M., 10
White, S. H., 20, 43, 88–90, 100–101, 109, 113, 116–117, 130, 186
Whittlesea, B. W. A., 14
Whittlesey, R., 158
Wible, C. G., 35
Wiener, Jan, 136–139, 143
Wilkie, C., 148
Williams, J.: *Eyes on the Prize,* 98
Williams, J. M. G., 22, 52, 205–207
Williams, William Carlos, 65
Wink, P., 198
Winograd, E., 20, 110–111
Wolfe, Jack, 29
Wolfenstein, M., 37

Wong, Jade Snow: *Fifth Chinese Daughter,* 199
Wong, P. T. P., 84
Woodworth, R. S., 72
World War II, 1–2, 25–29, 31–33, 156, 158–161, 169
Wright, D. B., 35
Wyer, R. S., 5, 81

Yi, S., 200
Yuille, J. C., 57

Zenker, Arnold, 44
Zimering, R. T., 166